OSI

Mewn Heddwch

Co-editor Hilary Rhys Osmond
Photo: Iwan Bala

Correspondence

I cherish those unconsidered moments
When we find ourselves unaware
Between things
Times of completion or of waiting
Rising, dressing, gathering, resting
We pause in disregarded places
Posed in unexpected correspondence
Irregular, tangential
Sitting, lying, walking
Strangely unaligned for customary communicate
Then, unconsciously between each other
But as one
We talk, think, dream and stare
The world seems vacated
There is no beginning and no end
Time has vanished
There is only us
And we, are one.

Osi Rhys Osmond

Hawk and Helicopter. Oil on unprimed canvas. 140cm x 160cm

ENCOUNTERS

IWAN BALA
HILARY RHYS OSMOND
IVOR DAVIES
DAVID ALSTON
M. WYNN THOMAS
JOHN OSMOND
CHRISTINE KINSEY
DAI SMITH
KARL FRANCIS
WYN MORRIS
DAVID PARFITT
MICK AND THEA ARNOLD
HEDLEY JONES
NOELLE FRANCIS
SUSANNE SCHÜELI
TEILO TRIMBLE
BELLA KERR
STEVE WILSON
SAM VICARY
TINA CARR
SIÂN LEWIS
NATHAN OSMOND
SARA RHYS-MARTIN
LUKE OSMOND
SIMON THIRSK
LYNNE CROMPTON
GWENAN RHYS PRICE
LINDA SONNTAG
ROLF JUCKER
CHÉ OSMOND
MACSEN OSMOND
COLIN BREWSTER
BEN DRESSEL
MEGAN CROFTON
LESLEY DAVIES
BEVERLEY OOSTHUIZEN-JONES
JOHN BARNIE
MENNA ELFYN
RICHARD PAWELKO AND MARY SIMMONDS
BETHAN JOHN
MERERID HOPWOOD
ANN OOSTHUIZEN

First published in 2015 by the H'mm Foundation
The H'mm Foundation, Grove Extension, Room 426, Swansea University, Singleton Park, SA2 8PP.
The rights of the Contributors to be identified as authors of their contributions has been asserted
in Accordance with the Copyright, Design and Patents Act, 1988.

ISBN 978-0-9927560-9-3

A CIP catalogue record for this book is available from the British Library.

Cover painting: *Hawk and Helicopter.* 2011. Oil on canvas. 60cm x 45cm
Front photo: Osi in the front room of Bristol House, Llansteffan, 2104. Photo Siân Lewis
Back photo: Kitchen shelves. Photo Siân Lewis
Every effort has been made to provide details of all the paintings that appear in this book, however,
in some cases, this has not been possible at the time of going to print.

Design: Andy Dark
Typeset in Freight
Printed and bound by Gwasg Gomer, Llandysul, Ceredigion, Wales

www.thehmmfoundation.co.uk

Osi Rhys Osmond, Mewn Heddwch

26.6.1942 - 06.3.2015

As we began the process of assemblage that went into the making of this book, we were all, as contributors, aware that Osi was living on hard-won, but borrowed time. Unfortunately he did not live to see this book published, however, he had been able to read all the texts that appear in it, and seen the first stage draft copy of its design. It is rare for a person to get an opportunity to read the tributes, obituaries and eulogies written about them. But then Osi was a rare person. He also gave directions, made corrections and expressed opinions, of which I am glad and which, of course, were adhered to, because, as usual they were wise and relevant. I know that involvement with the book and reading the texts gave Osi comfort and poignant pleasure.

I am grateful to Hilary for her collaboration and invaluable help as co-editor, in sometimes difficult, but always stimulating times.

Finally, I wish to thank Ali Anwar for his support and generosity, without which we would not have this book in our hands today.

Iwan Bala

Contents

Osi in his studio, Llansteffan
Photo: Luned Aaron

Osi Rhys Osmond

"*My work is predicated on nature, disputed territories and the human condition. I paint on canvas in my studio as well as making large multimedia drawings, which include language and that I refer to as graphic essays and work out of doors on paper and in specially made drawing books. Usually I work simultaneously in a number of books and always carry a drawing book, although in the case of a particular journey or body of work I will create a drawing book specifically designed for that purpose. I have exhibited across the world and held one-man shows in Wales and abroad. My work is in many private and public collections including the National Museum and Galleries of Wales.*

Describing myself as a cultural activist, I contribute articles to a range of magazines, books and periodicals and broadcast extensively in subjects related to culture, the visual arts and the history and social life of contemporary Wales."

Llansteffan, April 2013

Foreword

To Osi: The Colourful Internationalist Druid
ALI ANWAR, CEO H'MM FOUNDATION

'Peace be upon you', my friend, the Mexican-looking man said to me in a confident Lebanese-Arabic accent accompanied with a firm handshake and a smile that lit up his face. 'Peace be upon you too', I replied. 'I am Osi Rhys Osmond', he said, 'and my real surname is "Othman" in Arabic.' Nigel Jenkins who introduced us, mischievously said, 'well, Ali Anwar is from Iraq, and we all know that his surname means "uncultivated" in Welsh!' 'Croeso i Gymru', Osi said, laughingly. This first meeting was over five years ago at the Dylan Thomas Centre in Swansea.

Osi Rhys Osmond is one of Wales's most respected artists, authors, broadcasters and commentators on art and culture in both Welsh and English. His own work has always involved the close examination of nature and the human condition. Osi characterised himself as a Graphic Psychogeographer. This type of art involves making large drawings, which include maps, drawings, collaged photographs, writings, history, dates and contours to produce two-dimensional layers. It is not just about the beauty of the landscape, it is also about the people who live there.

His political activities have been an important part of his work and life as an artist. He was an activist in the peace movement and a member of the CND, an active campaigner for the Welsh Language, served as a County Councillor and stood as a parliamentary candidate for Plaid Cymru.

He was brought up in the mining community of Wattsville in the Sirhowy Valley. His father and mother were both born there, his father, uncles and grandfathers on both sides worked as miners. This fascinating history was curated in an exhibition at the Rhondda Heritage Centre in 2012.

He was elected to the Gorsedd y Beirdd in 2006 in recognition of his contribution to the arts, education and the promotion of the Welsh language. He was a member of the Arts Council of Wales, and an honorary fellow of the University of Wales Trinity Saint David.

He was Head of Foundation Studies at Carmarthen School of Art between 1988 and 1996 before becoming a lecturer in Painting, Drawing and History of Art at Swansea Metropolitan University between 1996 and 2012.

Osi held many one-man exhibitions and has been amongst other eminent Welsh artists exhibiting their work at venues in Wales, London, Lithuania, Denmark and the USA. A prolific writer, he was the editorial consultant and contributor on visual culture for the *Encyclopaedia of Wales*, and was a regular contributor of reviews, criticism, and articles on art and culture for such titles as *Planet*, *New Welsh Review*, *Golwg*, *Barn*, *Tu Chwith* and *Taliesin*.

His broadcasting career has enabled him to contribute to radio and television programmes for the BBC. For the Welsh-language TV Channel S4C, he fronted a twelve programme series called *Byd O Liw* (World of Colour) in 2005, *Art of the First World War* in 2008, and *Lliwiau* (Colours) which explored the meaning of colour in different cultures. He visited a number of countries, including India, France and Australia, to make the six-part documentary.

Osi was obsessed with colours. 'I'm interested in the whole notion of colour – it's been critical for me throughout my life', he says. 'I've had an awareness of the power and wonder of colour since I was a child. I remember always feeling an appreciation of colour. I don't know whether colour attracts you to a painting initially but it adds to your appreciation of art. Colour is the basis of my craft - I talk through colour, I speak through colour, I use colour to express myself and convey my ideas.'

Osi asked: 'Why is snow white, the sky blue and orange is orange? Do we all see the same colours? And why do cats and dogs see the world in blue and yellow and bees see everything in ultra violet?'

He said: 'I always enjoyed working with red, it is very angry and passionate. I used to favour orange when I was younger but moved on to deeper reds. I'm quite interested in browns now

Hilary, Ali and Osi in Bristol House, Llansteffan
Photo: Iwan Bala

whereas I would have dismissed them when I was younger. The most colourful place I visited was India, where colour compensates for a lot of poverty and deprivation. It's in the costumes and the buildings – it's extraordinary to see', he added.

Osi's exhibition *Hawk and Helicopter* in 2011, an account through drawing, painting and text of the artist's experiences, thoughts and observations, was created while watching and painting the sunset from a high point facing south west, overlooking Carmarthen Bay which is designated by the Countryside Council for Wales as a Special Area of Conservation, as well as housing a military testing ground on its estuary edge.

Osi said: '... vast flocks of wading birds, migrants and residents congregate, roost, feed, preen, hunt and breed. Foxes prowl shorelines and rabbits tumble in cliff top warrens. Mad hares strut high fields. Cormorants guano their red roosting rocks a rancid pink. Ravens clank and tumble, blackly. The rivers pour down as the moon-drawn tide ebbs and flows. This is the normality of the place.

'Occasionally, this is disturbed by unexpected sights and strange sounds, for here hawks hunt and sometimes helicopters hover; peregrine falcons and Chinooks appear and disappear, fly, rise, descend, hunt, patrol, attack and retreat. The sudden raucous voice of the Chinook bruises the sky, assaults hearing, the blade's violent clatter shatters the clear estuarine light.

'The innocence of coastal land, suddenly becomes something else. This is the hawk's home and he kills to live. The helicopter comes to rehearse killing for strategic reasons, the land, sea and air lose their virtue, and beauty becomes conflated with terror.'

The Queens Hall Gallery, Oriel Q, in Narberth, featured a powerful and moving exhibition in 2014 by Osi. Entitled *Ymateb/Response*, Osi's work is in direct response to the conflict in Palestine and it questions the cultural acceptance of war and violence. He travelled extensively throughout the Middle East and has spent time in war-torn areas, such as Palestine and the Sudan. He was fascinated by the landscape and its colours. People in these places call him 'Rassam' which means painter in Arabic. Some of these places have the same names as in Wales; Salem, Bethlehem and Bethesda.

In this exhibition, he brought his personal experience of war and conflict quite literally onto our doorstep, with three drawings depicting large, chaotic scenes of war on Llansteffan beach and coastline. 'When they started bombing Gaza I realised that the Gaza strip is about the same size as the coastline and water that I see from my garden in Llansteffan, so I was struck by the image of a million-and-a-half people down there with bombs and rockets falling on them', said Osi.

I feel privileged that Osi contributed to the *Encounters with R.S.* volume published by the H'mm Foundation. He also launched this volume in February 2014 at the Oriel Plas Glyn-y-Weddw exhibition celebrating the life of R.S Thomas.

I have fond memories of working with Osi on this volume. I met several times with him and his lovely wife Hilary at their home in Llansteffan where we enjoyed the warmest welcome. Seeing some of Osi's paintings on the walls gave me extra pleasure. I also had the pleasure of meeting his children, Ché, Luke and Sara, and grandchildren, Gwion, Osian, Macsen, Aled and Caio. I'm delighted with the quality and variety of the contributions people have made to *Encounters with Osi*. I'm most grateful to all contributors, especially to Hilary Rhys Osmond and Iwan Bala for editing this volume and to Andy Dark for putting it together. I hope this volume will contribute towards promoting and celebrating Osi's name and his work.

On March 6th 2015, I caught the train with Jon Gower from Cardiff to Carmarthen to attend Osi's funeral. It was a sunny spring day, and Llansteffan, with its white houses and Norman Castle, sitting majestically across the estuary of the River Tywi, was preparing itself to say goodbye to Osi.

To be a Pilgrim was the first hymn sung at Osi's funeral at Moriah Chapel. The hymn is associated with the allegorical novel *The Pilgrim's Progress* by John Bunyan, written in 1684. It is about Christian's undertaking a pilgrimage in search of the Celestial City. This hymn is popular among Christian Arabs too, and sung in Aramaic and Arabic and other languages in many churches in the Middle East. The last time I heard it was at the Armenian Santa Maria Church in Baghdad over 40 year ago; hearing it sung at Osi's funeral made me feel quite emotional.

Llansteffan Village Hall which hosted the reception, was absolutely packed, and, on that day, Wales won against Ireland in the Six Nations rugby match to give Osi a good sendoff. Osi selected a few young men from the village to be among his coffin-bearers. When these men were children, and he was busy painting in his studio, they were continually breaking his windows while playing football outside his house. He would reprimand them in Welsh, they had by now become his friends.

My last visit to Osi was only a day before he passed away, and although I felt guilty for causing him some stress and pain for coming downstairs to welcome me, I was grateful to have the opportunity to spend a bit of time with him. Hilary made us one of her special herbal teas with honey. He was apologising for not being 'so responsive' and asked about the deteriorating situation in Iraq and the Middle East, and the safety of my family back in Baghdad.

Before I left his house, Osi said to me in his confident Lebanese-Arabic accent accompanied with a very firm handshake, followed by a warm hug and a smile, 'Peace be upon you, my friend, I mean every word of it.' He added: 'Mewn heddwch' (in peace). 'Peace be upon you too, Osi', I replied.

Osi was a unique person and a very dear friend who inspired so many of us.

Osi, the Colourful Internationalist Druid, will be greatly missed.

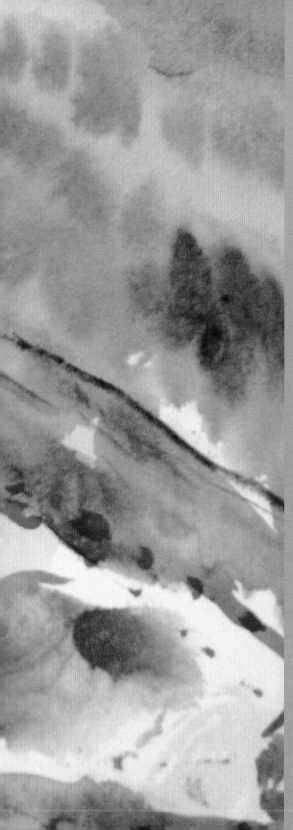

Overviews 1

Iwan Bala
Ivor Davies
David Alston
M. Wynn Thomas
John Osmond
Christine Kinsey
Dai Smith

Detail: *Chwarel mynydd y lan.*
1992. Watercolour. 10″ x 16″
Private collection

8

In chains/Mewn cadwyni. 1992. Oil on canvas. 72"x60"

Worker of the word and the image
IWAN BALA

Osi is irreplaceable. We are taught to think that such a statement is a fallacy, that all of us are dispensable (like everything we surround ourselves with). We can easily be replaced by others with the same qualities, whether in work or social circumstances, sometimes even within a family group. But not so Osi, there is only one man with the qualities Osi has, and it will be difficult for anyone to match them. The man who emerged from Wattsville in the Sirhowy Valley is irreplaceable and irrepressible. Where to begin, in an attempt to assay the qualities that make him so? This volume of short essays, of '*Encounters with Osi*', attempts to do so.

If I had to explain what an ideal Welshman was, if I had to give a definition, it would certainly be Osi that would be the touchstone of my description, somewhat romantic possibly, but nevertheless, true to life. He is a Socialist who stood for Plaid. He marched at the Miner's Strike, and at CND rallies. He not only talked the talk, but also walked the walk, in all things. Osi is more self-aware than anyone I know; he knows all these things that are about to be revealed in this book. He has reached a state of understanding of himself that is for now certainly, beyond any understanding I have of myself. Quite possibly, he was born with it. He reminds me of John Berger (who gets a name-check in Karl Francis' idiosyncratic 'Notes' in this volume, as an admirer of Osi's acting style) an equally polymathic educator, a man who understood deeply and was able to translate that understanding into a language that educated others. They have similar qualities, both in appearance and in their abilities to impart knowledge as if it were a gift. I concur with M. Wynn Thomas in his contribution to this book; there is a need to collect Osi's writings into a published volume.

I was not amongst Osi's many appreciative students, some of whom contribute their 'Encounters' in this volume, not in a conventional sense anyway. But I learnt a great deal from him, and still do. I learnt that the political was intimately conjoined to culture, and that within culture, poetry, history, and the natural world, are as important to an artist as the theory and history of art. I also learnt to maintain an enthusiasm tempered with critical judgment, through our many discussions on art and artists.

My encounters with Osi began many years ago, sometime in the late 80s of the last century. I was a little in awe of his reputation and somewhat abrasive 'valleys' demeanour which, to a north Wales boy, seemed almost aggressive at the time. But I learnt to

Photo: Iwan Bala

sentence, building into an oration that is simply wonderful to listen to, so long as you forget that you are the recipient of such a hugely generous summation. He once opened an exhibition in Oriel Q in Narberth, a joint show called *Vessels* where I shared the space with a friend, the ceramicist Billy Adams from Derry in Northern Ireland. Ceramics has never been one of Osi's 'things to love', and so, after a long oration about the qualities of my work, I dreaded to think what might come next as he addressed Billy's work. This is what he said: 'And Billy's work, well, Billy makes the things that god forgot to make.' What more needed saying? Isn't that what every creative artist seeks to do? But of course, it also meant that he did not have to continue discussing the work.

Wales is a country that celebrates poets to the nth degree, but neglects its visual artists, apart from Kyffin Williams, that is. This has been seen as a shortcoming resulting from a 'colonised mind-set', and the newly revived Museum and Gallery of Wales, Wales in Venice, Artes Mundi etc, might well augur new relationships with global art, and art from Wales as a part of that global perspective. I think we miss the point that artists like Osi have consistently made, and made forcibly. We are artists of the world. Our unique condition makes us so, and gives us a particular voice. Osi is one such artist, with a strong voice, whose depth of understanding in art and culture can be breathtaking. We both gave brief lectures on the work of Anselm Kiefer at Mostyn in Llandudno in 2011, called 'From the Ruins'. The hour-long session can be viewed online, and looking at it recently brought back to me how he had understood the cultural conditions that created the work of Kiefer. His enthusiasm and depth of knowledge whilst talking without notes was remarkable. It is always difficult to follow after Osi in these talks, of which we did a few as a 'double act'.

accustom myself to this different cultural aspect that exists within the confines of this small, divergent, complex Wales, and realised early on that, despite some admonishments, he was an acute and not dispassionate observer of my work, who grasped what I was up to, and, on the whole, appreciated it although my methods were very different to his. He understood the work I was producing in its historical context and the implications of that. He saw it in the 'round'. The knowledge that, somehow or other, I had his support sustained me, and Osi made it a priority to attend my exhibitions. I will be forever indebted to him. I sometimes asked him to open exhibitions for me, and his speeches were characteristically effusive; sometimes I wished he would temper the palpable enthusiasm expressed, I never felt wholly worthy of his praise. He was like a preacher going into 'hwyl', each sentence engendering another, even more expressive

Fforest Fach. Oil on canvas. 41"x50"

A polemicist, a person who extols values as seamlessly as a river flows, ignoring all the rocks of reactionary obstruction in its path: I know no person like Osi. Importantly though, unlike a great deal of 'critical theory' in the arts, where it seems 'theories' are invented in order to bolster a critical writer's reputation or reason for being, Osi's critique and theorizing is always of relevance to the real world that we live in.

As an artist, Osi embraces this world. He does this in various key locations, Palestine, Africa and his beloved Llansteffan. And he delves deep, dealing with topography, landscape, figures in the landscape and deep history as well as recent industrial history. One of his many memorable aphorisms is that of 'Cultural Alzheimer's' where he compares the way we 'forget' the recent mining history of Wales as easily as the grass grows over the flattened slag heaps, and as his own father's mind lost its bearings in the 're-developed' landscape and under the cloud of onsetting Alzheimer's, no longer recognizing his own home. These pithy one-liners that Osi constructs sound spontaneous, but are deeply considered and poetic in their expressiveness. He referred to my work in the *Field-notes* exhibition in 2011 for example, as being akin to 'Crampons on the slope of a slippery culture'. Landscape and memory imbue his work with a sense of connectedness to place, to an intense observation of that place, both through the eye and hand and with the intellect. He is no mere painter of landscapes, but a psycho-geographer. Like his friend, the late poet Nigel Jenkins, he shared that deep love and passion to dig like an archaeologist, to observe like an anthropologist, and to articulate his findings to the rest of us. Osi and Nigel often took a busful of American students on a cultural trip around Wales, talking all the way. I wish I had been on one of those excursions. A poem by Nigel published in *Hotel Gwales*[1] (incidentally with a cover image by Osi) called *Advice to a Young Poet* has these words in it:

> Know your place. What legends and myths
> Have their shaping here?
> What stories, novels and histories?
> And who have been denied a voice?
> And how, in this place, worker of the word,
> Might you make yourself useful?

The same criteria can be applied to the obligations of the 'worker of the image', and Osi fulfils all of these listed above to an extraordinary degree. Not only in image, but in word also. He and Nigel were *compañeros*, 'cyd-deithwyr'. They were friends and companions on the same journey, examining and extrapolating Welsh culture and identity as they went, and working towards its projection into the future, enriching us all in the process. But he could also 'Know' the places of others; only his perceptive mind could have drawn the conclusion that Halloween as practiced in New England, with all those frightening masks facing into the woods, was the remnant of the settler's fear of the native people. As a friend, he is honest and trustworthy, and a man you would be glad to have next to you in any embattled situation. In the trench warfare of cancer, he saved me from a killer bullet. It was his experience of the disease that made me wake up and ask a reluctant GP to send me for tests in late 2012, which found a tumor in good enough time to be successfully treated. Without knowledge of Osi's condition, and his very open conversations about it, I might have left it too late, which, as men, is our wont. So, more than anyone else, I owe him my life.

Everything that Osi undertakes, he does with a consummate mastery, whether it is constructing sketch-books, making a lily

12

pond in his garden, working on his allotment or drawing from life. In writing, teaching, lecturing on any subject, presenting for television, cooking or being the auctioneer at a fund-raising event, he never fails to impress. He is a cultural activist 'par excellence'.

It gives me great pleasure, both professionally and personally, to be able to help compile this publication, and my thanks go to Ali Anwar and The H'mm Foundation for providing the opportunity for me to do so, and to publish this necessary compendium. This book is a collection of recollections by friends, family and colleagues, and they follow the pattern set up in previous 'Encounters With' publications by The H'mm Foundation. It is in the nature of such a collection of reminiscence, that there is an element of repetition, but I have edited only lightly, because each voice brings something different to the story. Some essays are about personal encounters with Osi, some are about his influence and some about his art. I emphasise that this book is not an academic treatise, but is a collection of views and reflections, 'fragments' that build a picture, by some people who have been fortunate to have Osi Rhys Osmond as a shaping and influential part of their lives. I count myself as one amongst those fortunate people. Ali and I are grateful to all those who have contributed, and to Hilary Rhys Osmond who has co-edited with me. The book concludes with an interview with Osi by Ann Oosthuizen that puts flesh on the bones of the previous texts, illuminating all that has gone before with his philosophy, thoughts and reflections on life. The Welsh word for culture is 'diwylliant', which can translate fancifully as to 'de-gloom' ('gwyll' being the word for darkness or gloom). Osi, as usual, brings light to the darkness as he talks.

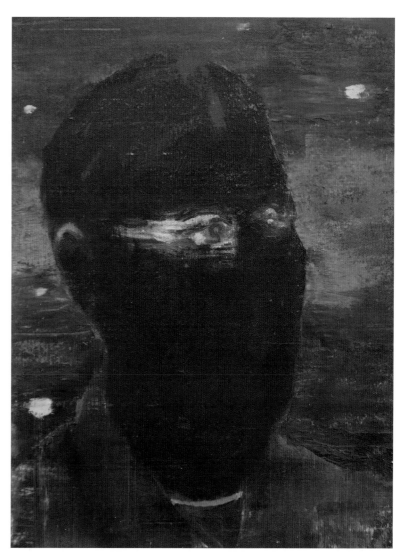

Masked soldier. Oil on canvas

13

1. *Hotel Gwales*, Nigel Jenkins. Llandysul, Gomer Press 2006.

Pages from sketchbook. Watercolour

15

Pages from sketchbook. Watercolour

Pages from Sudan sketchbook. Watercolour

Hand-made sketchbook

18

Allforio/Exporting. 2013. Oil on canvas

The Life and Works of Osi Rhys Osmond
IVOR DAVIES

Like many south-east Wales mining villages, Wattsville has one main street. Nearby, the New Risca Mine, opened in 1878, was 855 feet deep. One of the gems that 'the dark unfathomed caves'[1] did bring forth was Osi Rhys Osmond.

The Sirhowy Valley has heard many laments, from the poet Islwyn (1832-1874) to the Manic Street Preachers' bass player Nicky Wire's 'Wattsville Blues'. But more positively, Osi's exhibition *Landscape and Inheritance* at the Rhondda Heritage Park in April 2013 recalled his childhood in Wattsville, the history and geography of the valley. It was a tribute to his family, boyhood friends and predecessors, who bequeathed to him 'a mystery and a wonder at our brief eternities and where and how we spend them'.

His work also demonstrates the converse of 'hiraeth': namely Welsh and world-wide problems and politics, as manifestos of action rather than melancholic thoughts on loss.

He draws skilfully, composes from nature and the imagination dynamically and with precision. Charcoal views of the derelict colliery, some stained with watercolour are superimposed with other drawings as *papiers collés*. His fluent and loose lines disguise skilled draughtsmanship and suggest loss and abandonment. He has eschewed the clichés of 'the Valleys' and wishes that the word 'Valleys' could be banned. The Gwent or Monmouthshire valleys were not unlike the Glamorganshire U-shaped colliery stretches, and, just as Osi had gone to Newport, I saw the dynamic Rhondda painters with their daily train journey to and from Cardiff College of Art in the early 1950s. The Glamorgan painters later crystallised in the art-historical memory as the 'Rhondda Group', broke new ground for representing their ordinary everyday scenery, people and places. But later 'the Valleys' in less attentive hands came to

mean job losses, low morale, or the yearning for miners' lamps, coal-black clouds and weather, a picture imposed on us, which we came to accept and by which we came to be represented. Rejecting ready-made ideas of the valleys, an export so willingly embraced elsewhere by those who had neither heard of pneumoconiosis nor seen the pre-industrial landscapes, even as eighteenth-century topographical prints, Osi chose to look up. His gaze was towards the 'steep orange mountains', not as a Welsh story in the outworn fashion, but as an elevated and positive view of a world beyond these stereotypes. He 'looked heavenward' with a Rothkoesque feeling, dissatisfied with the way we have been documented.

Paradisiac blue

Over thirty years ago he and his family moved to the still unspoiled Welsh-speaking Carmarthenshire village on the west side of the river Tywi estuary; Osi and Hilary's house is literally in the shadow of the church of Llansteffan, which was almost certainly founded c. 650 by Ystyffan or Styphan, traditionally believed to be a follower of St Teilo, son of Mawan or Mawn ap Cyngen ab Cadell Ddyrnllug, Prince of Powys. Ffynnon Styffan, his holy well, is near the church, walled over today, but tradition ascribes healing properties to it. A more recent and perhaps ingeniously inventive text (Iolo MSS., p. 252. 2 Myv. Arch., p. 776) declared that one of the seven questions of Catwg the Wise to seven wise men at Llanfeithin or Llancarfan was to Ystyffan: 'What is the greatest folly in man?' Ystyffan answered, 'To wish evil to another without the power of inflicting it.'

But there are demons even in paradise: at the 2009 National Eisteddfod I toured and visited many eligible works, considering who should receive my award for a work which conveys the spirit of activism in the struggle for language, culture and politics in Wales. At the last, about a metre of unframed ordinary cartridge paper, distressed by the pressure of rapid and direct drawing, smears and scratches and scribbled notes, had been fixed to the wall like an afterthought, but all too urgently for smart presentation. Two strips at top and bottom of the work, show moons against indigo watercolour sky in a complete mensual phase. Watercolour, ink and pen, applied as *papiers collés* overlap edges, show the beautiful Carmarthenshire landscape around Llansteffan, where over half his life so far has been spent, and which has been used as a bombing range over the years. Troop transporter helicopters and a dark bird share the sky; wading birds look for food in the mud flats while explosives are tested on the shores of the estuary in preparation for sales of heavy armaments to Israel, Saudi Arabia and former Syrian insurgents. Entitled *Llanw* ('Tide' or 'Fill'), it accompanied a similar concentrated piece, *Llwch y Ser* ('Stardust'). For his life-long sacrifice of beauty to the cause, the least that Osi deserved was my award.

Five years later I saw a more developed and composed version of that landscape whose many wide land-planes ran horizontally below the gentle and menacing aeroplanes. It was a broad dry mat oil painting on canvas about 100 cm. by 160 cm., facing a wall in a closed off, shop-like, room in his house.

As a friend visiting the artist's house, thoughts like 'earthly paradise' and 'Aladdin's Cave' may come to mind. But trying to remember it clearly I keep thinking of the famous poem by Iolo Goch (c.1320-c.1398), known as 'Llys Owain Glyndwr', a precise description of Owain's court, its structure, architecture, and those who frequented it. It begins:

Llys barwn, lle syberwyd,
A baron's palace, a place of generosity,
Lle daw beirdd aml, lle da byd.
Where bards often come, a good place.

and ends
Gŵr meingryf, gorau mangre,
Man of strong good looks, the best place,
A phiau'r llys; hoff yw'r lle.
Who owns the court; lovely is the place.

It would be a vanity to emulate Iolo's *Cywydd* in describing Osi and Hilary's home, a dwelling where every inch of space is well utilised and made spacious. But the position of their home and its layout have the look of a medieval palace which has been rebuilt and modified over four or five recent centuries. And whether it is a medieval palace or this house, it is an installation of the designs of those who live in it. Here is the expression of Osi's soul, the whole interior being very practical but going towards the extension of his art into theatrical space and time. There is a moment of transition from the outside world into the narrow hallway carpeted with two finely knotted Turkoman runners. A dense tropically foliated garden lies beyond, whose series of intimate spaces are concealed, paved in part with clear cut slate and dolorite blue-tones. A pond of exotic fish in one of the arbours, with a few pebbles naturally incised and encircled by calcium-white lines and alabasters etched by rain.

The floor and stair boards are painted in many ultramarine, indigo, azure, cerulean, Prussian, Egyptian and phthalo blues. Osi's paintings that adorn the walls are mostly oil or raw pigment with a minimum of oil, sometimes spread by a plastic credit card as

20

21

The lily pond in the garden, Llansteffan

squeegee. There are dark silhouettes in Africa; a sense of hostages (Operation Cast Lead in the Israeli attack on Gaza) a background of indigo to light blue with a deep red head and touch of orange hair; a complicated entanglement of figures in earthy and dense brick-red colours. What is the significance of the dark running figure, a Sudanese 'walking boy' against the deep tungsten blue and light cobalt? A dark, black-and-red lupine dog stoops, and in another picture the simple dry painterliness brings out the same animal against a yellow scumbled ground. A human shape appears alone as if in a sauna, the simplicity emphasised by the invisible basic infrastructure of the figure drawing in a profound dark red to orange interior. Figures and people are often reduced effectively and successfully to two colours or tones by a chiaroscuro, especially one from which a smiling schoolgirl in a white slip and pink background becomes a familiar personage.

A porcelain plate depicting Ché Guevara hangs up high in one corner of the corridor. There is a resemblance. He has always been brave in defence of Welsh culture in the guerrilla struggle against its marginalisation.

Eryr
Up I forget how many storeys is his full-scale attic reached only by a simple, almost vertical wooden stairway, passing through a trap door. It has all been made by the artist as a place to spread his wings. In the wide space under ancient beams, the most simulating books, drawings, fabrics, aides memoire, plans, and other souvenirs of the future provide material for thought and meditation.

Down the hatch by the ship's ladder again, is a smaller room immediately below, a drawing studio, tiled up almost every wall and across a large table with many layers and overlapping piles of drawings and sketchbooks of all sizes and shapes. No room on the table for anything else but the tools of his explorations. The half-open plan-chest drawers contain open drawing books protruding, displaying half-finished watercolour sketches or observations of half-seen movements.

Here is the profoundest and perhaps the most important work, no ordinary sketchbooks, but evidence of the heart of his way of life. Many, perhaps most, of his books are sewn and bound by this versatile Silurian, with some of the larger ones revealing the carefully sewn thick cord and bold regular knot of masculine beauty. They are bound with the same strength and imaginative materials and various kinds of paper, some hand-made with rich textures, others well-chosen manufacturers' cartridge. He probably keeps a diary, but these heavy and voluminous art works in their own right become his travelling companion at home and on his many worldwide journeys.

Near home, at Y Wyrle, he looked at the same view from the same place before dusk every day for a year and recorded what he saw of where sky and land meet. Watercolour impressions are spread across his very long horizontal sketchbook, tailor-made to receive double pages of broad washes. The idea comes neither from Monet nor from Turner but from his own penetrating performance of perception and change. He will have chosen the format of the very wide narrow horizon before making the book into the only shape that would receive the variations and transformations of his repeated notes of different dusks. Elsewhere there may appear Welsh Black cattle or other distinctive breeds in their ordinary lives, but the most dramatic are very large bindings he took abroad to many parts of the world. 'Sketchbook' is hardly the correct description of these. And then there is the finely-sewn compilation of long envelopes, some with windows, paper bags and folded items, all opening very horizontally. I wish he could have been my teacher in school. But perhaps he is. He has compiled and bound a demonstration book for students, collected together from drawings – drawings he has made to demonstrate points for students. These have been picked up from the floor of life-drawing rooms after students had rejected them.

What he calls his studio is a rotunda outside, over the road, and, somewhere beyond there may be a vineyard, but this is another story.

La Langoureuse asie et la brulante Afrique

One very large sketchbook, which he took everywhere he went in India contains elephantine scenes, people of all kinds and some slightly Cézannesque translations of single hills. The structure is delineated like a net, and short strokes of *terre verte* and earthy watercolours describe the feeling of its mass and solidarity.

An Arts Council grant to visit the Holy Land in 1985 allowed him to see ancient cities, notably Jaffa where he sat and drew at length whatever appeared before him. Arab refugees, mostly from Iraq, offered him thousands of pounds for his works.

A red-bound book was drawn from his visit to Spain, another from Tuscany and one from Australia, but the most dramatic compendium was for his African drawing tour. Measuring about 60 cms high, 45 cm wide and 5 cm thick, the papers of various kinds and bound as elsewhere with a hard cover: a deep burnt

Hand-made sketchbooks

Bananas Sudan. 1997. Extract from drawing book. 24"x24"

sienna suede of coarse texture run through by a single irregular cerulean blue fine leather strip, to suggest the Nile.

Using his book as a parasol and a seat, he explored and drew the south Sudanese stretches, enormous grasslands, and tropical rain forests on both banks of the White Nile. The newly independent Republic of South Sudan, established in 2011 after the 2005 peace deal ended Africa's longest civil war, is very diverse, ethnically and linguistically, and traditional religions are followed. Besides the oil problem and the droughts, there are border disputes, conflict and disagreements between the South Sudanese Dinka Ngok people and cattle-herding Misseriya Arab tribesmen. These and other feuds, resettlement of population and wars occur in the tropical savannah and the Sahel. But the Llansteffan citizen was neither there as a journalist-anthropologist nor as a documentary photographer. His drawings of the land and its inhabitants show the one-legged victims of earlier British export manufacturers, people hiding and fleeing, and the 'walking boys', escaping from the army and horrors of war: eternally on the run. The variety of drawings also includes fine schematic likenesses of people who live naked except for bows and arrows; villages of round stone-built houses with thatched roofs like our bronze-age settlements, as well as boulders reminiscent of the same age, appear in the heat of the Fabriano cotton papers. One page is entirely covered with red Sudanese earth mixed with gum Arabic. Sapling stems, rounded and tied in a perfect circle about a foot in diameter, are thrown into the air while spears are aimed to pass through them. Equally great precision is achieved with graphite and charcoal in the target practice of the drawings in this giant book.

It would take a long time to go through all the stratified layers of these hand-made pieces of stored memory without entering the reality of each. But the time would be well spent. How would it be possible to exhibit them all, replicating or transporting or translating the whole room? Each would be exhibited half-open, or closed, or as one double-page spread. And how would it be possible to recapture the private drama without the intimate act of turning over all the pages and perhaps gradually damaging the vulnerable material? The impossibility of such a challenge is appealing. This mysterious room is quiet and contained. It contains a medium much more direct than painting in the conversational pages, bindings and sewing. The elusive, the concealed, half-revealed or temporarily opened leaves characterise the art form itself, the very aesthetic at the core of his personal production.

The palace at four a.m.
Drawing may be an exercise, 'press-ups for the brain – The landscape is earthed and drawing is a philosophical exercise' not self-expression. Osi sees the 'singularity of Giacometti' stripping away exterior life.

In pursuit of Alberto Giacometti, Osi stayed in the Italian Alps and drove into La Stampa. There, where he had made landfall, his journey began in the Swiss sculptor's birthplace. He chanced to stay at a hotel whose proprietor happened to be the child of Giacometti's cleaner, and would stand and stare at his studio. Like a detective carefully following the whole of Giacometti's life in Europe, Osi's long journey began.

In 1932 Giacometti, in the early hours one morning, constructed a fragile fantastical palace out of matches aided by? a female companion. Later that year, his famous construction, made of wood, glass, wire and string, and measuring only 63.5 x 71.8 x 40 cm, suggests the bare bones of a building with a female figure; vertebrae in a skeletal case and a prehistoric bird in flight. The small work, now in the Museum of Modern Art, New York, describes a large space and the concentrated, pared-down method that characterises subsequent work gives it surrealist presence.

In the same street where Giacometti had discovered a woman's arm still wearing a bracelet, Osi found a bracelet in the gutter.

Osi and R.S.

The versatile Monmouthshire draftsman has brought his thoughts and deeds together in relation to the poet R.S. Thomas, out of his opposite far corner of Wales. He recalls marching with R.S. on campaigns for CND and in support of self-government for Wales. The painter has written about the poet in 'The Ornithologist-Poet as a Bird', in *Encounters with R.S.*[2] with prose that reveals long acquaintanceship with much poetry. The artist, as lucid with words as with paint or pencil, uses his writing as he would any other medium. On page 49 he considers the bird as a metaphor for the gaunt poet:

> In his three parishes and in his retirement at Rhiw, he seems to personify four distinct phases of bird-like character and as he moves there is a change, a change in the poetry and a change in the man: places affected him deeply, party from expectation and subsequent disappointment and partly from the new reality...

> He begins in Manafon as a hawk, patrolling the bleak uplands, becomes a stalking harrier on the marshes and against the buttresses of Foel Fawr at Eglwys-Fach, stoops like a falcon from the sea-cliff parish of Aberdaron, and becomes the majestic sea-eagle of Llŷn. In his most productive creative home, the cottage

at Rhiw where he lived until shortly before his death in 2000.

The painter here penetrates the work of the writer. And he brings all media together in the series of 'graphic essays', or 'graphic psycho-geography', on the poet, which he began in 2013, using ink, pencil, words, watercolour and collage. 'Drawing, mapping, collaging, writing, and layering past and present – examining the poetry, life and landscapes of R.S. Thomas' (p. 49). The painter researched and visited the landscapes and people of the ornithologist-poet's four 'habitats' and traces the writer's changing engagement with them. The visual complexity of clear, fine, direct non-academic drawing and map-making, topographical and bio-graphical depictions appear for Thomas's four locales in these pictures, together with poetry written at each period. The most significant with regard to the poetry was his 'final metaphysical parish of Rhiw' (p. 50). At the earliest parish, Manafon, the poetry had been more directly related to the place and its inhabitants. Osi made many sketches from life at the spellbinding poetry readings R.S undertook, and some are included in these four large compositions.

A major exhibition entitled 'Correspondences', curated by the poet and artist Christine Kinsey at Plas Glyn-Y-Weddw in early 2014, celebrated the centenary of R.S. Thomas's birth. Fourteen artists were invited to create works inspired by his poetry and Osi was amongst them. He did not exhibit there the earliest of this most positive and productive struggle of his life, a torn landscape with sheep which included a church. But his interpretation of Manafon has an almost classical grandeur; it includes a collaged picture of R.S's church, St Michael's, above a river of fish and dragonflies, a heron, a kingfisher. Welsh Blacks graze there and a *papier collé* of the poet in his youth is top centre. A predatory bird and aeroplanes, 'Blood Spillers', fly in the night sky above in this visionary ordnance survey of the world in which Osi and R.S. are one.

R.S.'s life in Eglwys Fach is shown as a map detailed with place-names, beautifully drawn herons, a blackbird and his wife's face. It includes the poet profiled top left as 'Nimrod the Mighty Hunter' near a hawk's profile with keen eye and beak. In the third painting, celebrating R.S. in Aberdaron and Plas-y-Rhiw, an intense undercurrent flows through the calm watercolour washes. Over a crown-shaped peninsula is a horizon with aeroplanes above and yachts below. These three large pieces were exhibited and rapidly bought by a perceptive audience.

Writing and broadcasting

As an artist and activist, Osi has published critical texts and reviews, presented successful features on radio and television, and articles on art and culture for *New Welsh Review*, *Planet*, *Golwg*, *Barn*, *Tu Chwith* and *Taliesin*. He is the author of *Carboniferous Collision: Josef Herman's Epiphany in Ystradgynlais*.[3] His essay 'Visual Voices and Contemporary Echoes' appears in the catalogue-book *Imaging the Imagination*.[4] You can glimpse his erudition in an audio-visual recording, *From the Ruins* in a discussion with Iwan Bala at the Mostyn gallery, Llandudno in 2012 about land, memory and history in the work of Anselm Kiefer and how it relates to contemporary art in Wales. One of the most imaginative and widely admired of his many forays into television broadcasting was *Byd o Liw* (World of Colour) directed by Richard Pavelko for S4C. Certain artists were invited to make new visual interpretations or responses to earlier well-known painters' works of parts of Wales. He would find the exact spot where an artist had sat to draw the view, do a careful pencil drawing himself in his sketchbook dedicated to this exercise, then bring the living Welsh artist to the

place to do his own version. Osi's personality as a television presenter, his insight, his able performances and good looks attracted many who may not have been interested in art before.

*   *

From antiquity Chinese writers have avoided repeating the name of an eminent person in their texts. Named once, he may then be called 'the one-word poem author', then 'the dweller among mosses'. What Fowler terms 'elegant variation' may even enlighten the subject. By now the device may seem odd, contrived, antiquated, or surreal. So I have used it wherever possible, although my text is not a prose poem about the various aspects of a personality. Nor is it an analysis using art-historical methods. It is a description of some pieces of a jigsaw puzzle which are parts of an infinite picture. Or, like glittering glass smalti or tesserae for a mosaic, incomplete because decisions will never be made.

How is it possible to discuss, understand and reveal the reality of a person or to write about an artist and his activities? There is no limit to the number of observations, of his many works and other activities and thoughts. No matter how many thousand words add up, no story of a life can be complete. He is changing from moment to moment; his reality is also in other people; it is not quite possible to read his mind through his paint, though his sketches show something about his way of looking, drawing out and transferring a reality from the chaos of real life. He will surprise us. The virility and passion of a flame-bearer is in his work. Osi Rhys Osmond has lived through it and will go on.

1. From *Elegy Written in a Country Churchyard* by Thomas Gray
2. *Encounters with R.S.* ed. John Barnie. The H'mm Foundation, Swansea 2013
3. *Carboniferous Collision: Josef Herman's Epiphany in Ystradgynlais* Institute of Welsh Affairs, Cardiff, 2006
4. *Imaging the Imagination* eds. Christine Kinsey and Ceridwen Lloyd-Morgan Gwasg Gomer, Llandysul, Ceredigion, 2005

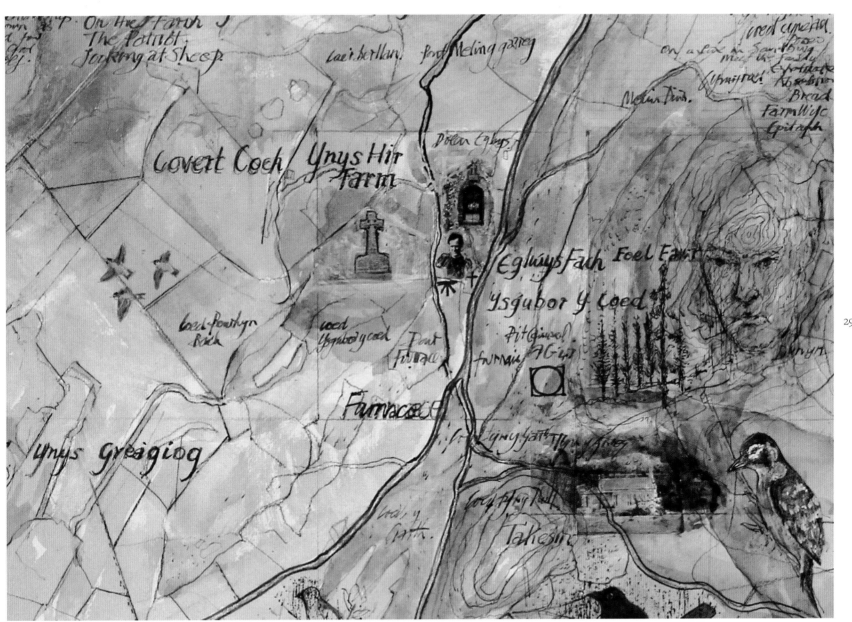

Detail: *Eglwys Fach*. 2013. Mixed media. 100cm x 100cm

29

Detail: *Aberdaron.* 2013. Mixed media

Detail: *Aberdaron.* 2013. Mixed media

Detail: *Manafon.* From R.S. Thomas series. 2013. Mixed media

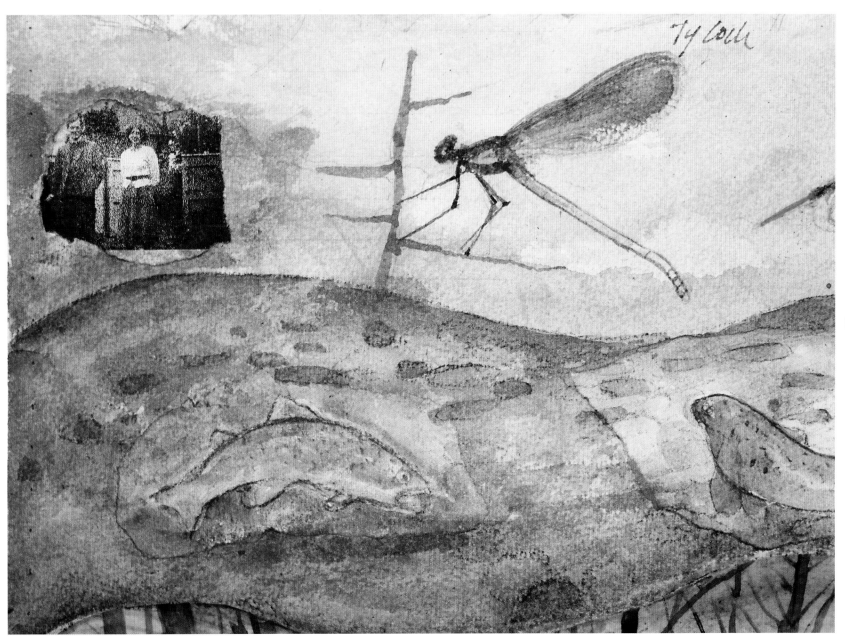

Detail: *Manafon*. From R.S. Thomas series. 2013. Mixed media

33

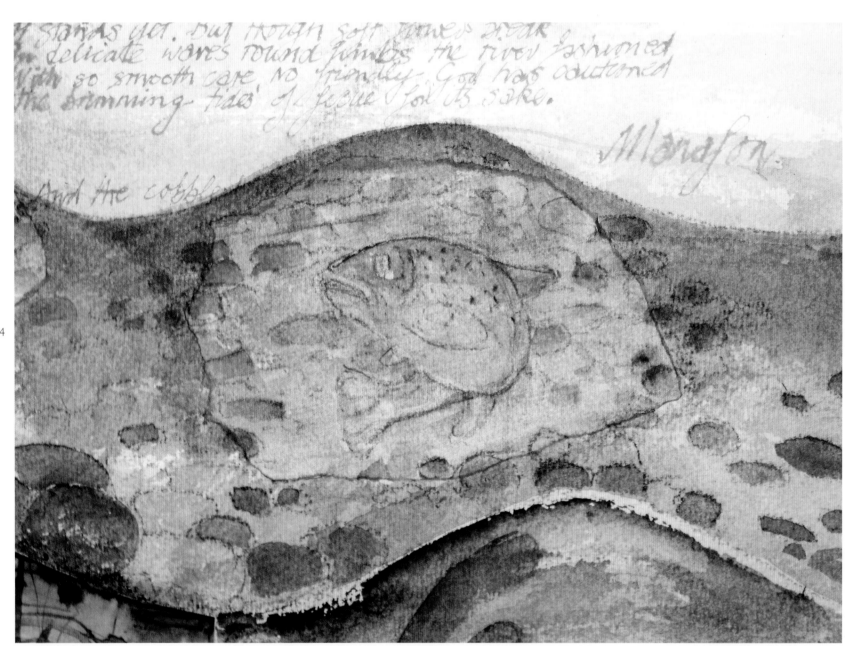

34

Detail: *Manafon*. From R.S. Thomas series. 2013. Mixed media

I could believe in angels,
owl
Those feathered overtones.
in Love's rafters I have heard.
him scream, too, fastening
his talons in his great
adversary, or in some lesson
denizen, maybe, like you and me.

No Truce With The Furies.
geriatric.
still point. Fathoms.
Jura.
Christmas Jr. The Lost.

Mynydd y...
Rhiw
Plas y Rhiw.
Gwern Saer
Mynydd R...
Bryn Hyfryd.

Detail: *Manafon*. From R.S. Thomas series. 2013. Mixed media

A 'Wales' Internationalist

DAVID ALSTON

Osi is regularly turned to as the 'colourful' empathetic cultural commentator for the media when it suits the media to have a Wales portrayed rebelliously but deliciously, talking to itself. This is to my way of thinking, a one-dimensional characterisation of somebody with a much bigger sense of Wales's hinterland. In this Osi shares some of the sort of outlook from Wales of a writer like Robert Minhinnick.

The move west in Osi's life into a Welsh-speaking heartland, more rural than urban, has not displaced his sense of a bigger picture. He will revel in the particularities and indeed the rugosity, the texture of this passing life of rural Wales and what it held. I once shared a train journey with him from Barmouth, and for all his growing care, increasing in recent years, over diet, I can still hear and see in my mind's eye an Osi rejoicing in the sight from the train window of Welsh blacks against a tussocky marshland edge, his resonant words on these cattle thrummed like a guitar chord from a Manitas de Plata, looking over the Camargue at St Marie de la Mer.

Rich associative power from things that are 'ur-Welsh' have always sustained him, and at the same time fuelled his passionate polemic. It is not some inverted UKIPism to wonder what a Wales will be like when patterns of current moneyed immigration produce a conservative, with a small 'c', 'retired' comfortable population with no active sense of solidarity or proactive citizenship. For Osi, this contrasts with the successive waves of assimilation and energies of all past immigrations particularly those of the Industrial Revolution onwards. For Osi these are also part of the warp and weft that has had its dynamism for culture. His large exhibition back in the Rhondda focusing on recent and long-standing work done in his home Sirhowy valley, was not

ultimately parochial, but stretched on the one hand from a deep sense and intuition of geology and time, to those worlds linked and traversed by the mining of coal.

Not surprisingly his template for the future is communal but international in feel at the same time. Take Wales's natural resources in sustainable energy...Osi would support the literal idea that Offa's Dyke should be just that, a Dutch dyke with water so that Wales can be an island...it is already surrounded on three sides by the sea, and this heralds, from his vantage point, an exploitation of natural energy based around community needs and corresponding supplies, and an undertaking of this against a background of international responsibility derived from an acute sense of the threat of global warming. Wales, from his credo's position, can act in self-sufficient ways to row back from the tsunami of consumerist culture. Osi will acutely feel that Wales, if it assumes its mature self-determining responsibilities, can take initiatives this way, act in its own interests but be globally responsible, internationally aware. He will point to Costa Rica to encourage us to think of similar possibilities in Wales. He will applaud charging for plastic bags as a small first step in changing habits, but his painter's eye will still have an image of the great clogged mass of an irreducible plastic Atlantis, a mausoleum for seabirds in each of the great oceans now.

This global imbrication of Wales is for me too, indicative of how his art has shifted in recent years, from a sort of colouristic Celtic mysticism (I'm thinking of a glowing but almost, in the end, anecdotal set of paintings I experienced in the 1990s based around the Venus of Machynlleth) to the powerful story of a traduced landscape of palpable eye-watering beauty, palled by the shadow of the Chinook pulsing over it, in his Mission Gallery exhibition in

Osi at the Rhondda Heritage Centre Exhibition, *Landscape and Heritage.* 2012. Photo: Nathan Osmond

Swansea. Narrative invades in complex topographies. Osi has visited conflictual landscapes abroad, notably in Palestine, but in recent years he has seen the sublime expanse of Carmarthen Bay as the fearsome site of a limbering up for global policing; but not in his name.

Osi has been the go-to commentator for the likes of *Planet* magazine (The Welsh Internationalist) looking for a frontline correspondent to send dispatches from the international cultural skirmishes of places like the Venice Art Biennale.

It is precisely because Osi is not the backwoodsman but the Wales internationalist, that his commentary here has been provocative. His chairing of the Arts Council's Advisory group on the Wales presence in this international arena has been passionate to achieve the most for the venture in all its dimensions, particularly and at his express insistence, for the Welsh public back in Wales to gain some pride and engagement with Wales being a Wales on the international stage. His biggest reservation would consistently be for this opportunity not to be 'carpet-bagged' artistically, or for Wales to pander to international art world 'fashionistas'. He vociferously pleaded the case for John Cale's piece, seeing it as, bar Peter Finnemore in a previous Biennale, one of the first Biennale presentations from Wales that was speaking of Wales but communicating in such a way as to network Wales into international concerns and attention.

For Osi, Wales's representation however deeply desirable, would always be a secondary matter in the biennial Artes Mundi, when placed against the position gained by the exhibition in projecting Wales and its context and concerns into a new and potentially powerful international network of artists linked by Artes Mundi's reflection of humanity in its richness and diversity.

So an abiding memory for me will be Osi, ebullient and in celebratory mood for Tim Davies's powerful and beautiful representation at the 54th Venice Biennale in 2011. Tracy Emin's offering in the British Pavilion two year's previously had essentially been a dealer's show, neons for your penthouse living room or bedroom, or, how daring, your onyx-clad capacious bathroom. In reaction, the British pavilion in 2011 had needed a wholesale makeover curtesy of Mike Nelson. But the thematic threads of the meaning of armistice and on-going wars were bubbling away that year. An upturned Sherman tank was doubling as an exercise treadmill with live athletes working out at regular intervals in Allora and Calzadilla's *Track and Field*. Tim Davies's opening two works in the Wales pavilion frenetically and incisively investigated the pomp and circumstances of Remembrance.

Such points and links to our situation, post-invasion of Iraq and with continuing involvement in Afghanistan, Osi could extrapulate to the succession of international visitors, particularly over those opening days.

One of the strengths of the Wales pavilion's new location being established that year between the Giardini exhibition site and the Arsenale, very much on a route between the two, was the fact that a clutch of other ventures and pavilions had gathered at the head of the Via Garibaldi. There was a temporary ecologically-driven exhibition across the way and just over the nearby bridge for the first time in Venice, an Iraq pavilion. When you scratched the surface of this, the Iraqi presence was in effect underpinned by some New York art agents and dealerships, but nonetheless, in a ramshackle almost derelict property across from Wales, with light coming through the floorboards, the Iraq pavilion had set up shop and because of the contested legacy of our UK involvement in the invasion, the art was proving a talking point. Ed Vaizey, the urbane and supportive UK Minister for Culture, visited the Wales pavilion officially in an itinerary to take in Wales and Scotland, having started out from the British Pavilion in the Giardini. With him was his small posse of DCMS officials and his ministerial civil servant escort. He had been impressed by Tim Davies's exhibition, taken it in. The exhibition had included a set of enigmatic sanded postcards where landscape is obliterated leaving suspended bridges in non-relational space. The works can look superficially like beguiling eighteenth-century architectural watercolours, before some of their other metaphorical considerations surface.

Osi engaged the Minister in conversation on the bright threshold of the Santa Maria Ausiliatrice church, home of 'Cymru yn Fenis'. His was a carefully triangulated argument. Some opening pleasantries about the international gathering of nations, the importance for Wales to have its artist in such an international constellation and yes, to present distinctive voices and not the homogenous. Maybe there was a passing reference to the British pavilion having really become, over the years, the London pavilion or at best the M25 pavilion (there were some twitches now from officials in the background). Maybe the briefing to the Minister had indicated just how positive it had been to have 'the nations and regions' on hand in Tracy Emin's year, if for no other reason than to deflect criticism of a certain meretricious vein in the presentation of her work then.

But then Osi moved in mischievously and continued his gravelly banter. They were, actually, as is Ed Vaizey's wont and Osi's

39

Osi with Arts Minister Ed Vaisey, Venice Biennale, 2013

affability, getting on really well. Osi returned to the United Nations aspect of the Biennale and cordially invited the minister to join him, cross the bridge and visit the Iraqi pavilion. 'I'm afraid the minister is on a very tight schedule', or words to that effect were probably offered at that point and with a final welshcake the Minister, in the twinkle of an eye, was gone. Osi's eye.

Two figures. Oil on canvas

The Music of Colours

M WYNN THOMAS

When I think of Osi Osmond I think of song. There is a simple personal reason for that. When arrangements were being made for his daughter's marriage, Osi asked my daughter Elin, a professional soloist, to record some Welsh folk-songs that could be played during the ceremony. And in return he kindly presented her with a striking painting from his *Hawk and Helicopter* suite of images that reflect graphically on the sinister co-incidence of bird and war machine over the beautifully estuarine landscape of Llansteffan.

But, of course, this was no arbitrary exchange of painting for song. For Osi – a lyrical painter, enchanted his entire life by what the artist Ceri Richards, following the poet Vernon Watkins, termed 'The Music of Colours' – image and song both belong to the single circulating currency of vivid imaginative apprehension of the world that we so casually, and too uncomprehendingly, term 'the arts'. That, though, is not to deny each art form its precious singularity. As he has piercingly written during the course of an impassioned advocacy of painting (that 'inconvenient means of being an artist' currently so scorned by 'the art-speak freemasonry of curators, academics, critics and administrators'), 'paint takes us into places where we would never normally go, simply because those places could only be brought into being by the process of painting.'

'Places': Osi is an artist who has always been passionately concerned to 'know his place,' and who has consistently used his painting to precisely that end. Visit the Welsh Writers Database section of Literature Wales's website and you'll learn that he was born in 'Wattstown'. Except that he wasn't. He was actually born in Wattsville, and is therefore native of a spot in the Sirhowy Valley very different from that in the familiar and fashionable Rhondda Valley where Literature Wales seems anxious to place him. From

Osi's point of view, the confusion could be said to be indicative of contemporary Wales's ignorance of itself; its insecure hold on the map of its own identity; its self-alienating unfamiliarity with the myriad places and location of which it is in fact composed. He, by contrast, realised from his very beginning as an artist, that painting would involve him going to places in Wales he hadn't previously even known existed. And such excursions began with the emblematic journey he, along with many other valleys arts students, undertook in his youth, 'down to the coastal towns, the journey by train and bus becoming psychogeographic artistic seminars in descending and ascending from colliery landscape to painting studio.' From the very outset, then, painting began to take him to regions, both geographical and psychic, he might otherwise never have visited.

And as he travelled, he began to sense there were extensive areas of Wales that didn't speak his language, even though their inhabitants did. His was the experience memorably voiced by R. S. Thomas in his seminal poem 'Welcome':

> You can come in.
> You can come a long way;
> We can't stop you.
> You can come up the roads
> Or by railway;
> You can walk this country
> From end to end;
> But you won't be inside;
> You must stop at the bar,
> The old bar of speech.

Osi became disturbed, as an artist, by his lack of inwardness with some of the localities to which he was attracted and came to appreciate that 'the morphology of place is deeply affected... by language loss.' In works such as David Jones's *The Sleeping Lord* he found a form of art dedicated to celebrating 'through text and inscription how the land holds a hidden spirituality of place through its naming.' Learning the Welsh language became for him a prerequisite for his progress in painting, and he came to share R.S. Thomas's hostility to such visitors and incomers as tried to impose their own 'foreign' language on Welsh places, in the process damaging their deep geo-cultural structure; affecting what Gerard Manley Hopkins might have termed the quiddity of their 'inscape'. On one occasion, when visitors to the west Wales locality in which he eventually settled asked for directions to 'Windsor', he directed them back across the M4 and advised them to head for Reading, although he knew full well they were searching for a local farm whose ancient Welsh name had recently been changed by its new monoglot English owners to that of the celebrated royal residence.

Through the medium of paint, he has developed a principled sensitivity to the psycho-geography of landscape. He scrupulously respects the precious integrity of place, both at the aesthetic level of its delicate ecology of shape, texture, plane and colour and as a socio-cultural environment instinct with the life of the particular past that has shaped it. His educated artist's eye has made him an impassioned global investigator of threatened sites. Visiting the USA to sample Halloween and the incomparable New England Fall, he happens upon an exhibition of Native American cultural artefacts – which he suggestively identifies as 'the tribal memory made visual' – at the Smithsonian Institute. 'This', he writes, 'was a show of immense riches, massive, shiny, glistening yet sombre, somehow heavy with grief, like the sad and solid sweat and tears

of strange gods.' And viewed from this perspective, the blazing autumnal colours of New England take on a deeply moving elegiac aspect:

> The botanists explain these changes by saying the more physiological stress a tree is under, the more colour the leaves will develop: the trees are in shock, even perhaps in trauma.

For him all those Fall colours seem different shades of Red – the colour of the 'Red Man' who once flitted through the forest glades. They are the trauma of the American land made visible.

His eye is likewise drawn, in Darwin, Australia, to the squatter Aborigines, lethargically fringing the beach with its sun-worshippers and lurking listlessly near the large casino. Soon he strikes out into their country:

> Green primordial landscape stretches beyond the placid water of the billabong in front of our cabin to the rusty red Injalak Hill, the place of the Long Tom Dreaming, mist rises with the dawn, the water's edges long and curving, like a giant fallen boomerang, teeming with fish and patrolled by crocodiles. Pelicans, ibises, egrets, geese, kites, parakeets and eagles pattern the shimmering morning air.

And with the help of a native artist, Gabriel, he gradually learns to read images from Dream Time, often recorded on rock in:

> paints ...almost all made by the artists; the pigments natural, white from chalk or the ash of particular trees, black from crushed charcoal, the reds, browns and yellows ground from

ochre, extracted from tree sap, juices, flowers, seeds, berries, insects, body fluids or blood, while natural gums fix the pigments. With limited colour, grass brush, bark support, the indigenous artists and the specific subject matter, these works have an extraordinarily powerful affinity with this place.

This is the kind of art to which Osi Osmond has himself consistently aspired, one which is grounded in such perceptions as that 'the red sandstone of Llansteffan, where I now live, is so different from the blue pennant limestone of my original Sirhowy valley home.' The remark occurs in an essay in which he sadly deplores the lack of any trace of the local, of the vernacular, in the materials out of which buildings across Wales are fashioned. The marble and granite that floor the new Swansea shopping centre, he notes, have been imported from China. 'Shop in Swansea', he caustically writes, 'walk on China.' For him these are the tawdry signs of what – recalling geologists' division of deep time into such eras as the Cambrian and the Pleistocene – he dubs the 'Peripatetic' age. And he contrasts the west's consumer-propelled globetrotting with the incessant travel of young boys from the Nuba people of the Sudan who have to keep moving in order to avoid being forcibly recruited by some sinister militia or other.

Osi Osmond once memorably described a prominent artist of the day as given to 'spelling by creative lunge'. He himself is as talented a writer as he is an artist, his essays – that cry out for collection into some more permanent form – bristling with barbed epithets and combative aphorisms. Museum assistants are styled 'sherpas for the uninitiated', Grayson Perry ceramics are 'sparklingly crazed with kitsch', London curators display an 'Ealing Comedy fear of that other, dark, uncharted Britain' to which Wales belongs, and postmodernism is derided for 'dining out on history'. But

astringent though his comments on the cravenly provincial, the smugly metropolitan, and the ephemerally fashionable may be, his imagination and intelligence (each an aspect of the other, of course) are invariably hospitable to the genuine in whatever guise and in whatever place it might appear. Thus, in the midst of an otherwise less than enthusiastic review of an exhibition of British Art generously 'toured' from London to the provinces (Cardiff), his attention is arrested by an image entitled 'In the House of My Father'. This takes the form of 'a large photo of a hand cupping a tiny model house made from skin.' Instantly responding to the deep, resonant humanity of this example of a conceptual art that is normally not at all to his painterly taste, he is further moved to discover that the artist was Donald Rodway, 'who had suffered from infancy with sickle cell anaemia and had died two years earlier at the age of thirty-seven.'

Art may, then, be fashioned out of the colours of personal, as well as cultural, trauma. Osi Osmond, who has himself had to struggle recently with life-threatening illness, has always been aware of this, which is why he has remained confident of painting's capacity to take the full measure of life. Of the New England Fall, he further wrote:

> It is the scientists say, the result of the dryness of the air, the colours are frozen, the leaves do not simply rot, they shift colour at different rates, some are still a deep living green, while others on the same tree are moving more quickly through the spectrum of autumnal change.

But vary as they may, to reflect the different conditions of living, the colours of the Fall, like the colours of Osi Osmond's painting and writing, sing out their magnificat of life to the very last.

Osi's brief eternity

JOHN OSMOND

Although we share the same surname and are from the same corner of Wales we think it unlikely that we are genetically related. But there is a stronger, spiritual connection between us. I think it is to do with a passion for language and the way it interconnects with the landscapes of our country. Osi's great gift is that he is able to complete the circle of these connections through the images he creates.

His most intensely visited landscape is the coastline where he has lived for many decades. He has constantly drawn and painted it from various vantage points on the Llansteffan peninsular. Depending on the direction he looks he can face out to sea east over Cefn Sidan and across to the Gower, south over Pendine to Lundy and Caldy Island, and west towards Laugharne. Every day I encounter one of the hundreds of images he has made here. Osi gave it me on my sixtieth birthday.

Another of his paintings I have is a lovely view of a sunset from a high place overlooking Laugharne, one of many he executed at this point. If you could put them together you would chart the movement of the setting sun across the horizon. For a number of years he regularly visited this spot at dusk, regardless of the weather. He seems to have painted instinctively and intuitively, without any pre-drawing. Each time he found something new and realized it with a remarkable series of flowing brush strokes and flashes of colour. As he once put it, 'these watercolours of the sunset are my way of holding on to the beauty of the Earth and the wonder of life itself.'

Osi is a great enthusiast and a great teacher. Of course, the two go together. My encounters with him invariably prompt an outpouring of words as he senses a receptive audience for his preoccupations of the moment. At these times I have learnt most of what I know about the enthralling renaissance in Welsh landscape painting in recent decades by artists such as Iwan Bala, Mary Lloyd Jones and others.

Invariably I would meet Osi, a member of the Gorsedd of Bards, at the various peregrinations of the National Eisteddfod. One I particularly remember was at Ebbw Vale in 2010. That year the encampment was built on top of what had once been the town's steelworks. Underfoot was a mixture of gravel, compressed coke and concrete, a dustbowl inheritance from the first industrial revolution. Not long before it had been a vast elongated mass of towers and sheds spewing flame, steam and smoke, a veritable Dante's inferno. Osi told me he remembered travelling to Ebbw Vale by train when the steelworks was still open. 'You passed through a cloud of steam and sparks before arriving in the station', he recalled. Looking around the Maes he said he felt a terrible, painful energy in the concrete beneath our feet, a kind of gasping and groaning of a different, suppressed culture straining against the lightness of what was being created upon it. In place of the steelworks now sat a gentle billowing cornucopia of all that is gentle and good about Welsh culture, the arts and the creative industries, a metaphor for modern Wales. 'There's a bit of psycho-geography going on here', Osi observed, a mischievous glint in his eye.

In 2005 he embarked on an exploration of Josef Herman, a Polish artist and Jewish refugee who settled amongst us in the middle of the twentieth century. Herman taught us how to look again at what has been a central image of the Welsh experience, mining and the mining valleys. As part of a project we were undertaking at the Institute of Welsh Affairs, on cultural connections between

Drawing. *Pentowyn*. 2008. Charcoal. 18"x16"
Private collection

Eastern Europe and Wales, I asked Osi to write a monograph on Herman's life and work. In the late 1930s he had escaped persecution by moving to Brussels. After the war broke out he fled first to France, and then Britain. But the family Herman left behind in Warsaw all perished in the Holocaust, a tragedy that conditioned the remainder of his life.

At first he settled in Glasgow and then London but eventually in 1944 he found his way to Wales and Ystradgynlais. There he went through a transformative experience, what Osi described as an epiphany. Herman arrived on a hot afternoon in high summer, and was impressed by the light from a copper sky that reddened the stones of the cottages. Nearby a stream flowed under a bridge, emerging from darkness but surrounded by a rich sparkling light. He was gazing at this scene when suddenly a group of miners appeared on the bridge, stood and talked and then turned and went their different ways. Here is part of Osi's account of the episode:

> Josef Herman might have spent the whole of his thirty-three years waiting for that one moment on the bridge at Ystradgynlais. The refugee from intolerance looked up and saw the sun set spectacularly behind the homecoming miners. In an instant all his anxious musings on life, humanity and subject matter seemed resolved in an overwhelming but glorious revelation that here was a way forward for his practice as a painter. The sun had silhouetted the men as great monolithic blocks, throwing into clear contrast the dark and essential matter of mankind and the life giving force of the sun setting behind them.[1]

In her Introduction to the essay, Herman's widow Nina quoted from the catalogue to one of his exhibitions in the 1970s:

> One does not seek roots: one grows them. And one is able to grow them only when one owns an organic energy, a capacity for inner development, which in turn owns as its necessary counterpart a capacity for response to the outer world, to nature and one's fellow beings...[2]

This describes very well Osi Rhys Osmond's own outlook and attributes and explains why he responded so warmly to Josef Herman's work. Of course, the work focuses largely on the experience of a Welsh mining community that again, is central to Osi's own experience. He was brought up in Wattsville in the lower Sirhowy Valley (not Wattstown in the Rhondda, as some have stated) and his whole life and work have been affected by that inheritance. His father and mother were both born there and his father, uncles and grandfathers on both sides worked as miners. It is somewhat puzzling, therefore, that we had to wait until 2012 before Osi decided to devote an exhibition, at the Rhondda Heritage Centre, to work that derived from this essential background. The exhibition vibrantly demonstrated the influence his people and their collective memories and landscape have had on his outlook. In his notes on the exhibition Osi observed:

> I have always been obsessed by the landscape in which I grew up and the pure abstract beauty of the changing colour of the bracken covered hills surrounding the valley that became perhaps the dominant factor in making me as an artist.

So how could he have ignored this important terrain for so long? In part the answer was contained within the exhibition itself since

Coal and Impressionism (detail). 2011. Collage and charcoal

some of the drawings and paintings went back many years, and had been waiting for that moment to see the light of day. More trenchantly, I think Osi had been waiting for the right moment when he could gather himself to say something fresh and arresting about a landscape that has been trodden upon by countless artists and photographers in search of a certain received image. This is confirmed by his exhibition notes, which continue:

> As an art student I resisted the vogue for a certain kind of image of the mining industry and sought to create something that spoke more about the eternal qualities of the landscape in which I found myself. The more sentimental view of the mining life that had become the accepted norm in the visual arts was something that I felt had been done and added little to any understanding of how that community lived, worked and socialised.

Open cast working. 2011. Water colour. 30" x 24"

It was a highly political exhibition. It was art that kicked with a vengeance. For me the most striking large-scale painting in the exhibition was of Nine Mile Point colliery, at Cwmfelinfach, where Osi's father and other relatives had worked. At its peak it employed 1,105 men who lived mainly in the surrounding villages of Cwmfelinfach and Wattsville. Constructed between 1902 and 1905 it was originally known as Coronation Colliery, but renamed Nine Mile Point because that was the distance of the tramroad to the colliery from the edge of Lord Tredegar's boundary in Newport.

Osi's painting focuses on the most significant moment in the colliery's history, the 1935 'staydown' strike when 164 men protested against the use of scab labour. This was the first ever 'staydown strike' in the history of the south Wales coalfield. Osi's

Grandfather, a Baptist lay preacher, led the service during the Sunday the miners spent underground. The painting uses typeface and newspaper headlines to drive home the politics. And, for sure, this was a struggle to bear comparison with anything that happened in the history of the labour movement across Europe during the first half of the twentieth century. The stay-down strike followed riots that had broken out in the colliery some years earlier in protest again at the employment of blackleg labour. More than 700 miners and villagers rioted and it took days for the police to gain control.

All this should be an essential part of our collective memory and inheritance, indeed a warning for our own times. Yet Nine Mile

48

Point and the heroism of its class-based struggles and tragedies – seven men were killed during the construction of the mine in 1904 – have largely been forgotten. Osi's painting, now in the collection of the National Museum of Wales will serve as a constant reminder of this part of our inheritance.

The stay-down strike was provoked by Davies Ocean's private union, the Gregory Union, a group of violent mercenary thugs, mainly ex-miners, who were shipped around the coalfield to terrorise the coalfield's recalcitrant miners. They went down and ripped the miners tools from the bar on which they were locked after work; this was a red rag to a bull, tools were personal, and the miners bought their own tools. The miners of Nine Mile Point resisted by staying underground, and so a new and revolutionary tactic in the struggle for justice was born.

And interestingly, what is never discussed in Wales or anywhere else for that matter is the fact that during the late nineteenth century around fifty thousand tons of carbon particles from the fireplaces and ovens of Paris were suspended above the Paris basin, which has its own distinct atmosphere. After the loss, in the Franco-Prussian war of 1871, of the coalfields of Alsace Lorraine, much coal for Paris came from south Wales, generally house-coal from the mines of Ocean Davies. The suspended carbon particles from the coal created iridescent skies, rainbow effects and an atmosphere that deeply influenced the Impressionists. Hence the title of the picture, *Coal and Impressionism*.

Later in the 1920s Davies's granddaughters bought some of the most important Impressionist paintings that now adorn the walls of our National Museum and Galleries in Cardiff. So the circle turns; this is a personal theory, not born out by research but by careful consideration of the facts. I should like to see a deeper examination of this theory.
(*EDITORS NOTE*. The last paragraph was added by Osi himself)

Osi sets out ambitious objectives for this and other artworks he has created around his valleys inheritance:

> The large-scale drawings layer the historic, geological and social phenomena of the area with contemporary observations, creating what I refer to as 'graphic essays'. These drawings combine images and words: landscape and memory, facts, figures, friends and family among speculations on geology, social history and genealogy. They endeavor to establish a sense of time compressed, a concatenation of dense time reflected in a current moment; acting perhaps as a kind of visual psycho-geographic document.

I think these works achieve even more. As Osi goes on to say, they reflect the community that made him and those who went before him. But above all, they bequeath, as he puts it, an essential mystery – 'is a history and a wonder at our brief eternities and where and when we spend them'. In that phrase Osi captures how, through his unique combinations of images and words, he has been able to convey our own special place and identity in the eternity of time's passing.

1. Osi Rhys Osmond, *Carboniferous Collision, Josef Herman's Epiphany in Ystradgynlais*, IWA, 2005, page 25.
2. Jack Lindsay, 'Introduction' to the catalogue of a touring exhibition, *Josef Herman: Paintings and Drawings*, Summer 1975.

49

Colliery winding gear. 2011. Charcoal

Colliery winding gear. 2011. Watercolour

51

Risca Colliery. 2011. Charcoal on paper

Risca Colliery. 2011. Charcoal on paper

53

Rhondda 48 Rock vein. 2011. Charcoal and mixed media

Risca Colliery. 2011. Charcoal on paper

56

Dazzled / Llachar. 2002. Oil on canvas. 24"x18"
Private collection

On painting

CHRISTINE KINSEY

> Painting is both lucid and miraculous coming as it does
> from knowledge, sensibility and intention.
>
> Osi Rhys Osmond.

Osi studied at Newport and Monmouthshire College of Art between 1959 and 1964. The landmark building with its green copper dome had been built as a Technical Institute, opening in 1910, on the banks of the River Severn in Newport, Gwent. It was an Art College between 1958 and 1975.

The Edwardian marble entrance hall and sweeping staircase led up to a hierarchy of floors that accommodated students studying a range of visual disciplines. These culminated on the top floor Antique Room that housed the Fine Art Painting students. It had a corridor lined with plaster casts of figures from Antiquity, and the Life Painting room under the green dome was where the human form was studied through drawing and painting.

The Art College attracted students mainly from the eastern Valleys of south Wales, who were supported by local authority grants to study the four-year course for the National Diploma in Design. It was here as a seventeen-year-old art student, who had recently enrolled on this course, that I first encountered the eighteen-year-old Osi. He was walking with a group of male students through the main hall that was used as a canteen. We were in the Beatnik era and the perceived attitude and dress was dour and bleak. The effervescent enthusiasm of Osi's voice and persona were in overt contrast to those around him.

Art education at the time was changing, moving away from the academic influence of the Royal Academy and Slade Schools of Art to an interpretation, sometimes a misinterpretation, of the ideas and concepts of the German Bauhaus. But in Newport, it was still the monochromatic world reflected in the traditional (representational) subject matter that we were encouraged to paint. Osi chose to specialise in painting for the final two years of the NDD, which was awarded after completing an examination that included painting a composition with three figures in it. Newport College of Art had garnered a substantial reputation for Fine Art, especially painting, under the tutelage of the painter Tom Rathmell. We were encouraged to paint and draw our environment, and since most of the students came from the coal-mining areas, this naturally became one of the main subjects. The paintings of Joseph Herman were influential on how students portrayed their environment. He had lived in Ystradgynlais for eleven years from 1944, some of the time using a derelict 'pop factory' as a studio. Student paintings often followed similar colour and composition to those seen in Herman's paintings: miners walking up a hill, with their backs to the viewer, with strategically placed telegraph poles on the right and left of the picture and telegraph wires heading into a distant landscape. Sometimes these monochrome images were punctuated by a red neckerchief or a setting sun.

Osi had grown up in Wattsville in the Sirhowy valley, where his father and grandfather had been miners, and his paintings portrayed a very different picture of this coal mining community. As Osi says:

> As an art student I resisted the vogue for a certain kind of
> image of the mining industry and sought to create
> something that spoke more about the eternal qualities of
> the landscape in which I found myself. The more
> sentimental view of the mining life that had become the

accepted norm in the visual arts was something that I felt had been done, and added little to any understanding of how that community lived, worked and socialised.
(From the catalogue *Tir a Threftadaeth*)

The first large painting of Osi's I saw were of the hills surrounding his home. They were painted in strong oranges, reds and yellows; the colour, he said, of the hills in Autumn. He had been aware of and had appreciated the power and wonder of colour since childhood, and the sheer joy of colour in this painting has stayed with me from that time. He says:

> I have always been obsessed by the landscape in which I grew up and the pure abstract beauty of the changing

Red Greyhound/Milgi Coch. 1997. Oil on canvas. 51cm x 61cm
Private collection

colour of the bracken covered hills surrounding the valley that became perhaps the dominant factor in making me as an artist.

During the NDD course we were taught to make drawing books of all sizes and to draw at every opportunity and Osi, to this day, constantly draws in his hand-made books. His creative process has been based on 'thinking visually' and 'paying attention' to the world around him in all its forms by gathering information for further consideration when creating images. On occasions, drawing in his book had unexpected consequences. The Sculpture Department of Newport College of Art was on Bolt Street, in the dockland area of Newport. After class (and some classes started at 9.30 am and finished at 9.00pm) Osi and friends would go to the local pub for a drink. Often the pubs were full of dockland workers and their reactions to Osi taking out his book and drawing in it meant that sometimes these drinking sojourns concluded in unexpected ways.

When Osi and his family moved to Clunderwen in Pembrokeshire he taught in Narberth County Secondary School. It is a cause of pride for him that his name was on the same plaque as the poet Waldo Williams, who had also taught at the school. Osi's great love of poetry includes that of Waldo's as well as many other Welsh poets writing in both languages and international poets whose writing he has 'experienced' and which has nourished his visual language. He has written about the relationship of the word and the image, particularly in the culture of Wales. In the chapters 'Visual Voices and Contemporary Echoes' and the 'Conclusion' in the book *Imaging the Imagination*[1] as well as in other essays such 'Taking Welsh sensibility out into the wider world – Welsh artists of the century' in *New Welsh Review* and most recently in *Encounters* with *R.S.*[2], 'The Ornithologist Poet as a Bird', he contributes an original insight into the culture of Wales.

The breadth of subject matter in his paintings, his drawings and prints range from evocations of his immediate environment to responses to international events. In one of his earliest solo exhibitions at Chapter Art Centre, Cardiff (December 1975 – January 1976) the titles of his paintings suggest this range of concerns, from watercolour paintings of St Govan to paintings in gouache about Joe DeMaggio and J.F. Kennedy as well as oil paintings called *Odessa Steps* and *Sharpsville*. The inter-relationship between the local and international was epitomised in his exhibition *Cymru a'r Wlad Sanctaidd*. Osi's father and grandfather had been lay preachers in Wattsville and Risca. He had grown up in a home where the chapel was an integral part of everyday life. He heard stories from the Bible that described Middle Eastern places and landscapes. He felt throughout his childhood that he knew these places as clearly, if not more clearly, than those places in Wales that bore the same names.

Between 1984 and 1987 he visited the Middle East and the result were paintings of landscapes depicting places with the same names in Wales as the Holy Land, names like Hermon, Salem, Peniel and Bethlehem, Nebo and Bethesda. The contrast of colour between these paintings was extraordinary. I first saw the paintings in an exhibition in the circular gallery in the Library of Haverfordwest. The juxtaposition of the cool, deeply velvet colours of the landscapes in Wales against the searing vibrancy of the colours of the Middle Eastern landscapes, created a tension of colour that usurped accepted orthodox Christian religious imagery of Biblical lands perpetrated by many of the churches and chapels. He says, 'Colour is the basis of my craft – I talk colour,

I speak through colour, I use colour to express myself and convey my ideas.' This obsession transported to the Holy Land and Southern Sudan, in 1996 under the auspices of Christian Aid, gave us a personal vision of remarkable beauty. His experience of meeting the people living under the dominance of colonialist violence left an indelible mark on his political thinking.

Osi's involvement in the political life of Wales has engaged with both local and national issues as has his commitment to the cultural life of Wales. His paintings in the series 'Ar y Graean' painted in 1999 incorporate an image of a rusty tank with it chains trapped by the rocks on the coast near his home in Llansteffan. The tank has been creatively transformed in his paintings, through the alchemy of paint and the imagination, into an object glowing with colour and becoming a metaphor for Wales. 'Ar y Graean' was printed as the cover of poet Mererid Hopwood's book *Singing in Chains*[3] which explores *cynghanedd*, strict-metre Welsh language poetry, and how these rules of engagement could, in fact, rather than being restrictive, create a freedom in writing. The painting was also shown in the exhibition META accompanied by Elinor Wyn Reynold's poem *Mae 'na ddynion yn gorwedd mewn caeau ym mhob man drwy Gymru*, an example of how the conjunction of word and image in the culture of Wales has powerful resonances.

Osi has, sometimes, chosen to paint the same subject matter in a variety of ways which can be seen in a series such as 'Ar y Graean' and 'Fenws Machynlleth'. The series of paintings, 'Machlud/Sunset', which he has been working on for many years, are watercolour paintings of the sun setting over Carmarthen Bay, made in his handmade painting book. The significance of this engagement with a single subject offers the viewer an intense experience of this landscape in all weathers and at specific times of the day. The result of this engagement is an exploration in time, where light and dark exist at the same time as light transforms into dark, day transforms into night, where opposites coalesce; life and death, creation and destruction, inner and outer, microcosm and macrocosm, presence and absence. This can be equated with the Jungian concept of the Nigredo as he described it in his Mysterium Coniunctionis lectures; the dying of the light in order that it is reborn, bringing life back into the world. These concepts imbue the paintings of Mark Rothko, and the later paintings of Anselm Kiefer. Osi's paintings in this series portray a deeply meditative process but also, as always, he is 'paying attention' to other informative connections to the world around him.

His exhibitions *Ymateb* (Response) and *Hawk and Helicopter* were created while observing and painting the 'Machlud' (Sunset) series from a high point on the coast looking south westerly towards Carmarthen Bay. These paintings highlight his engagement with the natural world and also his response to the violence and destruction taking place in the Middle East, Europe and Asia. He says of this time:

> Sitting quietly in the same place I see many birds and animals, the Peregrine falcon holds a particular allure for me and I often see and hear military activity, the manoeuvres of planes and helicopters bombing and shelling the target area of Cefn Sidan. Witnessing this I sense the beauty of nature, land and sea compromised by these violent, aggressive intrusions, momentarily the Earth loses its virtue to man's madness but nature and the sun redeem and these watercolours of the sunset are my way of holding onto the the beauty of the Earth and to the wonder of life itself.

In *Tir a Threftadaeth*, Osi returns to imagery that depicts his childhood family and the mining community where he grew up. In his most recent work he describes himself as a 'graphic psycho-geographer' and his images are a form of 'deep mapping' that includes 'images and words, landscape and memory, facts, figures, friends and family among speculations on geology, social history and genealogy'. He refers to these works as 'large-scale drawings that layer the historic, geological and social phenomena of the area with contemporary observations, creating what I refer to as 'graphic essays'. They encapsulate a 'history and wonder of our brief eternities and where and when we spend them.'

Osi has asked the question 'What is art for?' in an age of ubiquitous visual imagery. He answers the question through the wealth of visual imagery that he has created through painting which he says 'brings into physical form, painting and poetry, those thoughts, images and realisations for which no other means of being apprehended exists.'

1. *Imaging the Imagination: An exploration of the relationship between the image and the word in the art of Wales*, eds. Christine Kinsey and Ceridwen Lloyd Morgan. Gomer Press, Llandysul 2005.
2. *Encounters with RS*. ed. John Barnie. The H'mm Foundation, Swansea 2013.
3. *Singing in Chains*, Mererid Hopwood, Gomer Press, Llandysul 2004.

Osi: A palimpsest in persona

DAI SMITH

Re-wind

The Ruperra Social Club in Trethomas, adjunct to Bedwas. Still a mining village in February 1985 when I go there to see the final scene to be shot of Karl Francis's film *Ms Rhymney Valley, 1985*. I am writing a piece for *The Listener* that will appear when the film is made and released. It is one of Karl Francis's fictive documentaries, in which real people are placed within its frame rather than directed, and real people, like Neil Kinnock will appear as themselves. He will be there tonight on the 15th of February to be filmed. Neil, as leader of the Labour Party, will present a (real) cheque to the Rhymney Valley Miners' Support Groups in aid of the families who had members in jail because of the strike. And Kim Howells, Research Officer and Spokesman for the NUM, and Terry Thomas, the Vice President in south Wales, will be there, to cheer, to applaud, and to be filmed. The main room of the Club – dance floor, stage and bar – is abuzz with people, lights, music, a scurrying film crew moving amongst the scattered tables and chairs, and filming snatches of dialogue from the principal 'actors' who are part of the set-up of a Beauty Contest that will, in the end, be nothing of the kind. The real Ms. Rhymney 1985 will be a newborn baby. A future being conjured out of a receding past, but with values cherished. Even at this unfinished, sporadic level of bits and pieces, people sense they are at something special. The film will be met with acclaim. The strike will be lost. That is not far away and it is surely sensed, though few will say it openly.

Amongst the people I am introduced to by Karl is one of his 'actors', an old friend of his, so handsome I begin by thinking he is indeed an actor. Not so. This is Osi Osmond, not long turned forty, jet-black hair, a tangle of curls, a whipcord body and a craggy face, bisected by an aquiline nose. He behaves as if he was a rock star. I get the impression from his voluble conversational, buttonholing style that he thinks more of us from the Valleys should be strutting our stuff as rock stars. That we deserve it. That our places need it. That it all may be too late. That we have to do it anyway. No choice, see.

Fast Forward (1)

We are sat in company, Osi and me, at a table outside a very late-closing bar in a small campo in Venice. It is the Biennale of 2007. My first. I am there as Chair of Arts Council Wales. Osi has been coming for many years, to see what is truly new and what is merely new. We are putting a collective dent into a bottle of very good grappa, chosen by Osi, naturally. At midnight, in the stone-soaked heat of June in Venice, the conversation is lively, and gets livelier. Osi has long since gone west, to live and teach in Carmarthenshire and his search for what is older and truer, not just truly old, has along the way led him to elected politics (Plaid, naturally) and fluency in the Welsh language (*bien sûr*). I tell him he's gone Native. He tells me he always was. He explains the Biennale to me, its value and its crap. He thinks it's great that Wales has finally established its own Pavilion there. A national niche. He opines that most of what has been on show from Wales hitherto, is neither Welsh enough nor good enough. We discuss Art and the Nation. And Identity. No one agrees. Osi wins most of the time though, genial and informed. Osi is dressed for Venice. A blue-striped cotton jacket. An open-necked deep blue shirt. White cotton trousers and silver buckled black belt. No socks in his deck shoes. This time I do not think rock star. I think movie director onset. But if we drink any more of the grappa, I am sure we will have a terrible hangover. Osi says it will not be so. Not with this grappa since he, personally, has chosen it. In the morning there are no hangovers. Osi magic.

Aberdaron (*detail*). 2013. Mixed media

62

Fast Forward (2)

We are in the Welsh Pavilion on the Guidecca, Venice Biennale 2009. Osi had applied to become an Arts Council Wales member, saying it was against his better judgment, that he reserved the right to speak out, that all of it, none of it, any of it, was 'Welsh enough'. He is appointed. He becomes the Chair of the Council's Venice Biennale sub-committee. Plates move. Tectonically so. Wales is represented this year by a single artist. John Cale from Garnant near Ammanford and New York. He makes a piece of video work that condemns the familial 'English Not' of his childhood, and is seen by some who view the films to be 'dissing' Wales, making it melancholic and oppressive. It all ends with a video in which Cale is water-boarded. To indict those who do so to others of course. In America, directly so. And in Wales? Some, who like the quiescent enamelled sheen of most contemporary video pieces, think Cale is an imposter, an impersonator, and a fraud who is messy instead of highly resolved. I think it is moving. Its content is fierce – its execution is passionate. It is certainly 'Welsh enough'. Together, sipping Prosecco, Osi and Cale are brother rock-stars. Under Osi's guidance Wales has arrived in Venice, and in succeeding Festivals will stay there. Osi is pleased. We are in the future at last. I remind him of when we had both sat, some years before, in an invited audience at the National Museum to listen to their strategic plans and to give our 'expert' opinion. Osi had stood up and said that the glass display cases full of Nantgarw porcelain and Swansea china were like his grandmother's front room and that someone (he'd volunteer) should take a stick and smash them open, and all the china with it. I had applauded. I think we were alone in this view. Cale had laughed at the story. Osi asked had I noticed how the rock star's expensive walking boots had their laces untied all the way down, eyehole after eyehole, loose and free. You could trip over those, Osi said. Better watch out for the stairs on the way down.

Close-up

Rhondda Heritage Park. The gallery upstairs. A Saturday, early March 2012. Osi has asked me to open – though naturally he will speak as well! – his major retrospective exhibition entitled *Tir a Threftadaeth*. His land, his legacy. We arrive early to take it in. I have seen Osi's work over the years but not like this, so much of it, so varied in style, so glowing, so loving. Yes, that is the word I would choose for it, though the love might be as fierce and demanding as it is tender and yielding. Landscapes everywhere, all speaking of his south Wales. There is a long-distance capture in a wash of misty blues and rain-drenched greens of Abergwynfi, its slopes and copses and roofs that feels alpine. But the pre-coal Valleys were indeed often compared by the early Victorian traveller to the Alps, remote and untouched. As they are again in some places today like, say, Pen-pych at the top of the Rhondda Fawr. They are not, though, and despite the predatory instincts of pocketbook developers, they will never become Wales's next (and last) National Park. Not while Osi, and me too I'd add, have breath left to scorn the de-populators. Osi is astute enough, for all that, never to sentimentalise his subject, never to re-populate it with Lowryesque kitsch figures. He prefers the bleak truth, aligned with a tinge of defiance.

In front of me on a far wall, there is a piece that holds me immediately. I stand transfixed. There are Dufy-like ink scratches, vertical black lines for telegraph poles and a forest green grove of incongruous trees, then flecks of lime green on the far mountain slopes, fresh amongst the barren scree of rocks and grey shale, with patchy blemishes of coal where the industry had seeped to the surface. He has titled it 'Maerdy, Rhondda 1983'. The perspective is from halfway up the mountain road that plunges down from the plateau that would take you over and up to Aberdare. It is not a literal picture though it is, in its sweet, sharply drawn and delicately coloured sketch of tilted terraces and switchback roads recognizably that end township of the Rhondda Fach. For me it is heartbreaking. Because it is of Maerdy. Renamed by the coal-owner press in Cardiff as 'Little Moscow' after the 1926 General Strike, the base of one of Britain's greatest trade union leaders, Arthur Horner, Communist President of the South Wales Miners' Federation from 1936 until he became General Secretary of the National Union of Mineworkers in 1946, and in itself a site, real as well as dreamlike, of an alternative world. Because it is Maerdy in my native Rhondda. From the 1960s on I spent years researching its history and writing it up for the book I published (with Hywel Francis) in 1980, *The Fed: A History of the South Wales Miners in the Twentieth Century*, in which one chapter is called, 'The Fate of Little Moscow', and shows a photograph from 1926 inside the Workmen's' Institute, the cerebral centre of Maerdy, where billiards and books, and newspapers and debates, and dances and a gymnasium and a cinema, cradled the culture of a people. The photograph is of those people in December of the year of the lock-out when defeat had come to the British miners, and in Maerdy the men, and women and children of that distant world are standing in front of a full-length picture-poster of Lenin on one side and a gold embroidered red-silk banner on the other, a gift and a salute to Little Moscow from the working women of the Krasnaya garment District of Moscow. In the middle of his own picture, still standing in 1983, Osi has centred the largest building Maerdy had ever had – the Workingmen's Institute – solid, rose-pink, symbol of all that was once meant to be about hope. 1983. At the end of

the 1984-85 strike Maerdy will be the last pit in south Wales to go back to work. In defeat. But not broken. Not one miner from Maerdy broke the year-long strike. Within five years the colliery will close forever. Outside in the colliery yard of the Rhondda Heritage Park, a lone and loaded dram stands, with a collier's chalk message on it, a reminder that the last coal from the Rhondda came to the surface in 1990. In old Welsh 'Maer-dy' had meant 'The Home of the Slaves', a place for slave markets in the Dark Ages. The Workmen's Hall, its Home of Freedom, fell into disrepair and was demolished in 2009. Its lingering spirit is crucial to any eye focusing properly on Osi's picture. Landscape is about more than landscape, even when it is only implicit. Osi understands. From Wattsville in the Sirhowy Valley, Nye Bevan's valley, how would he not?

Everywhere in this exhibition of 2012 Osi's loving, forensic examination over the years of his landscape, in piece after piece, sees him transform what he has ingested into a mindscape. This is his interpretation of individual lives and a common history that has been as marked by where, as much as by when and how, it was experienced. Osi adds to this happenstance, however, a profundity of intent derived from his study and practice. He has a European sensibility, set within comparative traditions and practices, observed and absorbed. Osi is a graphic historian. Osi is a visual intelligence operating in the mode of a public intellectual. Osi is, within himself, a palimpsest of his subject, scoured clean and scrubbed over, until it emerges transformed, and made translucent by his hand and through his mind.

Nowhere is this more apparent than in the masterwork of that 2012 exhibition. It is Osi's own Map of Memory. In the end, as at the beginning, and I mean in and for itself, it is simply entrancing as a picture. Kestrels flying, again, into blue swatches of sky, pierced by funnelled tubes of light, above the red and burnt orange mound of Mynydd y Lan whilst, at a distance, the unlikely turquoise ribbon of Afon Sirhowy winds across the bottom of the picture and the latticed greenery of trees softens parts of the mountain above. Almost pastoral. Yet never so. Or not since other marks were made on this landscape. The bottom third opens it up with the precision of a surgeon's knife. Inked and etched collieries, stacks and winding gear, overhead cables from pylons lifting coal up and away, lines of coal trucks waiting, the purple and blue leaden heaps of muck and waste, the domino rows of terraced roofscapes, the industrial settlement of Wattsville, the livid pink and washed-out light that follows the human scavenging of the land.

Up close, really close, there is something else. If the landscape's mineral exploitation is what pulled a population in to work, so those people made lives that were humanely shaped, in dimension and in purpose, in values and growth. That sense of them has been conveyed usually in other forms – in words, in music, in gestures – more so than in visual form. And if visually, then mostly in portraiture, single and collective, taking them out of rather than melding them into their world. Osi does it differently. Look. Snapshots pop up amongst the houses. Family photographs are squares and oblongs on the mountainside. They are smart and tidy, these people. They are in their Sunday best. They are Osi's family and friends. It is Osi Rhys Osmond himself. His sister talks to me as I stare and stare at the art he has made. She tells me, though I did not ask, that his name was Donald then. The artist, in 2012, is a persona long since transmuted into a self-created Osi, but his is a creativity formed by these memory traces, which he writes in a spidery hand, as signposts and indicators, onto his map.

Little histories. Incidents. Markers of a life. I think he is as imprinted into this landscape of upbringing now as much as if he was as native to it as stone or grass or tree or bird. His is a painterly calligraphy of belonging.

A Loop
For this film will have no ending. It forms and re-forms, and echoes. I think of this whenever I see Osi at the Arts Council: in committees or in conference. He is, of course, a unique presence. When he is not talking, in measured or in passionate deliberation, he is drawing. The heads of his colleagues, I think. I do not ask to see them. They seem, as he does them, proof enough that we have an artist, a maker, amongst us. To say that he has been brave in his illness is to tell the simple truth, and to hell with the clichéd prose. This is no time for fastidious elegance. I tell him, with his colourfully embroidered Afghan hat on his head when his hair fell out, that with his eyes screwed up in amusement he looks like Lenin. He seems pleased. When his hair returns so does the look of the rock star. I guess he never went away. Osi gave me a small, coal black and silvery white picture he made, in dry-point, of the imprint of a fern, the kind that appears when you break apart the shiny fissured coal that has been squeezed underground for aeons to reveal the sprayed out fronds of a fern. In every detail just as it was, just as it will always be. Real. Vivid. Unchangeable. Defiant in the shape it holds and the story it is telling.

Fellow travellers

Karl Francis
Wyn Morris
David Parfitt
Mick and Thea Arnold
Hedley Jones
Noelle Francis

Red Horses. Oil on canvas

Notes, prose and poetry. An essay of sorts.

KARL FRANCIS

May 1959 From notes

FLASHBACK   SCENE 1

K: Alright mam?

M: How was London? Have some tea.

K: Met this boy Ozi on the bus.

M: Where is he from?

K: Wattsville, over the top, not far. He swears he knows Uncle Billy the preacher.

M: Not your uncle, your second cousin once removed. What does he do?

K: He paints

M: Well if he knows our Bill he must have a big heart ...
Bring him home – does he talk; not one of your shy ones?

My mother said,
And when Ozi carried her coffin in 1979 you will understand the reader and the painter and the film-maker are all of one creation. And when he asked me to carry his mother's coffin in 2011, as he had carried my mother's coffin in 1979, then you will understand I have known his family also, and been wisely, kindly advised and loved.

I see his mother's heart, his sister's smile, and Nathan's strength and in Ozi's paintings I see the family.

Note 2012

His whole family has inspired him.
Stella and his dad Malcom
and his painting of them in the street –
Inspired us. Inspires me. I dream of paintings
Ozi land the sign

Having a valley boy for a lifelong friend is Mafiaesque
and of the kindness,
Jesus kind.

I talk to Ozi's paintings every day and they answer back in the angelic way all of Ozi's art speaks and teaches, the stillness of paint so peaceful to behold. The eternity of a painting. I feel the energy and love and conversation. Ozi's work brings me so much that when I wish to meditate with the God of Love there is a marriage of peace and hope that is what Art brings to us all. To make permanent what is by its nature evanescent as Ozi is – the evanescent man.

> Am sure she said the pebbles sing
> A choice I make, she talks to god about her heart, her shame, her joy.
> A pebble on a beach will come and go, the salty wave
> will love caress, the pebble roars and raves,
> Seashells will sing and whistle down the wind

Ozi comes from one side of the same mountain as me; he to the north, me to the south, and our dads mining coal under the shared tip, in two separate pits eight miles apart as the pigeon flies, and barely ten yards between them underground.
Except for rock and death and floods and dust.
Above us the earth, and they half a mile down.

Our friendship born deep
Compassion from the start
We honour, we conquer,
We defend, we forgive.
And always we love.

Clwyf/Wound. 2009. Hand-mixed oil on canvas

My father Malcolm. 1991. Gouache. 36"x 24"
Private collection

Having a valley boy for a lifelong friend is Mafiaesque.
Honour and courage among artists; as Ozi shares so he receives
and being valley Mafia brings with it a real critique not just an Oh
and Ah but with the why and the how. Friendship is based on
respect and love and humour. And being in the same fight against
mediocrity and greed.

    A Prydderch boy with paint in Oziland.
    And as the we,
    the she,
    the hymn that Ozi is.
    We understand,
    The wisdom of the RS Thomas man –

    Ozi who is
    so deeply loved.
    The Painter's hand
    who shares his life, his love.
    The we, the him the them create
    Intelligence
    and
    Belonging.

Add to that the gifts of St Teilo and Aneurin Bevan to a family; the
love of painting and poetry, the listening to a woodpecker peck
and the lady next door shouting, asking if Ozi was home yet.

The sound of Mario Lanza in the lanes. Ozi who is loved
Who shares his life, his love.
Nearby a street of stories, and a hill at the back as big a garden as
you will ever see – to go wild in, makes Hyde Park look like a
puddle of green.

Two miners' sons off to Higher Education met on a bus, seen him at a dance in the High Cross Youth Club. And on that bus we listen and we learn.

The wisdom words we Welsh create with ease. Belonging too.

Notes 1959 Newport Art School
The Tom Rathmel time.

He was a friend of Sandra Phipps, the wonderful artist from the Church House, Bedwas and all that she and Veena Morris, Dave Peterson brought me to – and Ozi tied the knot of teaching all - the me I am in part was a gift as Ozi nurtured love for us, always encouraging the warriors from Newport Arts School and Ozi always the teacher and friend.

When he first he became very ill with cancer we cried.

> And love herself cries out
> I am my own reward
> and garden gates creak shut
>
> The fire burns, the couple silent in the night-time smile of stars
> The seagulls sleep, the waves slip back
> to leave the mud alive with life
> Let love be that reward enough.

And this is the Ozi I know – not simply because our paths crossed again in 1966 and the wars against Enoch Powell and Racism were fought and my wife Jan worked with him in Newport.

Note 1966/8
A pilgrimage always sewn together by other friends – Christine

Kinsey and Wyn Morris, where we shared ideas with a passion that is lost on Wales today. Wales a lost land. Discuss. Do not leave but stay and fight we agree. Ozi is Plaid. We stay with Labour.

NOTES FOR BROCHURE, 1968
I got to know Ozi deeply when he worked with my ex-wife and Wyn Morris, and Ozi and I worked – we shared jobs then, sort of – in Newport Tech and the Queen's School, Stow Hill where I taught Pakistani immigrants English and Enoch Powell gave a speech. We had a fight with some Cardiff thugs, then shook hands. Went from Chapter to Butetown for the jazz.

A shared passion for Jazz and Africa and Justice has never passed away. It helped my work enormously and Ozi has appeared in about five films of mine.

1979 Narbeth
Alf Gooding the Welsh owner of Catnic – a Caerphilly Lintel producer – backs a film script that is to be made in West Camarthen and Pembrokeshire. Ozi gets a free car because he is our location man.
This first drama film was called *The Mouse and the Woman*, loosely based on a short story by Dylan Thomas. One could write a book about that.
Ozi found most of the locations and had a 'drink-all-you-can, eat-as-much-as-you-can' approach, and 'Can I suggest so-and-so for extras' – stories of the concussion – four times I think from bus to set, the stalker boyfriend, the beauty of west Wales.
If ever a film about a film is made this should be it. Everyone who was sober was fired and then returned next day knowing that memory loss would play its part. A Gay time with farmers using real truncheons playing policemen; the traffic to the beaches held

72

Islwyn Road (detail). 2005. Watercolour

up for 6 miles on Easter weekend because the children of the cops were 'in the film so wait..' Our office a bar room and old red telephone coin box, the film was it and Narberth was Hollywood. The making of a film. It ended up in the Director's Fortnight in Cannes in 1980. Ozi singing in Welsh to the French at the ICA.

Earlier 1975
And in Above Us the Earth – first film
I like turning ordinary people into actors – and Ozi got his big part as the young prophetic revolutionary – discussions about film form and culture discussed so easily with real people – you could say my theory is that you cannot turn luvies into coal miners, and as scripts are based on conversations overheard or plagiarised, or adapted and sometimes original, then the trick is to make a film. Ozi personified that and so began his career as a television broadcaster too – 'truthful and amazing' said Gwyn Thomas, the writer, of Ozi in his film column for the mighty *Western Mail*. Thirty-five years later in 2012 it was declared to be the choice of the BFI, made up of a French-English jury, as being the best-ever independent Welsh film. Thank you Oz.

Oct 21 1975 Notes after ICA showing
Later Prizes won at Mannheim Germany and other places etc.

And in this friendship of pit and art and family and love for Wales, the independent land we wish for deeply to be separate, in that film there was one scene of Ozi offering a new Wales.

> It was the cheapest of films to make and it won quite a few prizes. It needed subtitles because of the valley accents and Ozi played the juvenile son of the father lead, and his nationalist views, some say, as seen in the film helped Plaid

build a base in the valleys.
John Coleman *New Statesman*

Except for one scene of Ozi and Windsor Rees playing my father as he died – flashback – interestingly the proletariat all loved the scene but yes, it was theologically out of tune, but so was Picasso and the Lord's Prayer out of tune with the critic. I see this as all part of Ozi's creation, as an artist himself and every day I talk to one of the paintings I have in my small Welsh collection.

> That love is work is foolishness, is loneliness.
> A daughter told me that.
> And wave at waves because the wave waves back
> I never work at love, I live.

1985 The Miner's Strike
1985 BBC London
MAY. Notes on Ozi for BBC who ask 'who is this bloke?'

And then there is *Ms Rhymney Valley*. The style continued – real people not actors and there was Ozi again

The film opens with Ozi talking to an older, tired Betty, a single mom. They discuss Arthur Scargill. Betty likes him but Ozi is not so sure.

'What style is this, who is that bloke' – 'interesting man' says Peter Goodchild the head of BBC Drama who had commissioned the film that won Drama prizes when there were no actors in the film.

It's not acting, it's what was called by Sean Day Lewis and John Berger 'Modern Welsh Realism', a new art form, etc.

And for me it was all down to Ozi and Betty, Charmain and Margaret and Abe and Ray Davies and Kim Howells. And so many others, liberating women most of all.

Film-makers, like painters, use real people to sculpt, they say. The truth is that Ozi, like most valley people, projects himself. All I did was guide them and the drama is obviously in the event and in the difference of opinions.

Reality shows, shouts, screams.

Not this reality TV nonsense where the poor are abused by media ambition, but Truth. We hope our work is Truth. This was intelligence, more like Italian Realism – Bicycle Thieves – and, as John Berger had written and said, excellent.

OCT 2000
Notes from KF

His paintings I have bought – one must buy art.
Ozi is good with money. I took a photo once of him buying a round – a historical moment – but the prices were fair and the art beautiful.
Never a dull moment.
My house is full of Welsh paintings and Ozi is there, and I buy out of love of painting.
He works hard and we are different in that anonymity is part of my lifestyle and the more modern Ozi fits in with the modern sale.
Paintings speak.
There is one painting of a woman with her hand on the shoulder of another lady walking away, and I gave it away, so I remember

his paintings from most exhibitions because I have a memory for that. It's with Ruth Kenley Letts who produces *The Hours* for the BBC. Lucky girl.

Paintings speak for themselves – modesty and silence helps better than the competition of noise. To be told what a painting is by a curator spoils it for me because the curator is going to say the same about another painter the week after.

Ozi's paintings will live for me, not because I have many, but because they were part of our shared friendship.
I talk to Ozi 's paintings prayerfulness and Ozi land the angels have a job in hand
And hymn in him not far away
And all those nights of drink at Chapter bar with Jules and Mik and Brian always about art and democracy those paintings and the beautiful Erica Da 'Aborn – no chance says Ozi – pointing at Tony Davies her brilliant husband of the day – possessive love and alcohol the orders of the night.

OCT 2011 NOTES
It is also a fact that I have a secret life as a poet and essay writer, choosing anonymity usually.
I wrote a poem about Ozi when he was taken ill.

I took a photograph of his hands painting the Golden Mosque in Jerusalem from a distance of some miles on Palestinian territory – he has that photograph still he tells me – and it speaks mountains. Strangely enough I began writing about the Painter's Hand about a month ago – what I would give to the book is an observation more telescope than Windows 8.
I have collected his paintings for a lifetime.

And I will call it love, she says
this sober spirit love will smile
with seaside happy sand and western winds, she says
and strangers at the garden gate
who talk so much of love to love disdain and scowl
and so the listening begins.
The need to know
it all to understand.
A walking sandy rocky sweet and tender love she smiles.
He takes her hand
She takes his eyes and whispering
so still the day, she says
I never lose by loving you
I always lose by holding back.

As I write I stare at a painting of Hebron when Ozi's visit to Palestine and Israel on a grant from the Welsh Arts Council coincided with me working there with Joshua Sobol, the Israeli writer.

Palestine Israel 1990
Notes written on reflection

NOTE
Ozi paints the Dome from a distance
A Hebron day and nearby

Out of a stone house in a rocky cliff
the mother looks.
Her child so happy to see Ozi paint.
Rasin Rasin Painter Painter
The man

The child speaks Aramaic. She smiles
Ozi shows her his sketchbook
and she the child with a father not there in war or jail
I have a father for a day her voice will say
Two fathers her mother says smiling at me

The child disappears into the rock.
Tears in the mother's eyes
as her story unfolds
The mother waits 4 years for her husband
to return from the Lebanese refugee camp

His fate unknown as Mossad executes the voice of Palestine.
The child returns in wedding dress of white and silvering her joy
is in her shyness eyes
But she one day might meet an Ozi Arab man or Israel good

The MEMORY IS DEEP
Palestinian girl, her dress, the painter's hand, Moses and Arnie, the Brooklyn lawyer, etc. Asking us about girls in the old town – Jerusalem 1990, I think.

The marriage dress that shone so bright that day
A Hebron day I have the paint upon the wall
I see the Palestinian girl in Ozi land
His hand the painter's hand

On the Arab bus we both looked Semitic – me bald, big nose – Ozi with his face, got the looks.
Rasin, Ozi and I would say, just in case. Artist, artist, having seen the humiliation of Palestinian Israelis who were constantly

humiliated by the abusive Israeli police.

Or the farmer at Job's Well that Ozi painted. I would write some secret poem, the man asking who we are, we both thinking he was Israeli – propaganda said Israel was a desert, all sand until Israel murdered Palestine.

'My family has been here 2,000 years,' he said, and smiled. 'We understand Time, my friends.'
And he saw we were friends, as did the guy who laughed when Ozi said he was a teacher of art.
The Palestinian art work is Michaelango passed down orally.

NOTE
Apprentice art and pottery. Ozi listening – defining moments in his life.

NOTE
If you have a gift you find a master who pays you and you learn, and we sat and drank tea and drove back to our lodgings, passing the wired-all-over prison-like Israeli settlements full of Brooklyn and Odessa accents – speaking English.

NOTE
No fear of death, the optimistic paranoid
And Ozi strokes his face the way he does
when deep in thought his soul a busy day for him –
his art will never be that fig tree dead Gethsemane
The Olive mount a resurrection man is he.
Hope marries Love and Faith is spirit
bigamy delight

'The Poet as Ornithologist' (*detail*). 2003. Oil on canvas

NOTE

Ozi and the Jerusalem brothel cheap rooms and the burning bites of desert bugs and Ozi with his swelling eyes and going to the Dead Sea for the mud. To heal. Arnie the Brooklyn guy on the bus.

NOTE

Ozi bitten by bugs in that room we rented above the Russian brothel.

NOTE

Teaching Arnie the Jewish kind and so eager to fall in love and Ozi teacing him about our Mabinogian Wales, and about how he politely says the American Israeli is Buffalo Bill

NOTE

And Brooklyn sweet Arnie in shorts in a Palestinian café, and then the bus asking Ozi where is this in Jordan – women, Israeli and Palestinian smiling always at him...

NOTE

The Israeli Police man humiliating men
Good manners you need our Ozi tells the dark Sephardic cop with death in his eyes

JAN 1977 DIARY NOTE

I spent many days in Narberth and Clynderwen and when I and my wife split I went to the arms of Ozi and family in Clynderwen, but the caravan was too small and I was soon in Llanddewi Velfrey with Ms Morris.

1982 NOTE ON AA, BRECHFA

It is shortly after this when I stopped drinking that Ozi says I helped save his life – that is, we stopped drinking – and on one trip (must have been 1972) both unhappy and we talked in a way men do not. We were coming back from London, two valley boys outwardly, – we opened up about the heart and brokenness.

NOTES **1985**

Ozi agrees to be in *Ms Rhymney Valley*, my film on the miners' strike.

Someone from Cross Keys tells me that all women, all ages, admired Ozi for his valley voice, the boy soprano to the baritone man.

I had the habit of making sure any new girlfriend met Ozi because you would soon know if she liked him or me – like most, I fear rejection.

NOTES **1981**

Ozi and I walk home from that club near the Aldwych – or should I say Ozi is followed by 7 beautiful, dancing in the street, young ladies

There are deeply personal and family moments that do belong here but ...

MAY 2003, LLANSTEFFAN

Am so happy to be able to confide my brokenness with Ozi and Hilary – as it's none of the business of those in the mob who will read it – should I open up?

MAY 2004, BRECHFA

The mob misrepresents the goodness in film I share with Ozi and

Fissure/Hollti. 2009. Mixed media. 10" x 12"

I thank God for his gentleness – friendship is private and its longevity is honoured. For example, when my Swiss lover and I split up and Ozi had to listen to me for a few years. And the love he has found with Hilary so beautiful to see.

NOTES JAN 2014, LLANSTEFFAN

I ask Ozi to be in *Streic y Glowyr* using our archive material – he speaks Welsh brilliantly now – I am very proud of him. His hair is gone but it will return stronger than ever.

NOTES, BEDWAS, DECEMBER 2014

And this is my friend Ozi
All of Wales cried when Ozi had cancer
All of us
We cry
And then again
The rugby talk.
And he returns with hair, the curly smile
The bravery of man is Oz, who shares his life, his art,
Has time for all. He gives his heart,

Being there at the funerals,
at the wedding.
Is a gift of family

And he is there for me whenever I ask.

Being there, sharing the Ché and Luke years
and all the mother ways
we learn from Cymru Wales.
The valley education, mountain high,
and better than our luck and destiny.

And Ozi is in love
is honesty, is hiraeth, hwyl and Hilary and more
To feel their everlasting love
Their gift to all who knock their door

And Sarah's celebrating days,
the baby born
and being there when Stella passed away
bring deep the memories of love

and always hope in darker days when hope is food
and Love is God. And God is love.
And God loves Ozi and they will laugh and do and shall
no tense the gentle he our Ozi man
to argue more than Job and win God with a smile
of his integrity.
And blossoming
the He who shares has shared his life
we laugh
we pray we love

Fifty Years

WYN MORRIS

How can one think back almost fifty years and come up with coherent memories? I think its Montaigne who talks about finding that any sort of fixed point bolts off like a running horse. So it is with my memories of Osi or Oz as we knew him in those days and yet, although our period as colleagues was pretty limited, I still think of him as one of the most important friends that I have ever made. We were working together for three or four years at what was then the Newport and Monmouthshire College of Technology. This was a fairly new, utilitarian looking building up on Allt-yr-Yn Avenue, Newport, one of the posher parts. It was, at that time, a college that catered for and reflected the industrial and manufacturing dynamism of Newport and the surrounding region. Newport was not a very pretty town in those days either but was a rough, tough steel town with plenty of life and work in it. Nearly all of our students were male, studying for various qualifications in Civil, Mechanical and Electrical Engineering and Metallurgy with a much smaller contingent studying Business and Management. Getting the necessary vocational qualifications in these subjects was their main reason for being with us, and many fitted their studies into a pretty crowded working week.

Somebody, somewhere had decided that, for an hour or two a week, full-time and day-release students had to experience something called Liberal Studies. What this consisted of was largely up to us, the staff appointed to do this work, with very little help or direction from anyone. Doing this difficult/thankless task, which did not go down very well with some hard-pressed students, is how Osi and I first met. I have no doubt that there was much sterling and heroic work done in this field. However, if you want a good if zany picture of what went on across the land, pick up Tom Sharpe's hilarious but oh so near the mark novel, *Wilt*. Things were very much easier for us because our students were older and better qualified than were the majority of students in colleges of further education.

Whatever his impact on his students, and I only infrequently had brilliant little glimpses of this, his impact on those of us who worked with him was electric. He had a way of looking at the world, which was totally at odds with the mainly instrumental and vocational preoccupations of the college. Newly qualified from Newport College of Art, his views were also frequently at odds with the social science orientation of most of his Liberal Studies colleagues. I, for one, always welcomed his refreshing slant on things as it always provoked and challenged.

This was in the late 1960s and some of us, involved in this work, must have thought of ourselves as some sort of an outpost of that decade's counterculture movement. Not that we had very much time for middle-class kids who played at dropping out of society, depending on daddy to get them back on track again. I remember that Osi and I had an argument along these lines with ex-public school students, who had taken us in to sleep on armchairs when attending a weekend course in Bath. More usually on such courses we and our students stayed at the Royal York Hotel. Since the hotel's brochure showed a blonde draped over one of the beds, Osi's tongue in cheek response was to leave his bedroom door open. For me personally, not only was he a breath of fresh air, but he also gave me the opportunity to connect with people, places and communities in Newport and Gwent which were comparatively new to me. This was local experience that served me well over the following years.

Once in 1968, after taking my eight-year-old daughter to visit Osi in his flat in Newport, she told me that he was the 'most amazing

D29 Llansteffan. 2002. Watercolour on paper. 24"x18"
Private collection

person in the world' and that she was also amazed that her boring dad had such an interesting and exciting friend. This is not surprising for, at the time, Osi looked more like a handsome Welsh gypsy than anything else. When we got near the house we could hear *River Deep, Mountain High* by Ike and Tina Turner booming from inside his flat. My daughter Sian was smitten!

Through Osi I got to visit various places up the valley from Newport. After work on Thursday evenings, we used to go up to the Welsh Oak in Pontymister for an hour or two. Here Osi not only regaled us with stories about the historical links that the place had with the Chartists, but he also knew many of the local characters who drank there. I particularly remember one of his friends, an old ambulance driver, telling us that part of his job was the disposing of diseased miners' lungs after post-mortems to determine whether or not they had died of silicosis. Further trips were made up to Ebbw Vale, where a friend of his lived just across the way from the very noisy old steelworks.

Most importantly we visited his home village of Wattsville, lovingly described by Osi as 'the Bournemouth of the Western Valley'. Here we met his lovely mam Stella, his dad Malcolm and all the family, along with various friends and neighbours. Here also Osi and Mark Duffield, with me tagging along uselessly, made a short film about the village of Wattsville, which has been shown in at least one of his recent exhibitions. I don't know about Bournemouth, but every day up there remains sunny and magical in my memory, even if it meant lugging our filming equipment up Mynydd Machen, over towards Ochrwith and back again. Although the film, documenting the detritus left in the village by mining and other industries, was in black and white, what has stayed with me is a summer in glorious Technicolor. I remember

82

Ymdrochi/Bathing. Hand-mixed oil paint on canvas

that we spent one afternoon on the hill behind Osi's mother's house searching the skies through his binoculars for kestrels. On another occasion, we visited Nine Mile Point, famous for its stay-down strike in support of the Miners' Union.

All too soon our working days together came to an end when Osi and the family moved down to west Wales, where he has lived ever since. There is a story about his early days down west when he was stopped by the police for riding his bike the wrong way up a one-way street. When asked for his name, he replied that it was Donny Osmond, and as a consequence, he ended up in the Police Station. His first name is of course Donald, and therefore his answer was technically correct if rather mischievous. Policemen don't always appreciate people who take the proverbial.

Before he went down west I have one claim to fame in that I taught him his first few words of 'the language of Heaven'. Not that they were particularly heavenly words for they were mostly choice Welsh swearwords (perhaps the only way to start learning a new language but perhaps not?). It makes me proud to think that Osi, a man of Gwent, as well as other members of his extended family, are by now fluent Welsh speakers.

Although as miners' sons we came from different ends of the south Wales coalfield, we had been brought up in similar traditions of Welsh nonconformity (not that that side of us was much in evidence back then). We were also steeped in the political and industrial militancy of the south Wales coalfield, both of us coming from mining villages and families. In those early years however Osi was more of an anarchist than anything else and was once described by one senior member of the college staff as that 'rebel rouser Osi'. We had a great sense of optimism back then and felt that we were going to change everything. Who has this optimism nowadays?

Another young man from the same sort of background and with a similar political outlook, who joined us at the college to do the same sort of work, was Karl Francis. Some years later we would meet up when Karl was working on his groundbreaking films based on different aspects of Welsh life. I think Osi would have been quite happy to take the leading roles in all of those films. Karl missed a trick there; Osi would probably have been a star. Later, during the turbulent years of the Miners' Strike in 1984/1985, we all went down a few times to my own home villages of Cwmgors and Gwaun-Cae-Gurwen with Karl and some of his film crew. I remember how bemused my father was when one day we all turned up on his doorstep. Even then we all knew that if the strike were lost, then very soon there would be no mining industry left in south Wales. This would have disastrous consequences for valley families and communities, and so it proved. Margaret Thatcher was given a sendoff in St Paul's for goodness sake. Long before that, she should have been put in jail.

I know very little about art but, along with other philistines, I know what I like, and I like and am proud of the few paintings that Osi gave me in those early days. Osi, Karl, some others and myself still meet now and then when he comes up to Cardiff. He injects into our conversation the same highly-charged energy and enthusiasm with which he has always put over his ideas and which makes him such a marvellous friend and companion. Some friends make life worth living. For me, Osi is one of those.

84

Marwolaeth/Death. Oil on canvas

Hostage (*series*). Oil on canvas

Hostage (series). Oil on canvas

Hostage (*series*). Oil on canvas

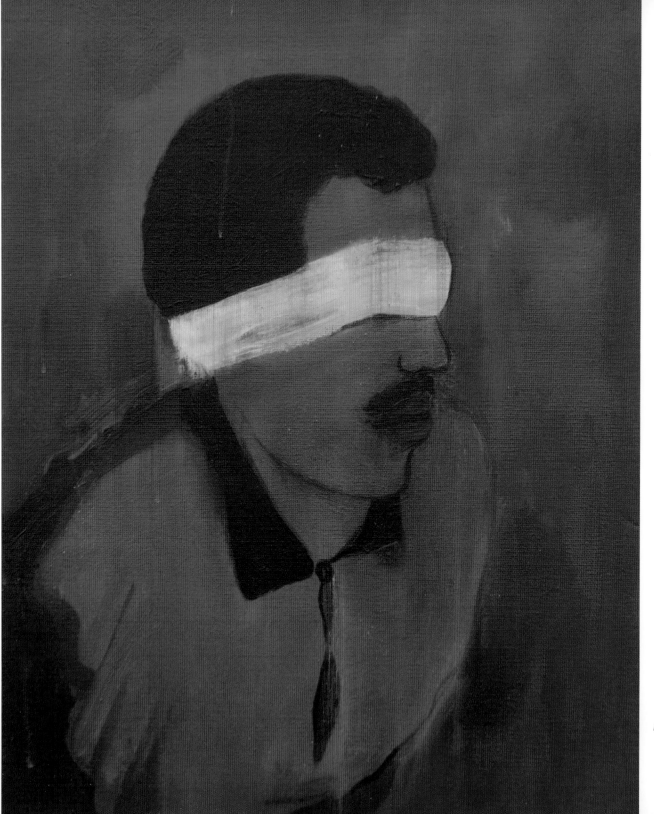

Hostage (*series*). Oil on canvas

Hostage (*series*). Oil on canvas

Pam?/Why? 2009. Mixed media on canvas

Thinking about Osi

DAVID PARFITT

Two funerals. Elizabeth Rathmell's twenty years ago and Roger Evans's four years ago. I met Osi at both. At Bette's funeral in Cwmbran I hadn't seen him for more than thirty years. Almost the first thing we said to each other, in unison, was, 'We should have had that fight.' We met again at Roger's funeral in Cardiff in 2010, both of us pleased to meet for the second time in many years, and we met again by chance for a third time later that year at the Picasso exhibition at the Gagosian Gallery in London.

In 1959 we were students at Newport College of Art. In those days my family lived in New Tredegar. I had digs in Newport during the week and went home by train on weekends. Osi lived nearer, in Wattsville. Many students travelled into Newport by bus or train from Abertillery, Abercarn, Risca, Pontypool, Abersychan, Blaenavon, all mining or steel towns in the mountains and valleys that lie behind Newport. Early each morning art students streamed over the road bridge spanning the River Usk towards their studios in Clarence Place while charabancs of labourers, bussed down the valleys to build Llanwern Steelworks, jeered and shouted at us. Crossing this bridge on the first morning of the first term I met up with Dai and Roger Evans and, later that day, with Osi Osmond.

'How do butt?' said Dai and Roger, both of them looking wild and exotic in their striped caps, draped jackets, skin-tight jeans (zips to get your legs in) and suede shoes soled with a thick crepe (Eton Clubman's); me dowdy in my grey tweed school suit. Up the front steps we went and then up a further three flights and on to the top floor. There, straight in front of us, Eddie Couch's store room of drawing and printing papers;[1] then right, along the corridor, past the Painting and Decorating Department and on into the beautiful Art School studios with their cool north light. Osi was

there, handsome, tough looking, funny, sharp and friendly, if always a touch dangerous, as the year group of 1959 assembled.

At Newport Art School the first thing we had to do was to learn basic bookbinding and make a sketchbook.[2] Then out into the streets to draw. Our drawings were subsequently tested by making paintings from them. On weekends we did the same thing, drawing and painting where we lived. For me that meant panoramic views of New Tredegar and Tirphil from each side of the Rhymney Valley. Drawings too – Black Beauties were our favourite pencils – of Elliot's Colliery, its winding gear and shunting yards beside the Police Station where my father was the Inspector of Police. Dai Evans started using gouache as well as pencil in his sketchbook, causing a revision of our ideas about what to draw with. We tried out many kinds of instruments and materials: sharpened sticks, writing ink diluted with water, Indian ink, dip pens, quills and brushes, coloured inks, conté crayons, watercolour and charcoal. We were competitive in a friendly way, and on Monday mornings there would be an eager inspection of each other's weekend work. Our drawings grew in size, often covering two pages of an open sketchbook.

This pleasure in looking at and talking about each other's work triggered many discussions about European, American and British painting and led us to make regular trips to Cardiff and London to see major exhibitions and to check out the commercial galleries.[3] To get to London we caught the early morning Newport to Paddington train, returning home on the 1 am milk train. We bought brushes from Lechertier Barbe in Jermyn Street and oil paint (in tins!) from Brodie & Middleton in Long Acre. Nor did we neglect buying clothes in Carnaby Street, looking at the bookshops and record shops in Charing Cross Road. We scoured

Fenws/Venus. 1994. Oil on canvas

them for biographies of painters we liked and for records of our favourite jazz musicians,4 after visiting the nearby National Gallery. Geoff Grant discovered Vlaminck, Derain and the Fauvists, Bette the quiet paintings of Gwen John and Paula Modersohn-Becker, Osi was inspired by the colour and defused edges of Mark Rothko paintings, Dai by the self-portraits of Stanley Spencer and the grey slabs of Nicolas de Stael, myself by Bratby and the Kitchen Sink School. All these influences were filtered and understood in the context of working in the street, up the mountain, under the pithead – painting and drawing always from life.

One or two days a week we worked in the Life Room. One morning perhaps twelve of us were painting the austere Miss Probert. She was naked and standing, one knee on a chair, and supported by both hands holding the back of the chair. We were crowded around her in a circle, as close as possible but still able to see the whole of her from head to toe. Your view of her, front, side or back was a question of first come first served. After much jostling and bickering to establish suitable working spaces the class was settled and quiet. Everyone was set up, easels placed so as not to get in each other's sightline, and our palettes, brushes, turps jars and bottles balanced precariously on stools and small tables. We were working steadily, making a mess to get ourselves out of it (killing the white) when the studio door is flung open. In comes Osi – he was often a bit late – whistling and full of beans. Chorus, 'Shut the fucking door'. Osi, 'Of course, what's the matter with you lot?' Osi shuts the door and then prowls behind us still whistling, in excellent humour and radiating good will, looking for a place to squeeze into, a place to settle and paint. People adjust, move up a little. We've only just started so it's no big deal – we can alter and change what we've done. The class settles again, all quiet, concentrating and painting, mixing paint, smoking and murmuring to each other – never totally silent. Osi starts whistling again. Me, 'For Christ sake shut up Osi.' Osi, all innocent, 'What have I done?' This kind of exchange goes on for a while. I pick up a paint rag off the floor. Osi flies across the studio shouting, 'That's my bloody vest', and crashes into me. One easel topples, and then the next one and so on around the studio, spilling turps, palettes and paint, a shambles in all directions as everyone tries to save their paintings and possessions. Miss Probert retires to her cubicle. Then Tom Rathmell5 looks round the studio door, just his head and half a shoulder. He doesn't say anything, just looks at Osi and me in a neutral kind of way as if he might be fixing us in his memory to draw later. We dust ourselves down and start helping to set the studio to rights.

Osi and his wife Hilary came to stay with us in London for the weekend in mid-November 2014. They wanted to see the Rembrandt and the Turner exhibitions, but also Anselm Kiefer at the Royal Academy and Sigmar Polke at Tate Modern. With astonishing stamina Osi and Hilary saw three of the exhibitions on the Saturday and the Sigmar Polke on the Sunday before driving back down the M4 to Llansteffan. I drove them across London on Sunday morning to Tate Modern. We parked easily enough opposite the Tate and just outside the restaurant where we intended to have lunch. Osi said that he had a Tate Friends card and could take me in for free. It became clear however that the card only allowed one guest to visit the exhibition, not two. I said I'd rather pay. Osi said not to be silly, I could go in with Hilary and then she could come out of the exhibition and take him in too. I said, 'No Osi, my father was a policeman and I hate doing things like that.' Osi said, 'My father was a Deacon, I'll buy your ticket.' I said, 'I don't want you to buy my ticket, I'll buy my own ticket.' Osi said, 'I'll buy your ticket.' I said, 'We can't fight in on the forecourt of Tate Modern.' Osi said, 'I'll buy your ticket.' I said, 'We should have had that fight.' Osi laughed. He bought my ticket and my lunch too.

1. Eddie Couch handed out three sheets of drawing paper to us each week, a free allowance for every student.
2. Osi still makes his own sketch books.
3. At Helen Lessore's Beaux Arts Gallery in Bruton Place, London, we saw paintings by Frank Auerbach, John Bratby, Lucian Freud, Edward Middleditch, Jack Smith; at the Tate, large shows of paintings by Picasso (1960) and Francis Bacon (1962); at the Whitechapel Gallery Mark Rothko (1961)
4. Osi and I shared a liking for West Coast jazz – Bud Shank, Art Pepper, Chet Baker, and saw the Modern Jazz Quartet concert in Cardiff circa 1961.
5. Head of Painting at Newport College of Art. He was a wonderful teacher, very quiet and gentle, never saying much, but always inspiring.

Roger Evans (1942-2010). Newport College of Art 1959-1963, Royal College of Art 1963-1966 to study in the newly opened Film School. He worked as a camera man for The National Coal Board Film Unit, Harlech Television, and the BBC and for the film director Karl Francis.

David Evans (b1942) Newport College of Art 1959-1962, Royal College of Art 1963-1965. Taught at Edinburgh College of Art 1965-1968, Granada Fellow, York University 1968-69. Senior Lecturer, Edinburgh College of Art 1969-1998. Member of RSA and RSW. Represented by the Open Eye Gallery, Edinburgh.

Geoffrey Grant (b1942). Newport College of Art 1959-1963. Elected Member of the Midland Group 1972. Head of Art and Design Courses at Cleveland College of Art. Retired from teaching in 1992 to paint full time.

David Parfitt (b1943). Newport College of Art 1959-1963. Royal College of Art 1963-1966. Senior Tutor Royal Academy Schools 1987-1990. Represented by Messum's, London.

Elizabeth Rathmell (1942-1994). Newport College of Art 1959-1963, Royal College of Art 1963-1966. Painted and exhibited throughout her career but never wanted to teach in art schools.

Thomas Rathmell (1912-1990). Liverpool College of Art and Royal College of Art 1935-1939. He started teaching at Newport College of Art in 1949 and became Head of Painting and then Vice-Principal before retiring in 1972. Welsh Arts Council Retrospective Exhibition at Oriel, Cardiff 1982. He was a Member of the Welsh Group and of the Watercolour Society of Wales.

Then and now
MICK AND THEA ARNOLD

In January 1969, on a bitterly cold evening at Newport station, waving me off to Germany where I was going to teach, Osi shouted, 'tell them about me' which I did and have continued to do to this day.

Where to begin?

Meeting up with Osi again is an enervating experience. First, the firm handshake then the direct gaze and embrace, before he launches into yet another enthusiastic discourse. The same gaze that he uses every evening as he watches the sun set over his beloved estuary at Llansteffan. For Osi that's another adventure.

First, there's the journey in the big white van, a mobile studio, up bumpy and winding country lanes until he reaches his usual vantage point, the same one every evening, where he captures the sun as it dips over the horizon on the estuary.

Every evening, a different range of colour, depending on the weather and the season. The journey in the van is an adventure too. Jars, brushes, canvases, tarpaulin jumping about in the back as Osi talks animatedly about the landscape, pointing out this and that, a colour, a shadow, a line of trees. His sketchbooks too, all handmade, will show a vast double page spread of vibrant colour.

Watercolour is a deceptively difficult medium. There is a formulaic technique, prescribed and predictable, but Osi has mastered his own. Armed only with his box of colours and his trusted Kolinsky sable brush, Osi attacks his work with vigour. His watercolour technique is confident and fluid. He hones it here, evening after evening, night after night.

As the light goes, he climbs back in the van and goes rattling down the lanes again, to Bristol House in the centre of the village of Llansteffan. His house is full of drawings and paintings and music, maybe Hilary playing the piano or the sound of a piece of opera in the background. In the winter, usually a large piece of driftwood, burns precariously on the fire in the front room and always, it seems, a delicious smell of some wonderful meal, simmering in the kitchen.

Towards the end of the evening, a more reticent Osi, after a high octane energetic day, the lowering of the voice, the long sinewy fingers twisting a piece of paper as he considers the events of the day, sifting through them, evaluating, rejecting, reflecting on ideas to be activated in the morning.

Osi; painter, writer, actor, theatre director, sage, Welshman and much, much more. Caring, moral, perceptive and curious. Curiosity, they say, is a Welsh trait, which Osi has in abundance, always trying to get to the heart of the matter. He respects and appreciates people but he is never afraid to speak up when he disagrees or when he believes something is wrong. He has always stuck to his ideals, honest and outspoken, a loyal friend. These qualities are firmly rooted in his upbringing and early life.

The journey from Wattsville, where he was born, to Llansteffan has been hard at times but he has remained resolute and single-minded.

Osi grew up in a mining family in the Sirhowy valley, in a devout chapel family. One has the feeling that the values he holds today, honesty, integrity, generosity are firmly based in that background. He has never lost them. There are many sides and facets to Osi's personality. He is very open and he externalises them all, each imbued with passion.

Osi is still very attached to the valley. Much of his recent work comes from here, linking the past with the present. His humour and commitment to all things Welsh emanate from here. Looking beyond the obvious, Osi always has an individual slant on things. He is a natural storyteller, and has, I think, been from an early age. He tells the tale of playing with a group of friends all day on the mountain and coming back down to the valley in the evening, the kids would say to him, 'Hey Osi, tell us a film'. I imagine he would keep them riveted, wanting more and more stories.

Starting at Newport Art College in 1959 gave him the opportunity to express these stories and experiences visually, giving him the freedom to explore his background. It was at times confusing, I'm sure, but, bit by bit, a more rounded view emerged. As with any generation of painters, there is always a quest for a new means of expression.

The curriculum at Newport Art College in those days was fairly traditional. It included perspective, calligraphy, often more endured than enjoyed, also bookbinding with Mr Dunn. Mr Dunn was a master bookbinder with a small shop under the railway bridge on Caerleon Road. This was something that obviously caught and remained firmly in Osi's imagination. To this day, he takes care and a great delight in making and binding his own sketchbooks. They are integral to his work, particularly his watercolours and drawings. He binds and sews by hand, a vast array of different papers and support surfaces, which present him with a different challenge every time he works on them. Those of us who had access to his Palestinian sketchbooks and more

recently to the work he has done on the estuary at Llansteffan, can only be in awe of the way he uses these surfaces. They become integral to the work.

Osi and his sketchbooks are inseparable. He carries one with him all the time and draws in it incessantly. He is a fine draughtsman and fills them with quick, perceptive and expressive drawings. They have accompanied him on many of his travels, memorably to the Holy Land, both Israel and Palestine, where he spent many months travelling, drawing and talking to the people. Growing up with evocative, biblical names, like Bethesda, Hebron, Bethlehem and so on, his curiosity needed to be satisfied. What did these exotic places that rolled off the tongue so resonantly in chapel really look like? Osi located them and painted them both in Wales and in the Holy Land.

Some years later, he also travelled to Africa as an artist-in-residence with Christian Aid. The effects of the strong sunlight there once more influenced his technique. The surface of the paintings changed, still the vibrant colour but more matt and gritty, the form more 'contre-jour'.

Newport, in the early sixties, had almost taken on the appearance of a Wild West gold-rush town. Llanwern, the huge new steelworks, was under construction on the outskirts of town. Massive foundations were necessary to raise the site above the marshlands. The town was vibrant, even slightly anarchic, the roads clogged twenty-four hours a day with lorries, carrying loads of shale used to shore up the site.

The architecture in the town was a strange mix. The Greek Classical Lyceum Theatre, Commercial Street with its Victorian

Y Cibl Coch/The Red Cibl. 1992. Oil on canvas

architecture, its large department stores and quaint arcades all still intact and busy.

The population, it seemed, had almost doubled, the pubs and clubs were awash with money. There seemed to be a perpetual energy that drove the town twenty-four hours a day. It was an exceptional time in many respects. There were coasters and barges still moored on the River Usk below Newport Bridge. Amidst this entire clamour lay Clarence Place and the Art College. It was a mecca for students from all over south Wales. The students too were an odd mixture at that time; many had already done their National Service. They had seen service all over the world, Malaya, Korea, Hong Kong. Then there was the younger element, like Osi and myself, who had come straight from school. It was a vibrant, dynamic time and from the painting groups, many personalities emerged, people like Bryan Jones and Christine Kinsey, founders of the Chapter Arts Centre in Cardiff. Alan Osborne, painter, playwright, musician, and Jack Crofton, sculptor and founder of the Meridian Foundry, were there also. Peter Davison who migrated to Canada and did well. There was also Dave Parfitt and the Evans brothers, David and Roger. The list goes on and on. It was an amazing few years with powerful groups who energised each other. Throughout all this, Osi's upbeat, catalytic presence pervaded. He was respected by all he encountered, always driving forwards, unrelenting in his desire to keep people on their toes and stop them sinking into apathy. He had a gift for engaging everybody, the tea ladies, Mrs. Waters and Mrs Chaffey, the barmen and the lecturers. Osi demanded good, solid, honest answers from all he addressed.

Newport at that time was much respected for its painting department under Tom Rathmell. Paintings of the miners and the mines were very much in vogue. They had captured the public's imagination. Many students were getting into prestigious London colleges on the strength of this work.

Osi burst on the scene with a slightly different take, moving away from the muted colours and many greys, Osi discovered Chrome Orange. He walked around proclaiming the virtue and the beauty of this wonderful colour. It was as if Provence had hit the valleys. He saw colour where no one had seen it before. His unbridled zest and enthusiasm fell to a large extent on stony ground. It did not fit the established perception of the valleys. Where tradition saw earth colours, soft rains and mist, Osi saw the sun bursting through, illuminating the pit head, the mountains, the sparse growth of trees and bushes. He saw the sun shining on Wattsville in pure Chrome Orange. His painting has changed and evolved over time, but he continues to paint with a passion as he always has and still to this day, his work is infused with strong Chrome Orange. Generally nowadays, he painstakingly mixes his own paint, using pure pigment, beeswax, and assorted varnishes to achieve maximum clarity and heightened colour.

Determined to carry on painting after leaving Art School, Osi took a studio in Commercial Street in Newport. There was one Chrome Orange painting from the many I remember of this time of a weightlifter or a wrestler, a large man, by dint of his profession and it necessitated a very large canvas. Living as he did in a small studio in Commercial Street, this presented many problems.

Curries were comparatively new in those days. There were probably only two Indian restaurants in Newport at the time. Osi availed himself of these but quickly moved on to create his own curries. In this, he was fortunate in having a group of Ethiopians who lived next to his studio down the docks area of Newport. They introduced him to a plethora of new and exciting tastes and smells. Many of these exotic spices, could only be purchased in tiny little shops tucked away in the depth of the Newport dock area. In those days, the docks were still fairly busy.

Osi moved on to do his teaching diploma in Cardiff. Here, he met what was probably a more cosmopolitan and urbane selection of people from all over the country. Many of them were demure, particularly the females. Within days, they had become completely enthralled by Osi, his wit, his confidence, and his perception, not to mention his good looks. He was fearlessly outspoken, always entertaining but there was a serious core to what he said. They followed him around as he continued to declaim about everything from Tamla Motown to the Welsh language. He was already sharpening his oratory, which he now uses to great effect.

A period of part-time teaching followed mainly in Newport until finally, Osi, feeling restless, moved to a more rural situation, first to Narbeth then to Llansteffan. Moving deeper into the hinterland of Wales itself, his feelings about his identity and his Welshness became more real to him, like the coastal undergrowth itself, more enclosing, more entangled, more rooted. He is passionate about the Welsh language. He moved to west Wales so that he could bring his boys up speaking their nation's language. His sons, growing up speaking Welsh, bit by bit drew Osi more deeply into the need for it. The need for the greater range for expression it would give him. This was a time of transition, leading him deeper and deeper into the quest for his beginnings. At times, no doubt, the confusion too of having to reconcile the richness of his Welsh valley culture, the blending of

his more distant past with the present, the tearing away of layers and peering through, the need to know and understand more fully, his sense of belonging. This was brought together so well in his recent exhibition at the Rhondda Heritage Centre.

I remember one evening going to his house in Llansteffan when he was extending the dining room to make a larger kitchen. A load bearing joist held up the separating wall rather precariously. He was preparing a lovely meal, as always, but in his one hand he held a sledgehammer. Breaking off from cooking every now and then, leaving the pot simmering on the stove, he walked over to the separating wall and attacked it with the hammer, dislodging yet another piece of masonry, all the time proclaiming about art, politics and the state of the Welsh nation.

A few years ago, arriving in Llanstefan with fifteen students after many hours' drive from Belgium, we pulled up outside Osi's house. They were due to spend a week working with him at the art school in Carmarthen. We were ushered into his studio, which was crowded with all sorts of artistic paraphernalia. He started talking to them and despite their long journey and lack of sleep, within minutes, all were mesmerized and raring to go. My colleague from Brussels, who is one of the most articulate and loquacious people I have ever known, was completely silenced by the oratory, the first time I have ever seen that happen. Some days later, as we sat in Osi's kitchen to yet another delicious meal, prepared this time by Osi and artist John Selway, he was once again silenced by the discussion and banter between Osi and John. 'I have never heard two people talk quite so much', he confided in me later. My colleague silenced, not once but twice.

The spin-off from this was, that many of these students from all

The Kitchen, Bristol House, Llansteffan. Photo: Siân Lewis

over Europe, were determined to go and study in Carmarthen with Osi. The story does not end there. Sensing that these kids might be a bit lost in this situation, Osi and Hilary immediately offered to put them up for a few weeks or months until they settled in. Some of these young people have gone on to do extremely well but they have not forgotten that experience. Throughout all these varied activities, his painting has remained the one constant. It encompasses the many facets of his personality and contains the diversity, the energy, the richness, the myth and the poetry that is his life.

Black Vein. 2010. Charcoal, coal dust, mixed media. 24"x18"

The circle

HEDLEY JONES

I first met Osi in 1978 at the Rhyddings pub in Swansea. I had been teaching part-time on the Foundation course in the West Glamorgan Institute of Higher Education for a couple of years and was lunching with some colleagues who said that a bloke called Osi was going to join us. Everyone knew him except me. In walked this good-looking man with a big black coat flowing behind him and a giant smile preceding him. We made an instant connection, probably through humour, and certainly through a firm handshake. That connection grew over several years of teaching together at Swansea and later, Carmarthen.

It was while teaching separate Carmarthen Foundation groups in a large room in Trinity College that Osi showed one of the reasons why he is such a magnificent teacher. Far from overwhelming the room with his renowned oratory and great voice projection he was aware of the needs of all students. He was constantly aware of my teaching methods and harmonised perfectly with his many incidences of eye contact and nods of the head, reassuring and encouraging.

His empathy with students and their needs on Foundation inevitably led Osi to the job of Course Leader of Foundation at Carmarthen. By this time I had left Carmarthen and was teaching at Swansea and Newport. I had a phone call from Osi telling me of his good news and also adding that there was a full-time teaching vacancy on Foundation. I got the job and Osi and I spent the summer of 1989 sitting in his small back garden in Llansteffan surrounded by colourful flowers, clothes pegs, wooden logs and artifacts working out just how we were going to teach the course. This is typical of Osi's generosity. He involved me from the beginning in planning the delivery and assessment and always said it was 'our course' when, in reality, he was the one who had

assumed the mantle and with it the responsibility.

This sharing of the course continued for six years and I and, of course, the students learned a lot from the great teacher. To witness Osi in full flow connecting and communicating with students was a privilege. There were several occasions that illustrated his skill. At one time he was stood on a table in a Portakabin (health and safety regulations were not his strongest asset) surrounded by over forty students, introducing a part of the course based on the circle. Using the Coliseum, a doughnut, a wedding ring, a car wheel and the anus as examples of a circle he had everyone's attention. Sensing the humour and slight shock of some students at the use of the word 'anus', there followed a ten-minute lecture on diet and why animals don't need toilet paper. 'How am I doing Hed?' was a frequent if rhetorical question flashed at me from his improvised stage. Everyone in the room was in awe of him and waiting like sponges to soak up more of his vast knowledge delivered in a serious but humorous way. The circle project was an outstanding success.

He cared strongly for the students and inevitably they responded by working hard and producing some of the best work ever by Foundation students. Osi's students set a benchmark by which Foundation work has been judged for the last 25 years and will, no doubt, be compared with for many years to come.

Osi's teaching was backed by a firmness of resolve that his methods were right and the results achieved were proof. He led his team by example but insisted on them following that high standard. 'Walk and Talk' was an Osi expression used on colleagues many times. Like many of his sayings it became embedded in everyday language and, probably as a tribute to him from a film director friend, was uttered in the film 'One of the Hollywood Ten'. He became frustrated by dalliances such as teaching staff talking 'too much' to students and not allowing them to produce the amount of work he wanted. 'What the Hell is she/he talking about for so long?' became a familiar exclamation of his. The fact that innumerable former students have achieved so much in the fields of art and design is a well-deserved legacy to his teaching and leadership. That many of those students have stayed in close touch with Osi is further tribute to the respect and friendship they have for someone who made such a positive influence on their lives.

As recently as November 2013, Osi opened an exhibition of the 'Best of Foundation'. It featured work of Foundation Art and Design students throughout the whole of Wales and parts of England. Although battling an acute illness for over a year, Osi delivered a truly memorable speech summed up by one highly experienced former Foundation lecturer from north Wales: 'That is the best opening speech I have heard at any exhibition. What a man, what an inspiration, what a teacher, what a motivator.'

I was lucky enough to witness this man in action over many years; thank you, Osi.

Swimmer. Oil on canvas

The Blues with Osi

NOELLE FRANCIS

Cardiff, 1964. I was studying for my Art Teacher's Diploma when I met this overwhelming , charming, engaging young Welshman. Osi was as passionate about art and Wales as he is now. He demonstrated an energy, fearlessness, and an ability to plunge himself into the world with a confidence I had not seen before. I was twenty-two and a few years previously had walked out of Convent school and straight into Art College. I felt divided by having a mother from Egypt and a father from Monmouthshire. 'Francis' means Border man, and I felt divided in two. I plunged myself into my art and never looked back. I always knew this was what I wanted to do, and Osi Osmond felt the same way.

I met Osi's family in Wattsville, a south Wales valleys village with just two streets, close to Nine Mile Point Colliery where he played as a child (I lived two mountains away, near Pontypool). I found that I could relate to his parents in a way that I never could to my own, felt accepted and at ease with them. I suppose it's easier to get on with friends' parents than your own sometimes, you don't have to try to meet their expectations. Here I could simply be myself and not have to worry about anything.

There was a big connection between Osi and myself. We understood each other right from the outset, partly due to our shared interest in the arts, but also in the way we both saw the world. I could have been swept away by him but I had to stay grounded. I had my own artistic path to take. Our tutor had the unlikely name of John Wayne and had set us a project based on the title 'Graffiti'. Osi had the idea that we would study and draw the sheep trails marking the mountains and valleys. The next two weeks saw us walking the hills and writing our thoughts and sketching what we saw. I still don't know what that had to do with graffiti, but it was a good experience, and I could see the beauty in the harsh landscape. I could see why it was such a part of him and he a part of it. We also went to Porthcawl where we photographed beachcombings.

In the early 60s, Cardiff was a melting pot of cultures. We would go to Butetown Jazz club and watch Victor Parker perform *Jelly Jelly Blues*, or head for the Quebec Club or Golliwog Café, which was the college café (political correctness had not been invented in 1964). Or we might check out the modern jazz performed at the Ghana Club. Osi's musical tastes influenced me hugely. We would choose songs on the jukebox ranging from The Supremes *Baby Love* to Tom Jones's *It's Not Unusual*, but it was his love of the Blues that I liked the most. We played Big Bill Broonzy and Dinah Washington endlessly. He says that jukeboxes were a great source of comfort to him.

Over the next fifty years we met, sometimes by chance, so now we still have an amazing friendship. He remains a charming, lovely friend who I shall always admire and respect. It's a real privilege to know him.

Osi with Noelle Francis 2012   Following page photo: Iwan Bala

Disciples 3

Susanne Schüeli
Teilo Trimble
Bella Kerr
Steve Wilson
Sam Vicary
Tina Carr
Siân Lewis

Pentowyn (*detail*). 2010. Charcoal, watercolour, mixed media. 12"x11"

Bringing out 'Gestalt'
SUSANNE SCHÜELI

In an introduction to the first drawing class with Osi, he stressed that drawing will change the way we see and perceive the world totally, that we will learn to observe closely and learn to see beyond the surface.

Osi was never interested in strong outlines of the models we were drawing or in a merely descriptive approach. He compared drawing to composing and wanted us to start by intentionally setting a few points, a mark; then develop the drawing by taking measurements, looking at the angles and how they correspond to one another: adding and taking off again, evaluating and questioning it over and over again. The aim was to draw what and how we saw it rather than what we thought it looked like. It almost led through a measured flow to a systematic arrangement.

Often he was saying that when drawing a person it was not just important to consider the shape and form, but also to see where the weight was and to capture the 'gestalt'[1] – a favourite word of his.

When we struggled to draw the life model in front of us, he always encouraged us to see and look again, to evaluate and re-examine what we were doing. For him, drawing was and is an intellectual debate, sometimes a struggle, on paper, and that debate needed to be seen in the drawing. It needed substance rather than superficial 'niceness'. He pushed us to bring out the depth, the essence, the relevance of what we were drawing; we had to make visible what he called 'intensity'.

This was true also for the approach to drawing which he lived and breathed and demanded of us: to insist and persevere, to

engage in it! It felt almost as if drawing was sculpting by other means. Osi had been trained in the old ways. For hours on end they had to draw anatomical drawings of the human body. This enables an understanding of what lies beneath the surface, but also gives the surface its shape, structure and physicality. He wanted that our lines on paper were not just lines; they were simply the means to bring out the debate about life and the world.

One of Osi's favourite artists is Alberto Giacometti. Looking at Giacometti's portraits or sculptures it became obvious to me what Osi had meant – what often had been difficult to grasp in class, fell into place.

I first met Osi sometime in 1999 when I enrolled at what was then the Swansea Institute to study for a BA in Architectural Stained Glass. I entered the department full of curiosity about my first drawing class. And there he was, eating his muesli, drawing me into a conversation immediately. He found out that I am Swiss and so he told me about his love for the art of Alberto Giacometti. It turned out that he was going to be my drawing teacher. And he was unlike any other drawing teacher I had encountered before or since.

The plentiful struggles I endured made me realise and discover the subjective beauty in these drawings. What I initially considered 'chaotic' areas in a picture showed over time, a certain clarity, an essence of purity.

His approach to drawing has deeply influenced the way I worked with glass. I started to use more and more multiple layers in my glass designs, each with its own characteristic of language, history, colour, directions, and texture. This interplay fascinated me

Ymddangos/Appear. 2009.
Oil on canvas. 24"x16"

because it allowed me to build up layers and take them off again. Through the translucence of the glass, I could bring sensitivity and harsh boldness together at the same time.

In these many ways Osi was a true teacher to me. I still am inspired – in whatever I do: drawing, gardening, drinking coffee, making glass or practising yoga – by his alertness, his accuracy, his energy and his way of 'going beyond'.

1. Gestalt theorists followed the basic principle that the whole is greater than the sum of its parts. In terms of visual perception, the whole (a painting for example), carried a different and altogether greater meaning than its individual components (paint, canvas, brushmarks). In viewing the 'whole', a cognitive process takes place – the mind makes a leap from comprehending the parts to realizing the whole.

We visually and psychologically attempt to make order out of chaos, to create harmony or structure from seemingly disconnected bits of information.

The prominent founders of Gestalt theory are Max Wertheimer, Wolfgang Kohler, and Kurt Koffka.

Fenws/Venus. 1994. Oil on canvas. 40"x30"

A man of quite different appearance

TEILO TRIMBLE

The National Eisteddfod in Sir Gâr, Llanelli 2014, a breeze blows through the Maes and relieves the thronged participants on this hot last day of Welsh Culture's crown jewel. I walk into 'Y Lle Celf', rolling out my paper onto the floor of the reception area, demonstrative. This time it is me who is unapologetic and uncompromising, making a public statement, as if rolling out a prayer mat. I face the entrance, my 'East', in this exhibition space of the art deemed 'worthy'. Is it disrespectful that I should take it upon myself to make this statement without prior permission? I begin to work on something that Osi Rhys Osmond called a 'graphic essay'. The subject is Osi Rhys Osmond himself.

Day 1 of Swansea Institute Foundation Course 1999, I along with about sixty other fresh-faced students are sitting in a long studio on the top floor of the Swansea Institute on Alexandra Road. It's the first day of term, the mulch scent from the tree-lined street that is also home to the BBC, the Glynn Vivian Art Gallery and the Library waft way up the cold, disability-unfriendly, concrete steps to the top of the building, reminding us of the turning of the seasons. Change is in the air; it's the first day of term and we are not wearing shoes shined by dad, and itchy shirts with the cellophane scented shop creases still lingering. Today brings a different and more daunting kind of nervousness in myself at least, for it's the first day of our Foundation course and my first day in a non-Cymraeg-speaking education establishment. The first day in a place where we cannot hide behind a uniform, and the rigid, yet comforting rules of school.

This awkward tension persists as we clutch to our "summer assignments". Late teenage awkwardness and hormones mix with the smell of charcoal, clay, 'Lynx Africa', ink, and pencil shavings. The tension is broken by the approach of the tutors; we have

already met Steve White, a balding, friendly man, who reminds me of an English vicar. The other tutors flank him as they sit on one side of the long desk as we straddle with arched backs our wooden stools, with rucksacks and handbags brimming with pristine pastels, colouring pencils and watercolours, trying to disguise our anticipation and trepidation as well as our assignments, behind yawns and baggy branded jumpers. Stephen White reassures us, he turns to his right to Osi, a man of quite a different appearance, acutely attentive yet somehow distracted. Osi is distinct in almost every way. He wears black from head to toe apart from a white T shirt which peeps from under a crumpled shirt, wooden beads adorn his berry brown arms, sleeves rolled up. Gypsy-like dark and peppered curls frame deeply pooled perceptive eyes. Sentences pour out of his mouth, strewn with big words like 'juxtaposition', and ebbing phrases like 'in the sense that'. Yes, he is Welsh; there is the familiarity and wholesomeness to his vowels, and Welsh 'ch's'. But not from here: the Swansea Valley. His speech is too rapid, too biting, rhythmic and industrial.

What he tells us does nothing to appease our collective fear of speaking in public; he talks of individualism, choices, growing and effort, in fact nothing that he says is really registering as we nervously anticipate presenting our work and ourselves. I clutch my Hyper Value plastic bag that contains my summer sketchpad or 'assignment'; I can feel a quickening of my breath as the first students begin to present their work. I had produced a page of my sketchpad each day of the summer as I worked in Pontneddfechan Tourist Information Centre. My sketches are dominated by landscapes of the upper Neath Valley. The lush rainforest-like gorges which inspired Alfred Wallace as he conceived his theory of evolution. The monochrome blue Rhigos

Wattsville (*detail*). 2010. Mixed media

mountain against the dark night sky pierced by the acidic lights of the opencast that twinkled at night.

Such was my sense of inferiority, that I had taken the pages of the sketchpad and mounted them head to toe on a large strip of paper which I then wrapped around a cardboard tube to resemble a toilet roll. I didn't think my work was worthless, but I thought that in the British political context, Welsh culture was, to put it mildly, not valued. At least this was the point I was attempting to make.

Gradually my turn came closer, Osi coaxing answers out of nervous students on this their first day. He would let them give yes or no answers to his questions and he found something interesting or noteworthy in everyone's work no matter how unimaginative and poorly executed they might have been. I was still an extremely shy and timid teenager, skinny and awkward. Suddenly it's my turn, I feel all the eyes in the room fall on me, including the eyes of Osi; kind and wizened like a sailor's yet at the same time fizzing with inquisitiveness and the playful cheekiness of a toddler. 'So what do we have here?' I feel tightness in my throat, and begin to mumble. He cuts across, 'Sorry, tell us your name first then?' 'Teilo...Trimble' I reply slowly. 'Teilo as in Llandeilo, St Teilo? Are you from Llandeilo? No? Where? Pontneddfechan. Okay interesting. So, Teilo from Pontneddfechan, what have you got for us?' The words flow from his mouth as if he were reciting his favourite piece of poetry whilst my words stick and stumble, tumbling out in irregular and untidy sentences. I manage to reach for my bag with a trembling hand and pull out my offering.

As Osi quizzed me and drew answers out of me, I felt that someone was taking as intense an interest in my work as I had given in producing the watercolours and sketches. He saw something interesting on a personal, political and cultural level in my work. As I later learnt, the post-industrial landscape and 'cultural amnesia' is a central theme in his own work. In that sense I felt as if I had found a kindred spirit that day. Until 'Tell us why you've chosen to present your work in this way?' I had a sinking feeling as I replied, stating the vaguely obvious. 'Well it's meant to look like a toilet roll.' 'Right. So it has the form of a toilet roll. And why did you choose that form?' 'Well', I begin to flounder, not wanting to reveal the bluntness of my real reason. 'It's kind of the way I see the image of south Wales, it's not really respected or given any importance in the British media.' 'Yes, very interesting, and that's a very Welsh response. However, I think you are being quite critical...in fact the quality of your work and the thought you've put into each piece needs and demands you to give it more respect. If you want others to respect your culture then you can't yourself degrade it from the outset, this is really very important.'

Swiftly he moves on, and away from the spotlight I am just another student on his first day on the Foundation course. I felt really quite naive. I was trying to be self-deprecating and clever but instead felt stupid and childish. In the weeks to come I begin to overcome this crippling sensitivity that just isn't accustomed to the straight talking that sometimes co-exist with this man's poetic empathy. His pithy remarks contain also an echo of his hometown of Wattsville in the Sirhowy valley, coal-dusted miners' hardness, humour and camaraderie. Thus begins the most imaginative and creative free time of my 'academic' life.

Osi is the Fine Art and life-drawing tutor for my year at Swansea Institute. I notice the sheer delight he has in talking, discussing and explaining art on an intellectual, cultural and philosophical level. Osi was and still is the most vital articulate and exciting cultural figure, and being around him in those formative years was like being in the radius of a furnace. Little did I realise that it was students like me, naïve, clumsy but irrepressible and full of cheekiness and possibilities, that provided the kindling for Osi's great blaze of creative, intellectual intensity and warmth. He told me 'some people are takers and others givers. I'm a giver, it's important to give.' In the life drawing class he told us to use our left hands, so we did. He told us to use our feet, so we did. He told us to draw with our eyes closed; again we did as he asked. All the time what we produced from these experiments and exercises was also vital and interesting, not 'interesting' which is today's cliché for 'I don't think much of it, but I can't tell you that.' He found what we did INTERESTING.

Osi is like a cultural superconductor; he took our energy and amplified it with his own limitless energy and shooting it back at us. Later, when I went on to university and then to study filmmaking, and even when I lived in France, I could still feel this energy remotely through his articles that my mother sent me, or through his appearances on television. He beams this cultural energy directly back to its source and illuminates us, in all our ugliness, our shadows and our loveliness. It is the same as it was, under his warm though often critical and good-humoured spotlight, on that first day of Foundation studies. Osi is a cultural giant in a Welsh context, truly internationalist in his outlook. His self-confidence scares the establishment, for good reason. We don't have enough culturally active, critical and confident Welsh voices; instead we have grey establishment figures that have divided the meagre spoils of devolution, keeping Wales in perpetual bureaucratic servitude to their equally meagre ideas.

Day 7 of the National Eisteddfod 2014, under the broiling hot sun of the Maes, he is still dressed in black head to toe, outside the Pabell Heddwch (Peace Tent). He urges the passers-by to sign the White Book of Carmarthen, with the same intensity of spirit and determination that I remember so well. 'We're not asking you to give your details or join we want you to sign that you agree to the principle that we should work towards peace.' He frogmarches confused Carmarthenshire octogenarians to the tent in the name of peace, with an energy that leaves me quite simply humbled. I tell him I've been asked to write an essay about him. 'I trust you to do it Teilo', he convinces me with his winning smile that suggests he well knows there are dozens who would paint a similar picture of his influence, his energy, and his force, this 'Osiness'. Later I feel it, this energy as I crouch and begin to draw and make marks on the paper prayer mat before me in Y Lle Celf. The eyes that fall upon me are not those of the critical Eisteddfod elders, or the grey flabby establishment figures who would have made me paranoid or feeling unworthy of their attention. The people who stop and talk are interested and inquisitive. 'What is this in aid of they ask?' I explain. Everyone knows him. I hear stories of how he spoke so eloquently on television or in a council meeting, or how he explained to one former student how women's bottoms looked like hearts, or that students were like 'beans growing' and that he and his fellow tutors were the sticks that made sure they grew straight and towards the light. I smile as I hear these stories, I look down and I draw my encounter(s) with Osi.

The life class and other things
BELLA KERR

Even to breakfast he did not arrive like other people from bed, but from the Atlantic... or from the wood, where he had discovered some rare, beautiful bird... We knew only the zest of his company and his example.[1]

On teaching days Osi ascended the staircase at high speed, arriving in his own weather (a strong breeze), flinging off his coat and scattering papers. We drank coffee and he ate with relish (hear noises of hungry pleasure) and declared his loves for the contents and maker of his sandwiches. And we talked – of the taste of a homegrown spring onion or an apple cut with a knife – about the precision of the poetry of J.H. Prynne – and the qualities of the paintings of Georg Baselitz, Gerhard Richter or Picasso. Osi saw beauty in plastics and packaging, a fine coat or dress, good posture and many other things. He questioned taxi drivers, mothers with pushchairs, caretakers and waitresses with tattoos – gathering material, building theories. Subjects such as masculinity revealed his insight, and questions about contemporary practice, such as the broadening of the means and remit of fine art or the role of photography brought forth Osi's scrutiny and scorn.

Joyce Carey's rich, semi-autobiographical novel *A House of Children* describes the author's father, a man whose visits to Donegal 'were less to a house than the neighbouring fields, hills, streams and oceans'. This dashing figure, threaded through a text dense with the intensity of living, has something of Osi – a glimpse of the energy that characterised his presence in the Foundation studios in the old art college building on Alexandra Rd.

Osi taught drawing and mainly life drawing. The person who teaches and the person who learns, and the exchange between them, this human contact is teaching, rather than the lesson plan and project with aims and objectives. In the life room it is a contact made around and through examination of the human body. It is about curiosity and the creation of meaning through drawing.

He sought the individual in each student and offered his knowledge and skills in return. The question of ego in teaching is interesting – in each encounter the finely calibrated expression of self is measured and adjusted to the student's need to learn. And when the exchange is balanced the student feels known and knows the teacher. This, and many other things, happened in sequence and layers throughout a day in the life room with Osi.

He started with conversation – chairs were drawn into a circle and Osi spoke and questioned. This broad discussion, about things beyond and within the processes of drawing, created the foundation for the class. The teaching considered much – looking and seeing – recording and responding – mark-making and measuring – technique and thought and feeling – the drawing and the person making the drawing.

He drew with the students and always carried a sketchbook and pencils. Some sketchbooks he made (beautiful, leather-bound) – all were filled with Osi's fluid, descriptive, precise and suggestive line. Two greyhounds float and dance on my bedroom wall, one in red chalk, the other suspended in blue.

Osi often speaks of love and this is a part of teaching that may be forgotten or obscured by our contemporary fears. The passion for a subject or practice, and affection for the student are threads that web the studio as we teach. The artist's and art school studio are spaces where emotion has a place – how to make anything otherwise?

Teaching is a form of parenting and so of immortality – our students are ours always and as descendants carry fragments of knowledge and experience into the future. In the time that I worked with Osi he taught hundreds of students, and none will have forgotten him. The skills of the drawing class will still be used by most – looking and seeing, and responding to what is seen with thought and feeling. Many are still drawing.

Osi often rushed from our studio to the BBC studios across the road to record an interview, or arrived with news of filming in Australia, his garden or at the top of a mountain. We fielded enquiries from young producers with piping Oxbridge accents and worried whether they would be presented with the abrasive or the charismatic (but always eloquent) man.

Osi is an ardent Welshman and passionate about the politics of place, borders, ethnicity and nationality, most particularly in relation to Wales and Palestine and the Middle East. Something seemed to soften, though, in the time that we taught together, as he came to an accommodation with this English foe.

Art education, and the Foundation Art and Design course in particular, is a broad education, about life, self and everything. In addition to life drawing Osi performed a series of lectures, vivid histories examining the decades of the twentieth century and the start of the twenty-first through art and design, politics and social issues.

Each year the Foundation course makes a study visit, often to Amsterdam, and Osi would speak of mud, war and the landscape as we approached Ypres on our journey home. We walked the city looking, eating, drinking, talking. Sitting outside the Kröller Müller Museum, drinking a beer with Osi while watching the birds and trees is framed as a moment of afternoon sunshine and happiness.

Osi sparked us all and stays with us as a voice we can conjure to argue with, to advise and guide. There is so much that could be said about Osi and teaching – these are just notes, a scrap torn from ten years, within a fifty-year span. Working with Osi as his colleague and friend has been and is one of the privileges of my life.

Over the ferny leaf – blades lying close to
the bank and now deeper green from the dry
weather a network of bright gossamer threads,
woven close together and catching the slant
evening sun so as to shimmer with a soft,
trembling brilliancy; we both remarked on it...[2]

1. *A House of Children*, Joyce Carey, Michael Joseph, London, 1941, pp.237-8.
2. *Poems: Pearls That Were,* J.H. Prynne, Bloodaxe, Northumberland, 2005, p.453.

Life study from drawing book. 2003. Watercolour. 10″ x 8″

118

Ar goll/Abandoned. Oil on canvas. 16"x10"

Cheese on toast

STEVE WILSON

The first time I met Osi was as a student in the 1980s. Art school was a joy and a boiling pot of all things weird and wonderful. From the moment I walked into the art school the nature of the educational establishment was obvious, plenty of colourful people, blue hair, green shoes; self expression in all its manifestations was evident. To some extent I was prepared for this, but it was Osi and his energy that overwhelmed me. He was passionate, busy and got straight to the point very quickly, with hardly a pause for breath. I remember the first few sessions very well. His quick-fire comments, observations and references were punctuated only to eulogise about his morning snack, cheese on toast, made the night before. A high-energy fuel for a lecturer on overdrive, it was hard to keep up. I can't but feel that his knowledge and breadth as an artist was to some extent wasted on us at that young age.

And yet, as an educationalist he has left a powerful impression on a generation of students. His message was simple: learn your craft, develop skills and understanding. Osi was never afraid to challenge and argue, at times, I thought, in quite loaded situations. I watched in quiet awe how he negotiated with edgy art students, treading this minefield with great panache and humour. His classes were lean, focused and thorough. There were no hiding places, everyone was expected to take part and make a full contribution and to justify their space and the attention of the tutor. That culture and reverence was always present, though importantly balanced with good humour and no doubt fuelled with his cheese on toast mid-morning snack.

I was lucky to have Osi as mentor; he didn't just talk on art he instructed on it. On many occasions over the years he illustrated a point by pulling out his sketchbook and sharing his work with us. I have very clear memories of that because it made such a big impact. For those who have been through an intense period of learning how to paint and draw, they will understand the significance of watching a practiced hand at work, of seeing a beautifully crafted image develop, witnessing the pattern and layers unfold. I remember the vivid colours and the underlying drawing; it was instructive and magical and in my experience very few tutors are either willing or able to demonstrate their craft in this way.

In more recent years I occasionally call on Osi. In 2011 I made a trip to Llansteffan and he gave me a tour of his studio. Before I knew it, he was hanging upside down from the beam, oblivious to the shower of coins falling from his pockets, so preoccupied was he with the point he was making, exercise the mind, exercise the body.

Osi is a driven individual, a deep thinker who is always making the argument that Welsh art, Welsh culture and Welsh communities deserve respect. Anyone making that argument needs a thick skin, it seems.

As a painter he uses powerful imagery to reflect his ideas, his outlook and experience. His images of the industrial footprint left in Wales leave a deep impression. Landscapes littered with more than industrial debris, but pollution too, often leaving diminished and ragged communities in the wake of the closed mines and other industrial works no longer in service. However, it is his work depicting the military presence in Wales and beyond that has left the deepest impression on me. Reminding us to be mindful of the active military machine that has wrought havoc in so many communities, particularly in the Middle East. To put this in context, a million people marched on London in 2003 to make it

Life study from drawing book.
1989. Gouache. 12" x 18"

contemporary rather than a Biblical context. So many of Osi's paintings are deceptively pastoral and gentle, but when you see the work as a whole, the landscapes have become increasingly punctuated with dissonant elements, the helicopters and jets act as a poignant reminders that all is not well, neither here in Wales or for that matter in Palestine. When Osi paints a Chinook helicopter, a red painting, ringing high-pitched with the sound and sight of the military aircraft hovering over the Welsh landscape, we know that he is not just painting 'landscape with helicopter', he is making a strong political statement. The MOD helicopter is making a dissonant sound in an otherwise peaceful country. This is a strong and defiant statement: 'Not here, not in my name'.

The apparent emphasis on colour in Osi's paintings belies the underlying drawing which is fundamental to the success of his images. At times his use of colour reflects a received and familiar naturalism, at other times, the palette is reduced, the colour intensified. Combined with stark and haunting images of figures and sinister aircraft, the result is powerful. Although his work is highly crafted, he manages to keep a freshness that allows the emotion to remain raw and tangible. Osi represents the views of many in his work; it resonates particularly with those who feel their voices are not heard.

It seems to me that there is little conciousness of Wales externally. We are perceived as minor and unremarkable; as a nation, our sensibilities are often ignored. Wales might be a small place, but it has a big and deep interior. It is my opinion that the big characters from Wales have helped to anchor our national identity and help preserve our sense of self worth. Osi is one such big character, an artist who as a celebrant of Wales, peace and equity, has left a colourful mark on this beautiful country.

clear that war was not acceptable, I saw the coachloads of protesters leaving from west Wales, I was present at the local vigils. Since then in a whole variety of forms many have continued to speak out in print, in performance, debate and in paint. In Wales as elsewhere there is a feeling that we cannot tolerate a military agenda to develop such momentum again, and that we in Wales have a part to play in resisting it. My own political awareness grew out of conversations with people like Osi, I was made aware that the whole story was not being told in the mainstream media and that we had to inform ourselves and see the world from other perspectives.

I remember Osi's work from the mid eighties. His paintings of Palestine and Wales were lyrical with flowing lines, drawn as much as painted. I think it was the first time I saw Palestine in a

Red Helicopter.
Oil on unprimed canvas. 171cm x 140cm
Private collection

122

Operation Cast Lead. 2009. Mixed media and collage on paper
Private collection

123

Operation Cast Lead (*detail*). 2009. Mixed media and collage on paper
Private collection

Hofrennydd/Helicopter. 2010. Oil on canvas. 60cm x 40cm

124

Helicopter (detail). 2010. Mixed media. 10″ x 8″

125

Knowing Osi

SAM VICARY

I am waiting in the college canteen with my new friends, gazing down from the first-floor gallery where they serve cheese pasties and cups of grey tea, looking at the heavy, double-door entrance.

I'm excited. Osi is paying a visit to Greestone Building on Lindum Road, Lincoln. He's bringing this year's group of Foundation students to see what the college has to offer. I'm hoping he will show up soon. And then he does, bursting through the doors and addressing the entire college:

> 'Hello Sam, where are you? Come to your Da!'
> I am blushing. I am at a loss.
> 'Is that really your Dad?' asks my friend
> And I'm quick to explain, 'No, no, that's Osi.'

Some encounters are important, it seems, and they are meant to last a lifetime. Although I've never recorded my time with Osi, never been one to keep a diary or make notes, my old sketchbooks are bursting with his teaching and my mind is full of images and stories.

In 1991 I left Wales to begin a degree. During that year my parents decided to divorce and the family home was no longer a happy place. There was every chance I could have faltered and abandoned my art education had it not been for Osi's motivation. He was my teacher, a driving force, and so I became the first person in my family to go to university.

When I started writing this, I opened my portfolio for some encouragement and found a stack of old drawings, monoprints and paintings. I remember the long, nurturing hours in the life room crunching charcoal into paper, and then progressing to paint and the wonderful world of colour and expression. I can see Giacometti's influence in the elongated drawings and blurred, energetic marks. I can also see Osi's. I watched him while he studied the model and suggested I made corrections to my drawing. He had been known to rip up work and get students to start again. We discovered nothing was precious in the classroom, except for those times when teacher and pupils were focused and learnt from each other.

It's a marvellous experience knowing Osi and there are lots of entertaining stories about the man and his manners. It's good to have a story to tell, and sometimes I forget which encounters are mine and which I've adopted. I like the ones where Osi is entertaining, such as the time he had lunch in a café near Cork Street and took the olive oil from the table to rub into his hair. I am sure I was there.

In 2009 I had the pleasure of working with my friend when he showed *Ymateb* at Oriel Mwldan in Cardigan, and I was the programmer. It could have been awkward, because there were decisions to be made about the hanging and installation and we might not have agreed. But Osi had experience in these matters and a plan to go with it. 'There can be only one boss' he said, 'let's see what you do with my work.'

The work was disturbing, uncomfortable, compelling and often very beautiful. It carried the harrowing message of war and the atrocities happening to the people of Gaza. The large-scale drawings and seemingly serene landscapes mapped the links between Osi's home in Llansteffan and weapon-testing sites along the estuary. It reminded me how close this was to my own home and how fragile our lives were.

The show opened with lively banter and plenty of reunions. People had come to see Osi: artist, writer, broadcaster and everyone's teacher. At some point he had probably offered them hospitality, reason, empathy and a taste of his natural wit. The exhibition was a huge success, the conversation was interesting and people left feeling like they had connected with the artist and understood his visual language.

I work in the arts, but I haven't always made my own. There were reasons for not practicing and somehow it became easier to hide behind an excuse, a distraction or someone else's achievement. Osi never stopped asking how my work was going and he wasn't talking about paid employment either. His belief in those early drawings and paintings astonished me and kept the fire in my belly.

Last year I made new work to show in Oriel Q in Narberth. The experience was liberating and during the process I remembered my practice. I was happy and went about day-to-day life with new eyes. I had conversations with people where I lost concentration and found I was studying their face, observing colour and tone and deciding how I would describe it. I read the names on the tubes of paint like they were old friends, stretched canvas, created a catalogue of reference, talked through ideas and dreamt of tomorrow's time in the studio. I suppose, in the back of my mind, I also wondered what Osi would say.

On the day of the opening it was hot and sunny and he arrived at the gallery looking very dapper in a hat. I'm transported back to my college days. I'm excited.

He approached the exhibition in his usual, confident manner, knowing exactly where to look and what to say. Incredibly he could

127

Helicopter (detail). 2010. Graphite. 10″x 8″

relate the new work to the past and spoke about the act of painting as if it were a special power.

There are many occasions when Osi has enlightened me, shared his knowledge, home cooking, passion for life and embarrassed me. It's all part of the game. I believe we find friendship amongst people we admire, because they are the ones that remind us of the qualities we possess and the need to work harder

So we can be
A tiny bit more
Like them.

Contagious passion

TINA CARR

I first came across Osi in the corridors of the Art School in Job's Well Road, Carmarthen. He was the head of Foundation and me a part-timer in the Photography department. I would always hear him before actually seeing him. His voice mellifluous in a way only Welsh voices can be – both loud and soft, rounded vowels and clipped ends – oozing the length of the long passageways between spaces like oil paint being squeezed from the tube.

His students, many of whom I also taught, were never ambivalent about him, he was 'clean off' or 'thinks a lot of himself he does'. Funny that, coming from students, but they loved him and he inspires them with his energy, his engagement with art, with politics and with life. Osi never merely walks anywhere; he processes like royalty, greeting whosoever he meets with the vocal equivalent of a 'high five'. Heads turn when he enters a room. His presence is felt in response to the airwaves leaving the space he now occupies and the intake of breaths as he is noticed by all and sundry. Osi responds with sparkling eyes and a flouncing of his Gypsy curls. He has arrived.

I love Osi's work as well as the man. His paintings, growing impressively larger over the years as the subjects he focuses on scale up. His dog series, small yellow dogs, larger red dogs all angular, looking lost and abandoned amid backgrounds of thick sculpted paint. The one I want is on wall in his front parlour, still waiting for me to stump up the cash.

Wattsville, the mining town where he was born, the culture into which he slid seamlessly and which could have engulfed him completely had he not fallen in love with the colours at the surface. The green of the valley, the bronze of the bracken, the red and gold of the sunset, debossed on his retina, informed his

sensibilities and kept him out of the mines in a physical sense. However mining seeped into his being by osmosis like beer absorbed through the publican's skin while he pulls the pints. And this is where Osi, my partner Annemarie and I come together. Our work too, almost without exception is imbued with mining. The reworking of the landscape, the spirit of the people, the physicality and community of the work, the terrible aftermath of closure and decline all of which we have recorded in our photographs and videos through successive projects in Wales. For our second book *Coalfaces* (2008) we asked Osi to write one of the accompanying essays, which he duly agreed to do. We could not think of a more appropriate or better qualified person to do this, Osi by then having become quite renowned for his writing skills, pertinent reviews in *Planet, The Welsh Internationalist*, and other such arteries of cultural in Wales, essays full of pithy metaphors. One that springs to mind, and will always be embedded in my brain as a milestone in the art-scape, is the phrase Osi coined to describe certain people in the establishment that he thought were missing something vital as suffering from 'cultural Alzheimer's'.

As part of Osi's research for his essay we all three went up to the location of the *Coalfaces* work – the Upper Afan Valley and the villages of Abergwynfi and Blaengwynfi in particular. We looked around to see what changes there were, if any, in the intervening eighteen years since the work was made – it was all depressingly the same or even worse. Then we went to have tea with Bert Ackery, a former miner, first as a collier boy aged fourteen, in the South Pit in Glyncorrwg, and later as a 'safety man' in the Dyffryn Rhondda Pit. Bert, by then well into his eighties, fell instantly in love with Osi and began to reel off his whole life story. He told Osi about how he loved his working horses. One in particular called 'Quack' had saved his life by sensing a rock fall in time for Bert to

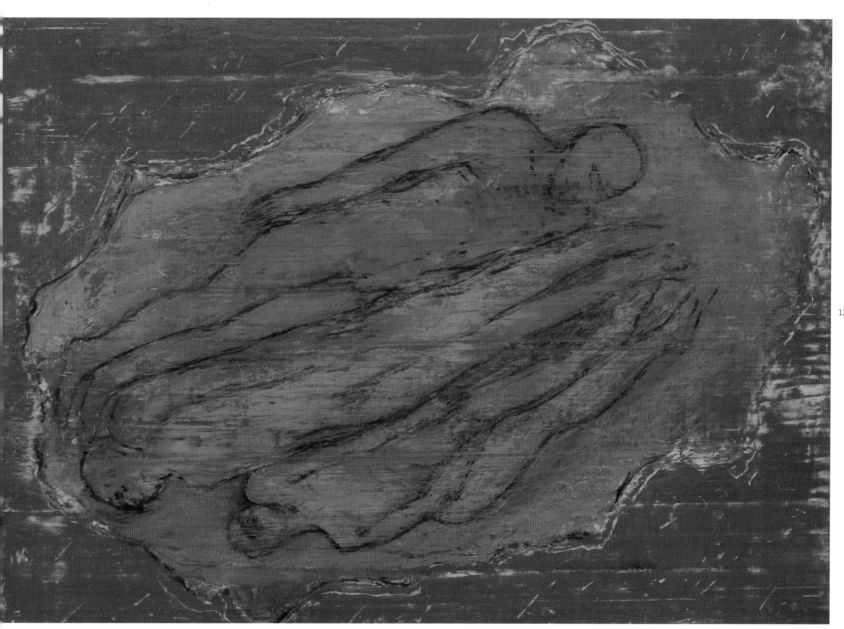

129

In evidence. Oil on canvas

get clear. He didn't know why they were called 'pit ponies' because they were really fully grown horses. How he graduated from horses to working the 'joy loader' and held the record for shifting the most amount of coal ever, a hundred and twenty tons in one shift. Then he became the 'first aid' man and was the only person allowed to administer morphine underground to men injured in accidents, and so on, an endless stream of consciousness from one coal man to another. Osi listened and learned, paced up and down the little parlour of the cottage looking at all the photos and the ephemera of Bert's life, interjecting when he could get a word in. Both men in full song were a joy to behold. We came away awash with tea and tales.

Osi wrote a fine piece for *Coalfaces* called 'Cul-de-Sac. Through a Glass Darkly'. It takes the reader through the photo documentary history of the coal valleys and contains some great plays with words that only Osi could have invented. Talking about the remedial landscape work undertaken in the valleys that remove any evidence of mining and superficially dress them up, Osi calls this 'post-industrial Botox'. Wow! Talk about hitting the nail on the head.

Another piece of wordplay that I enjoy again and again is this where Osi says: 'the smile has disappeared from the landscape and is replaced by the rictus grin of the unnaturally realigned.' Beautiful. And, talking about the now famous Glyncorrwg cycle trails Osi describes them as: 'adventure that utilises the wild landscape in a promiscuously short-term relationship with the geography that bypasses the social reality of life after coal for the local population.' Well, pinpoint accurate I say.

We were so pleased with Osi's essay that what ensued came as a major surprise. The day of the *Coalfaces* launch arrived. It was held at the National Library of Wales in Aberystwyth, in conjunction with an exhibition of the prints and videos. To a packed, expectant audience in the 'Drwm' Lecture Theatre, Osi proceeded to wet the baby's head in his usual courtly manner. First came the context. Next, extolling the merits of the work, then praising the artists for their consummate skill, their technical abilities, their commitment to their subjects – and then, the bombshell. With a rapier-like arm and forefinger extended, pointing directly at us sitting on the platform to his left, he pronounced that never in his entire career had he ever been asked to revise or make amendments to any piece or fragment of his work, that is until NOW. Annemarie and I had what can only be described as an OMG moment. What had we done? I remembered asking him to perhaps look at his essay one more time, tighten it up maybe, not to change anything, and all in the spirit of what Annemarie and I thought was collaboration. That day we saw another facet of the man, the tender, vulnerable side that could of course be hurt, albeit unintentionally. It is a standing joke between us now – the women who told Osi to go back and do it again!

On the beach at Llansteffan, Osi's territory, a beautifully warm afternoon, the tide completely out so that all the sandbanks are revealed, shiny and wet. The wading birds feed nonchalantly. Looking over the Sand Hills towards the Bristol Channel, the whole peace is despoiled by the firing range in line of sight and the massive noise of an unseen jet aircraft rehearsing for war somewhere overhead. 'Hawks and Helicopters', the series of paintings we love most in which Osi's gaze is fixed in the palimpsest of paint lain over with the graffiti of the war machine and sometimes birds. He attests to the fragility of life. His passion drives him forward. He is still very much in love with life.

Cysgodion/Shadows. Oil on canvas

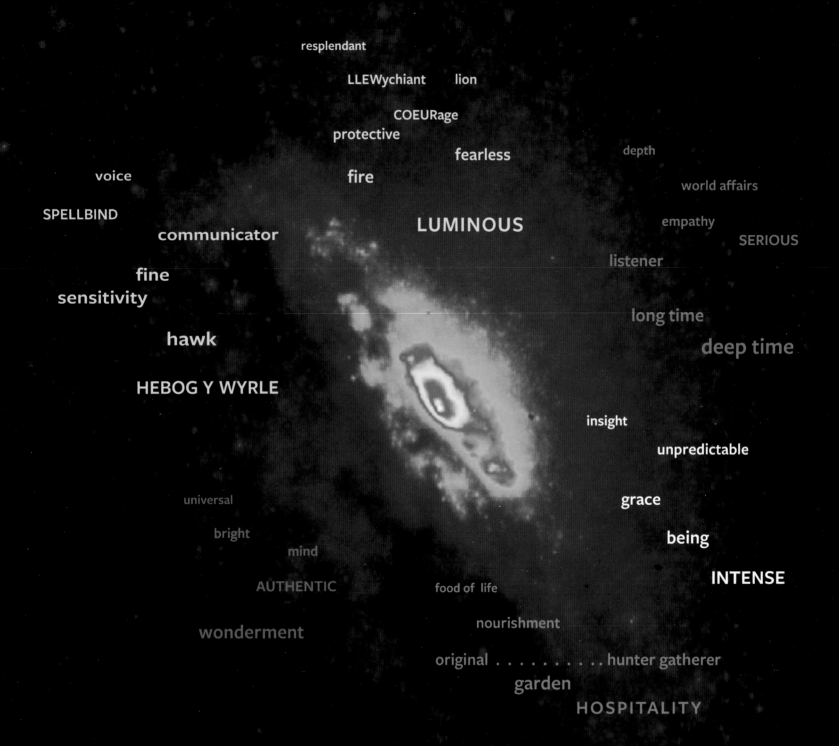

resplendant

LLEWychiant   lion

COEURage
protective

depth

fearless

voice   world affairs

fire

SPELLBIND   LUMINOUS   empathy

communicator   SERIOUS

listener

fine
sensitivity   long time

hawk   deep time

HEBOG Y WYRLE

insight

unpredictable

universal

grace

bright

being

mind

INTENSE

AUTHENTIC   food of life

nourishment

wonderment

original . . . . .hunter gatherer

garden

HOSPITALITY

Above: (background) Image of galaxy NGC 4945 - showing the huge luminosity of the central few star clusters. The colour-code corresponds to intensity.
Credit: ESO European Southern Observatory

Luminosity

rugby
passion
hwyl
Cymru
Warrior for Peace
calon
solidarity
artist
cultural activist

Stages of Luminosity . . . Siân Lewis

Initially you perceive something intense, mine was a kind of 'what was that tornado?' moment in 1983, as a Foundation student sapling at Dyfed College of Art, Carmarthen, where Osi taught. Some years later I tutored part-time on the inspirational Foundation Course run by Osi and Hedley Jones, which they 'led from the rear' with intent to trigger self sufficiency and independent thinking in the students. Random sketchbook checks, zero tolerance of synthetic shoes, e.g. odourous trainers (somewhat attributable to heated life-drawing classes), total ban on laziness and a stealthy encouragement of intelligent creative application pervaded this stimulating climate....with advice to hold the creative process lightly, 'treat it like a delicate bird - don't crush it'.

Stellar reverie

I have since had the great good fortune to know both Osi and Hilary in profound and treasured friendship. I've experienced their joyous, warm hospitality - it's like no other, with loving kindness and solidarity. This friendship was ignited around Osi's 50th birthday - June 28th 1992. I joined him with his family - Hilary, Sara, Che and Luke, for a magical day on 'the boat' - a traditional wooden sailing yacht. In many ways, it was exquisitely simple and uncomplicated but also an extraordinarily 'golden day' - a stellar reverie. We set sail from Llansteffan boat club, relaxed in warm easy sunshine, journeyed out into Carmarthen Bay where the anchor was dropped and we all dived into a scintilating clear sea. It was like swimming in starlight - breathtaking - followed by a delectable picnic of smoked salmon with lemon, Hilary's home-made bread and champagne....and to finish off an evening barbecue in the garden....a truly visceral, Llansteffan Riviera experience which, according to Osi and Hilary, was their very best day on the boat.

'Sauce or gravy?'

The 'sauce or gravy' question arose during a memorable Celtic feast of Samhain prepared by Osi, at home in Llansteffan and filmed as an episode of *TV Dinners*, presented by Hugh Fearnley Whittingstall, first broadcast on Channel 4 in 1998. This was an exceptionally atmospheric and fun feast to partake in. Osi excelled with culinary prowess and wit, 'turning' several of the vegetarian film crew into momentary meat eaters, as the aromatic roast rack of pork emerged from the kitchen, wafting of cider, bay leaves, cloves and garlic. Osi passed around the 'sauce or gravy' to which I enquired 'what's the difference?' Quick as a flash came his incisive retort: 'gravy is what my mother makes, who comes from the valleys - and sauce is what people make once they've been to college and read the 'Sunday Times etc...'
(To view the programme on Channel 4 - *TV Dinners*, series 3/episode 8: www.channel4.com/programmes/tv-dinners/on-demand/25046-008)

Luminosity as 'the intrinsic brightness of a celestial object'

I understand we are all made of stardust...through time and experience I've developed a fuller awareness of this exceptionally bright star in our galaxy and the effect of its radiance. My 'tornado' introduction has evolved into witnessing a Warrior for Peace with an 'unsplittable core' (ref: Giacometti)...he always signs off 'mewn heddwch / in peace'. This fully fledged, fully formed, flawed, reluctant role model keeps you on your toes though...won't allow you to indulge your deluded projections, but encourages a state of curiosity, engagement and intensity with 'who you want to be' as opposed to 'what you want to do' in life.

Luminosity in relation to my 'bioluminescent encounter'

It may not be evident immediately that something has rubbed off on you, but gradually there's a wellspring of thought, enquiry, memory, feeling that has been untapped and thereafter, like those fireflies or clock faces that glow after the lights go out, something remains illuminated, sparked!...a super positive contagion. This source of Luminosity has an integrity and freedom of being which engenders an unframed, ongoing, unpredictable, always surprising dialogue.

Ceffyl Glas

Andrew and I love this painting by Osi which we enjoy in our home. We are silently tuned in to this deep, blue, visual dialogue...

Time passes...and Osi finds a small black plastic toy horse on a beach in Greece; this becomes one of his favourite sculptures...we then reinterpret it for him in bronze. While it was in our care, a new dialogue developed between the the small toy horse and the painting. I photographed the 'scene' and posted it to Osi as a birthday card.

This image of communion represents an 'Encounter with Osi'...a conversation between worlds, dimensions, times, colours - in humour, tenderness and light.

Left : The painting featured in the image is *Ceffyl Glas* - Osi Rhys Osmond, oil painting on canvas, 12 x 16 inches, 2004

Images etc...

One August afternoon last year, as we in Llansteffan journeyed around the late tantalising sun, I danced around Osi and Hilary's home, camera in hand, foraging for rich pickings. The thing is, there's so much rich material - the artwork, atmosphere, objects, colours, the invisible yet tangible, special feeling of being there, both inside and out in the garden, which is very much an extension of the house...Osi and Hilary's home is such a pure reflection of themselves - their beautiful, sparky, intense way of living. This combined aesthetic DNA is a nourishing elixir...Some of those photographs I then wove into early concept layouts for this book.

luminosity
'In astronomy, luminosity is the total amount of energy emitted by a star, galaxy, or other astronomical object, per unit time. It is related to brightness, which is the luminosity of an object in a given spectral region.'
Jeanne Hopkins, *Glossary of Astronomy and Astrophysics* (*2nd edn.*)
University of Chicago Press 2012. ISBN 0-226-35171-8

llewychiant
[bôn y f. fl.+-iant] eg. ll. llewychiannau.
Y cyflwr o fod yn llewychol, goleuad, goleuhad; ysblander: luminosity, illumination; splendour.
GPC Geiriadur Prifysgol Cymru - A dictionary of the Welsh Language
© Hawlfraint Prifysgol Cymru 2014

Friends and family 4

Nathan Osmond
Sara Rhys-Martin
Luke Osmond
Simon Thirsk
Lynne Crompton
Gwenan Rhys Price
Linda Sonntag
Rolf Jucker
Ché Osmond
Macsen Osmond
Colin Brewster
Ben Dressel
Megan Crofton
Lesley Davies

Boys are primitive men (*detail*). 2012. Mixed media/collage

Manafon (detail) from R.S. Thomas series. 2013. Watercolour and collage on paper

My Brother
NATHAN OSMOND

When I look back on it, it was an amazing experience, having a brother who was seventeen years older than me. I was introduced to some amazing sights and sounds (of the sixties) at an early age. Although I was apparently a small guest in a pram at some wild artistic student gatherings (I can't remember), many of those moments of experience were not as you would first imagine. They were quite intense experiences of the landscape and environment. I have early memories of walking, crawling and being persuasively dragged (with tired legs) through overgrown woodland, bracken covered hillsides, rivers and streams that curiously invaded my shoes or boots (which usually had a hole in them somewhere). There were conversations about colours, textures, (that old favourite, dragonflies) and kestrels. And yes, I remember many of these as real conversations, not just the odd sentence delivered to quench the thirst of an inquisitive small person. All this and sheltering from thunderstorms and silently watching the natural world, it all sounds a little romantic, poetic and idyllic.

But it wasn't. We were not writing about it, we were experiencing it. The routes my brother wanted to take were not the official footpaths or well-trodden trails, but the places where 'you might see something' that others on the more manicured and sign-posted trails would not. We would sit and watch all manner of things from falling rain (he remembers me once asking if the rain was man's friend). I remember asking him at a very young age what the colour turquoise was, because he had mentioned it. Going into my father's shed, I recall seeing large pieces of white painted boards with black and red lettering. Again, I can't have been very old, I think he was doing some sign-writing for someone. I remember seeing these and thinking they were really clever. Just a few years ago, at Osi's retrospective exhibition, I overheard someone discussing the draughtsman-like qualities of some aspects of the mining images, and my thoughts went straight back to those very early examples of almost pure technique.

The remarkable thing is that whether I was 4, 14, 24, 34, 44, or now at 55, our meetings and relationship are always emotional and always educational. His ability to light a spark in a conversation, a room, or a relationship remains undiminished. To call him inspirational and passionate would be the biggest understatement. I am aware that as a teacher and mentor he has changed and still is influencing many people. As an artist and commentator he has done the same, but as a brother he gave me guidance and love that was unconditionally mine.

Yes he has always been a creative person, he had no time for ignorance and shallow views on subjects, or stereotypical views on any culture. Perhaps the WRU should have taken him on board as a cultural advisor to the Welsh team (and selectors) back in the 90s. By now, we might well have had a team with a sense of purpose and belief system to compete with the All Blacks.

Whilst I am on the rugby subject, my earliest memory of a game was when he took me to see Newport play the Springboks in the early 60s during an outbreak of foot and mouth. He was explaining why we had to walk through deep (to me) straw that had the pungent aroma of Jeyes fluid disinfectant. And back to the present time, he still enjoys going to matches but becomes (like me) increasingly annoyed at those supporters who are either engaging with social media instead of watching the match, or those who are just too drunk to know what is happening. More recently, it was lovely to see Osi enjoying the presence of a large part of the family at a match in Cardiff this year. I don't think the rugby came close to providing the enjoyment he was getting from being in a long row of sons, grandsons, son-in-law, nephew, niece and brother.

He still likes to disrupt any complacency, and has enough academic and cultural ammunition to do this with ease. His occasionally outspoken views may have been tempered of late but it is still fascinating to be around him anywhere, whether this is on the city street, on a mountaintop or at the dinner table. I would say that he has always been a man totally involved and immersed in life and experiences. He doesn't like to see people disengaged from the real experiences of life, as so many people seem to be at present.

He has been my official best man twice. When I was first married, it was in Norway, and he delivered a best man's speech which was memorable. The reception was in a large wooden mountain centre in the middle of the Trondelag mountains. The main course on the menu was reindeer. His opening words were, 'Well I don't know what Father Christmas is going to do this year.' His second best man's speech was many years later at my wedding in Llansteffan, where he engaged all of my English friends from London with his warmth and eloquence, whilst managing to humorously advise them not to spend too much time looking in estate agents' windows for second homes.

I remember being in a car with him in Newport one evening (I think I was about 14 or 15), and we had stopped at a traffic light when he noticed that an elderly man seemed to be in trouble on the pavement. Many people were avoiding his predicament (he may have been having a stroke), but my brother just left the car and went to help, getting him inside somebody's doorway and making sure he received attention. I suppose I am saying he was

always 'bothered', he was and is the antithesis of the current teenage phrase 'can't be arsed'. Always willing to listen and engage with people of all ages. Even when he was a young man I can remember him being fascinated by listening to the experiences of people even older than my parents. I have fragmented memories of the making of that black and white film that was shown in the exhibition mentioned earlier. He was interviewing retired miners and others for the sound recording to the film. It was apparent that his interest wasn't just in the sound recording, it was in them as people.

Over the years and on numerous occasions, friends of mine on first meeting my brother have been 'stunned'. For some, his enthusiasm and passion for life can at times be overwhelming. I remember in the early eighties someone asking him if he was taking any drugs or was he normally like that?

My wife first met him on a train not long after we had first met each other. This was an unplanned meeting before the days of mobile phones. We were getting on a train from Newport to Paddington and he was on it with a large group of his students on the way to London. We had a fantastic journey, full of questions, conversation, noise and colour. I remember my wife making a comment saying it was amazing to meet him, but comparing it to being caught in something like a tornado or hurricane of creative enthusiasm.

I suppose the greatest thing about this energy and enthusiasm was that it was not then, and is never now, just based on what we would now call a 'soundbite' from a shallow knowledge base, but a real belief in, and understanding of what he is talking about. As a brother I have him to thank for much of my development as a person, but also the development of my interests in the natural world and my photographic career, for sparking that early interest and just helping me find things out. I thank him for encouraging me with books and exhibitions, and always asking me how things are going. For being a rock when I needed it and a sounding board, an advisor when I asked for it.

In fact, he has been a constant inspiration and mentoring presence for me on all levels. I was with him and Hilary a few years ago when he was given his prognosis. I am amazed at how he has dealt with cancer. He said to me that he wasn't as much fighting it but applying a series of policies against it. Refusing to dwell on the negatives and having the support and love of his family and friends has undoubtedly helped, but his greatest reservoir has been supplied by the happiness and love his relationship with Hilary over the years has given him. As a young man he was always a 'bit of a tough cookie' and even now, if I was cancer, I wouldn't have taken him on.

So, there we have it! Perhaps the greatest thing about the last few years is that we've had them and will have more. I'm still talking in the present tense.

With family members – Rhondda Heritage Centre 2012

Osi, not just my mother's husband

SARA RHYS-MARTIN

How would I begin to describe Osi Rhys Osmond? Not only my mother's husband, Welsh artist, father, grandfather, writer, radio personality, TV presenter, traveller, gardener, creator, cook, sailor... the list goes on and illustrates his enormous personality and enthusiasm for life. If I was asked to provide instances to describe Osi (or on rare occasions, Donald, as I affectionately call out when, heedless of our slower pace, he leaves us behind both physically and mentally), such instances that come to my mind are these...

Although I always identified myself as being Welsh, I did not understand the full extent and meaning of Welsh identity until Osi started his work based on the Machynlleth stone graffiti. I joined him and my mother on a tour around Wales for research for his exhibition in the summer before I started university. Through my fascinating and illuminating discussions with Osi, my eyes and mind were opened to the history of Wales and the meaning of Welsh identity. Subsequently my passion for my own Welsh identity was stirred up, and a desire to learn the Welsh language, which continues to this day over twenty years later. Osi has huge amounts of historical information, which he retells in a captivating, moving and passionate way that becomes engraved on minds and remains for years.

As a teenager, I used to become acutely embarrassed at how vocal Osi can be when dissatisfied with service, food, places and his refusal to queue. However I would also be amused and impressed by his refusal to assimilate into most of society. Osi is not afraid to make a stand and to make a statement for what he believes in, whether it is the quality of service or people's behaviour. When travelling in Europe, as a teenager with him, I would be mortified by his insistence on walking into the kitchen if

142

In the flow of an impassioned address – Rhondda Heritage Centre 2012 Opening of *Landscape and Heritage*

he was not satisfied by his meal, and demanding to know which person had made it, then request for the food to be made again, which often required my mother to act as an interpreter, leaving me blushing with embarrassment at the table. He would also obtain fascinating personal stories from those around him whenever he showed his genuine interest in people's lives.

Another amusing memory is when we went to the L'Orient Interceltic Festival in Brittany. We were camping for the first time and I was a young teenager accompanied by a school friend. There were dogs on the campsite and Osi was quite rightly disgusted by the dog faeces dotted around the campsite (we are talking about over twenty years ago) and created little paper flags from his drawing book and twigs to put down next to the faeces with the words 'Merde de Chien!' written on them.

However, observing his refusal to assimilate has hugely influenced my subsequent confidence to develop my sign-language skills and become uninhibited by the use of sign language in society, whilst studying and in my workplace.

Travelling with Osi teaches me to view countries and sceneries as paintings, and to expand the use of my senses; not only learning about cultures and languages but to savour the sights, smells and textures of the country we are travelling in, absorbing the environment and atmosphere. Travelling with Osi almost always ensures meetings with interesting people, both new acquaintances and those from his past. Travelling with Osi typically consists of hectic, interesting and entertaining days, trotting after and with him on his wanderings, including driving off the beaten track to discover places he caught glimpses of while passing. Recovery was usually achieved by reclining on the ground while Osi energetically

painted, and in evenings consisting of eating and drinking delicious food and wine.

Art also became an intrinsic part of my life thanks to Osi's natural, passionate and enthusiastic teaching; as a teenager, I joined several art tours with his students at Trinity College, Carmarthen to London and the Netherlands. Through his fascinating descriptions of the art exhibitions we visited alongside explanations of the painters' personal lives, my passion for art and desire to understand the stories behind paintings and sculptures was fired up. That passion continues to this day. Our home has paintings that I've fallen in love with over the years from one of the most influential artists I've experienced, Osi Rhys Osmond. I think that one reason that my emotions become inspired by his paintings, more so than other artists, is because, through sharing his personal life, I understand the stories behind his work, which makes the paintings incredibly evocative.

These examples are only a selected few of many experiences I have had with Osi and continue to have.

It is not possible to summarise Osi Rhys Osmond in a few words. However, those words that come to my mind when I think of Osi are: intelligent, exuberant, enthusiastic, passionate, energetic, impatient, determined, extrovert, vain, generous, wise, loyal, memorable, supportive, loud, humorous. Osi is a strong, colourful individual evoking emotions in people he meets for various reasons, and always touching people's lives and minds.

Paintings on the wall of the front room, Bristol House, Llansteffan

Encounters with Osi

LUKE OSMOND

Whilst out on a walk with my own children recently, I was thinking about why I call my father Osi, or Ozi as it was before he Welshified it, and not dad, daddy or father. I cannot recall ever having called him dad. I have never really asked him about it and in some ways I think it should be left that way. Like many legendary people known by one name – Sting, Elvis, Picasso or Dalí – there is a touch of the showman to Osi. As a 10 year old I fondly remember sitting on the side of the stage at the Queens Hall in Narberth in the early 80s watching him belt out another Ian Dury number with his band 'The Philes'. This isn't to say he is a *complete* show off, it's just that he has a natural talent to entertain. And he always has something to say. He has always been very political. I remember going out canvassing in the general election of 1983. He was running as a Plaid Cymru candidate in Pembrokeshire, or Little England beyond Wales, and what a fight he put up against Nicholas Edwards who was the shoe-in Conservative candidate.

Osi let us grow up outside: incredible freedom to roam on adventures, learning practical skills from him, life skills from diving into any body of water with complete disregard to the dangers, and I loved being allowed to help him 'fix stuff', a pleasure that continues to this day. He allowed me to do things, try things out and make mistakes; to just have a go. Last summer we embarked on a project to landscape his garden, as we had done 30 years ago at Bryncelyn, digging a pond, building stone walls and even some steps up to the greenhouse. He let me do the lion's share this time around, but for a different reason.

My brother and I always enjoyed teasing him about his story telling, especially regarding his Davy Crockett-esque childhood. If you know Osi, or have heard him recount any one of his myriad experiences in life, you'll know he enjoys a good yarn. We took delight in chanting 'Jackanory, Jackonory!' when any aspect of his recounted narratives seemed to stretch his Celtic Storytelling License too far! It makes me chuckle as I write this, and I know Ché will do the same. If it is any consolation to him my children, especially Gwion, are beginning to do the same to me! There were of course more bitter times. When his marriage broke down, I remember shutting him out of my life; there were some very one-sided conversations on the telephone. I was 16 and I was protecting my mother, and probably my own feelings. Looking back, it might have been unfair in some ways, but it was how I saw it at the time. When I went to art college to undertake a foundation course he was running, at first it was a little awkward but I soon began to appreciate how devoted he was and how well he could inspire and inform. Not just art but in ways to think and approach one's life in general. I started out living with him and Hilary in Llansteffan but soon got the urge to move out and live as an art student in Carmarthen. I remember the other students were engrossed with his ways, his personality and charisma. That is one thing I believe he has in abundance. Charismatic, yet humble and true to his roots.

Or course I have always admired his art. He's been painting canvases for as long as I can remember. The earliest paintings I recall were of conflict and suffering, soldiers, images cut from magazines and newspapers and given an artistic treatment that is still as fresh today as it was back then. He travelled to Jordan and Israel to complete the series 'Wales and the Holy Land', landscapes from around Wales and their respective place names in the Middle East. He also began recording his new locality, Llansteffan, with watercolour after watercolour painted on location. I particularly liked the red box paintings, a somewhat ugly and brutal object that he transformed into a motif of beauty. When I finished my fine art degree from Cardiff we had the idea to collaborate for an exhibition in Narberth, 'Luke ap Osi'. I created a series of paintings documenting the changing face of Cardiff Bay, he included a selection from his expansive collection of paintings. It was a highlight for me to have been able to co-exhibit with him and it is wonderful to know he felt the same.

He travelled to Sudan with the Red Cross and created a series of paintings of the people and topography, huge colourful canvases with dark but happy figures which remind me of Matisse's dancers. I think my favourite series has to be 'Hawks and Helicopters', a record of the beauty and tranquillity of Carmarthen Bay contrasted with the underlying menace of the MOD firing range on Cefn Sidan sands. It is quite a sight seeing the fighter jets on their target practice exercises, though nothing can compare to the majesty and sheer excitement of seeing the peregrine falcons swooping over the cliffs on the headland. One of his later series saw him return to his roots, mapping his home village of Wattsville, its people, his family, and the essence of the area in what he coined as 'Psychogeographic Mapping' – large, collaged drawings documenting the land and his memories of it.

To coin Waldo Williams – 'Mynydd Islwyn, the backbone of his youth', Wattsville, once a scarred and traumatised scene now appears an almost idyllic landscape with its steep sides and ever changing colours. To me, Osi is a mountain of a man and nothing ever seems to intimidate him; no matter how big the challenge, Osi will always give his heart, soul and more. If I achieve a hundredth of what he has done I will have lived a full life. I thank him for all that he has done for me, for Wales and forever.

Hostage. 2012. Oil on canvas

Portrait. Oil on canvas

Osimosis: A kind of love

SIMON THIRSK

The first time I met Osi, I wasn't sure. Surely hanging out with a man so much better looking, more knowledgeable and eloquent than me – and, what is more, so unbelievably energetic – would be a big mistake for any man. But as soon as you get to know him, and his wife, Hilary – which, actually, you do immediately because what you see is exactly what you get – the rationale for all that charm falls perfectly into place.

Osi is a teacher, an extraordinary teacher who, whether he is reading, painting, gardening, cooking, driving, or walking through his beloved Wales, can never turn it off: he is constantly questioning, drawing lessons, tapping into his vast pool of knowledge and producing surprising insights for himself and those around him in an almost magical way. It is a way of life in which his wife, Hilary, plays a complementary artistic and musical part.

I always thought I understood a bit about art. (Well, we all feel something when we look at a painting or sculpture, don't we?) On this day we'd been talking about Augustus John, who spent some time near Bala where I live and whose proto-hippy lifestyle, rawness and fraternisation with gypsy girls seemed to me powerful and romantic, if not macho. I think I assumed Osi would feel the same. He didn't. A few months later, visiting the Glyn Vivian Gallery in Swansea with Osi and Hilary, I found myself steered towards a room where a painting of Augustus John's was hanging opposite Gwen John's *Woman in a Coral Necklace*. 'Look at the two paintings and tell me what you feel', Osi smiled. Then I saw – felt – the humanity. How gauche and egotistical Augustus looked then, even with all that power and talent.

Spend time with Osi and you come to intuit this sort of insight;

natural teachers make you feel somehow closer to the world, to think more deeply and question things more profoundly. I call it learning by Osimosis. A weekend with Osi makes me feel clever for a week afterwards. A week with him lasts a month. Three times I have been to the Venice Biennale with Osi and Hilary and each time I have returned feeling I have done a degree course in humanity – and maybe even scraped a pass. His and Hilary's insights are categorically different from mine. Osi's own artworks, whether they are of men in Ethiopia, landscapes in Palestine or the sea and sky and mountains of Wales, cast a similar spell, questioning everything: the beauty of scarred landscapes, the cruelty and kindness of mankind, the dignity of the oppressed.

Osi is now as well known as a commentator on culture and current affairs in Wales as he is as an artist. Though sometimes shocking in his views, and not always right, he is always stimulating and thought provoking – just as a teacher should be. His open and insightful attitude to his cancer speaks to self-exploration, a kind of Socratic exercise in questioning and learning about the role of human spirit in the physical body. To me, Osi's intellectual courage represents the possibility in everyman. Born without privilege, in a coal-mining valley, he has succeeded in both the art world, so frequently dominated by defensive cliques, prejudgements and pretension, and in life itself. To charm one's way through those stockades to the board of the Welsh Arts Council and into the media is surely something. But, to me, it is in the affection in which he and Hilary are held by their wide circle of friends that his true achievements lie, more in humanity than in artistry.

Osi has a particular interest in sketching the human form. Go to any event with him and out comes the drawing book; he starts sketching people, especially faces. His depiction of the human figure is grounded, he will tell you, on a thorough understanding of anatomy, like Michelangelo's. Any artist or casual critic who fails to recognise inaccuracies in bones and organs under the skin, risks instant enlightenment. Osi's depictions of Welsh landscapes, too, are schooled in a profound knowledge of its underlying bones, psychology and history, honed by weather, conquests, seismic shifts and exploitation. Some of his most recent work, such as the exhibition at Rhondda Heritage Centre gallery, exposed the human predicament of the culture he grew up in, drawn in cutaway and painfully depicting the cultural agony of capitalism's greedy scouring of the bones of Wales and the human cost of the process.

'The Welsh', Osi once told me, 'are blessed in the smallest of ways, by being not quite white'. A subtle idea from which I took the title of a novel and which gives me a gentle tingle in my chest each time I hear it. A kind of love. The Welsh are not as similar to the English as those ancient invaders assume. Over-run, integrated, conquered? I think not. The ancient language, culture and personality don't just survive, they sing through men like Osi.

Art, Osi has taught me, cannot be described as 'fine' unless it is also capable of failing. This is a test that condemns much of what passes for contemporary art, and, as with art, so with life and, indeed, people. Fine art can be based only on talent, technique, knowledge and understanding; skills and technique alone can never be more than craft.

Perhaps the English and those who forget these truths are victims of 'cultural Alzheimer's', Osi's intriguing notion that we become spiritually lost in a too-rapidly changing culture, even in the familiar landscape of home, alienated by the financially cynical imposition of retail parks where you could be anywhere, ubiquitous new roads leading to nowhere you wanted to go and the soulless clutter of cloned new homes everywhere – all destroying what was once imperfect, individual and loved.

Being with Osi – great friend that he has become – always makes me feel better, more knowledgeable and eloquent than I feel away from him. He and Hilary have a house stuffed with books and works of art, shouting wisdom and the urgency of art and humanity. What could be more energising and instructive than that?

And the big lesson? When I find myself culturally distanced from who I am and who I might be, I turn to art, often to Osi's painting that hangs on my wall depicting a huge rusted steel box with chains hanging off it that he found washed up on the sand dunes near Llansteffan – a beautiful picture of something that was used for RAF target practice, the man-made ugliness beneath the surface.

What greater lesson can a contemporary teacher impart about art or life? True Osimosis.

151

Cadwyni/Chains. 1992. Hand-mixed oil on canvas

Bethany. 1985. Oil on paper. 30"x40"
Private collection

Fragments from our past
LYNNE CROMPTON

Years later there were remnants of paint in the crevice of a stone on Llawhaden Bridge. This is where Osi had painted the view of the Cleddau and Sunny Hill, a few miles from where he lived overlooking the Preseli Hills, but more importantly or relevant to this story, overlooking The Old Mill where my good friend and his future wife lived. Hilary was also smitten and I accompanied her on 'so-called jogging' forays with the hope that we might come across this handsome artist who lived above our valley. The results are now history, and their passionate relationship continues to this day nearly twenty-eight years later, rewarding their friends with an interesting journey through trials and tribulations where loyalties were tested, broken families mended and eventually happiness descended on all parties.

Over those twenty-eight years our friendship has developed through happy and sad times. Osi's eulogy at my husband Brian's funeral was generous and poignant. Brian, being an English public school PE teacher and Osi a fervent Welsh art teacher, it would seem implausible that they would become friends, and yet through much banter and their shared love of nature, their sailing trips and their women's close friendship, they became firm friends. We shared a few trips to Ireland, looking at Celtic monuments and visiting churches before spending some happy times eating and drinking. Brian loved his pint and our visits to Osi and Hilary's usually began and ended in The Sticks, the pub opposite their house. After some fabulous meals, especially on New Year's Eve, we would adjourn the pub to finish off with a brandy and some-times the party would start again with singing around the piano or, on one memorable New Year's Eve, around the houses in Llansteffan.

Peeling back the years, memories and images tumble down. There are so many, and one that has surfaced is of Osi tucking into a pig's ear next to Ifor Davies who was demolishing a plate of tripe in a cavern basement restaurant in Vilnius while some of us chewed on black bread, smoked between courses and drank a lot to avoid the alternative offal choices. This was on a cultural trip to Vilnius, Lithuania in 2002 where my professional role as curator of Oriel Q Gallery involved eight artists and poets being invited to participate in the Exhibition *META* that had been initiated by Christine Kinsey through her involvement with the composer Bronius Kutavičius.

We had invited artists to choose a poet that they felt shared similar themes in their work and Osi had 'paired' with Elinor Wyn Reynolds. The relationship between the word and the visual is reflected in much of Osi's work and his writing has been a major development in his life, proving him to be a an intellectual figure in the cultural discourse of politics not just of Wales but also of the Sudan and in particular Palestine.

I first came across Osi's work at an exhibition where he had linked Welsh places with those in the Holy Land. Indeed, Bethesda, where he lived when I first met him and where he painted the hills every day, is the title of the first painting I owned of his – but is of Bethesda in Palestine. It hangs on my wall along with a sizeable collection of his work including some watercolours that I treasure, one of which was done on my birthday when Brian, Hilary, Osi and I had gone for a walk in Solva. While we retired to the pub and a big fire on a cold December day, Osi stayed at the end of the harbour painting and he presented his work to me as a birthday present.

I have invited Osi to exhibit at Oriel Q on a number of occasions and he has contributed to the Open shows annually. His series of 'Fenws Machynlleth' based on rubbings he'd taken from a grave, his series of images based on the washed up container at Scott's Bay seen as a metaphor for Wales in chains, his watercolours, 'Machlud', beautiful sunsets over Llansteffan, are but a few selections in his vast repertoire which I hope will be catalogued at some time.

When he was in the Sudan on a mission to record the disappearing way of life and collecting material for what was to be a exhibition shown in Oriel Q in 1998, I was on holiday and holding hands with Hilary in Florence. We were so worried about the risks he was taking, but he returned safely and with such a wealth of drawings and paintings in his sketchbooks that

led to another stunning exhibition.

Anther exhibition that stands out in my memory was the powerful response to the political situation in the Middle East, 'Ymateb' (Response). In these works you can appreciate Osi's intense and passionate concerns about the fate of ordinary people and his anti-war stance on situations around the world.

Wales, of course, is forever with him and in him, and his painted observation of 'Post Industrial Wales' was a touring exhibition that we took from Oriel Q to Wrexham and the Rhondda. In his writing Osi had first mentioned his father's confused state of mind towards his end, a condition Osi called 'cultural Alzheimer's'. This I believe was of paramount importance when Osi toured around

Wales drawing old mine shafts and bits of industry and landscapes that had been cosmetically enhanced but with the guts and soul still throbbing under the surface.

His passion for Wales could often be mistaken for anti-English rhetoric, but his views, anti-royalist and anti-establishment, are what give an edge to his rhetoric and sometimes furious speech. I would say that he is a man who 'does not suffer fools gladly' and not one to engage with in argument, since he believes he has the moral high ground on his side. For those of us who love him, we tend to believe that he has, and we all come under his spell even if it is with rolling of the eyes and shaking of the head. He is an irresistible force of nature.

GWENAN RHYS PRICE

Osi is vibrant, thoughtful and thought-provoking – and definitely the best thing that happened to my sister!
Could say more but I thought I'd keep it brief.
Cariad mawr.

Pages from drawing book.
Machlud dros Pentowyn/
Sunset over Pentowyn.
2009. Watercolour

In balance

LINDA SONNTAG

Work table. Photo: Iwan Bala

I went to collect a painting I had bought from Osi, and Hilary invited me to lunch. We were in the dining room – the door burst open and Osi staggered in, in a burst of wind and rain, water streaming off him – he slipped and dropped his sketchbooks on the floor – they fell open, raindrops spattering on to the fresh water colours from Osi's mac as he bent over to scoop them up. He was not at all distressed that they might get spoiled. He sat down in his wet clothes, rubbing his twisted knee, and spoke passionately about painting and the landscape – he pulled paintings out of a big drawer to show me – he was so vigorous, I was worried he would tear them. All the while, a huge log was burning in the grate, so big it stuck right out on to the floor and under the dining table. Rain rattled against the window – it seemed we might all catch fire or be drowned at any moment. The air was teeming with possibilities – we were poised between creation and destruction. Hilary was watching Osi with Mona Lisa calm but mischief sparkled in her eyes – exactly the combination needed to keep the whole thing in balance.

Who we are, not what we are

ROLF JUCKER

More and more I realise that sharing quality time with friends is some of the richest pickings life has to offer. During our autumn holidays, we went to see Osi and Hilary. As always we were spoilt by Hilary's cooking: her minestrone and her almond cake alone were worth coming all the way from Switzerland. And then there is Osi. I was just blown away by his presence again. I guess he had a really tough year, coping with several rounds of chemotherapy and radiotherapy. But you couldn't tell. I used to say that I very much liked to visit him because he is one of the few people I know who doesn't engage in small talk. This time again, he picked us up from the train station, ushered us into his beloved Jaguar and off we went into some serious discussion about the way the UK and Wales in particular are going to pieces. I really love this: he is not preaching at you, he is not off on a tangent, but he is cutting right through into the heart of the matter. And he does this with his whole being, his wit, sharp intellect, visual sensitivity, heart, passion, historical knowledge and visionary outlook. He is just so fully alive and present that the discussion immediately moves onto a different level, and it doesn't strike you as strange that you are, just two sentences round the bend, talking about the essence of being human (while gutting some fish a neighbour had brought in, as happened on a visit a couple of years back).

I actually came with some trepidation. Since I hadn't been to the UK for almost a year now, it just hit me when I arrived in London this time how run-down, dysfunctional and terribly lacking in life energy and future vision England was, an impression which was reinforced in Wales, in Swansea, Newport and Cardigan. But I was a bit hesitant to share these observations since I didn't want to be impolite to our UK hosts. But no need for false modesty with Osi: he himself openly complained about the incredible complacency and lack of understanding in most areas of life here.

When contemplating why this was the case, we quickly realised that it all started with Victorian clerks, trying to organise life into forms, processes, desk-based structures, cutting out all the chaotic and unruly and messy energy of real life.

For me, jumping like this into the midst of what really matters is like a revelation and a huge boost to inspiration. Osi, unlike most people I know, manages to be so interested in who we are, what life can yield if you are open enough to welcome it with both arms, that he fuses in himself what otherwise you have to seek out in different people. You know what I mean: some people are really fantastic artistically, but never dare to talk to them about science. Others are really emotionally competent and caring, but they have never understood the difference between war and peace, let alone capitalism, consumerism and anarchism. The fantastic thing of sharing time with Osi is that he does not accept any superficial socially received truisms for an answer. This forces you to 'up your game' as well, which is very healthy in our times of the so-called 'knowledge society', where anyone is free to utter any opinion, no matter how ignorant or ill-considered, and get away with it. I think what I am really impressed about is the breadth and depth of Osi's approach, something that becomes visible, palpable and intelligible in his paintings. This is the reason why I not only wanted, but literally had to buy his painting called *Pedair Oes y Cwm – The Four Ages of the Valley*. For me, quite apart from the sheer beauty of its vividness, colour tone, structure and visual depth, the painting is a prime example of an attempt to understand our current world in its complexity. Osi refers to these paintings as 'graphic essays', and indeed that is what they are: not just landscape and human-shaped environment, but also geological time; not just a particular industry, namely, mining, but also human society; not just memory and facts about coal seams, but windows on real people, family and friends. It brings alive the way industry, landscape, resources and environmental parameters shape and are shaped by the way humans interact with each other and with their environment. You can read the painting on so many levels and layers that it is literally a multidimensional, multidisciplinary and multi-perspective history of who we were, who we are and who we might become. It acts for me as a lens, sharpening my understanding of the world we live in.

With such a profound but also open and fertile view on life, you start to understand why Osi seems so disappointed when he sees how politics, how the way we do business, how our social and community interaction severely limits our human potential, and actually destroys our life-insurance system, planet Earth in the process.

But I am desperately and unsuccessfully trying to put into words what can only be experiences. This is why Susanne and I always try to go and see Osi and Hilary because the force of life can only be shared in real-time.

I guess poetry can express what I am trying to get at here, namely, the essence of who we are and what being alive means. But then again I am not a poet, so I will end not with my words, but with a recent poem by my favourite German poet, Volker Braun, called 'Wilderness'.

Wilderness

Aus dem Mutterleib kommend, kotgesalbt
Kennst du die Sensationen tosenden Bluts
Das Pochen der dunklen Lagune, den geheimen Farn
Dieser Nehrung, sinnerregt. Näher
                              kannst du dem Herzen
Nicht sein, Mitwisser schamloser Lust
Geängstet geborgen, im Uterusmeer.

Ausgetrieben, nackt
                    traumatisiert im All
Deiner Einzelheit: kannst du die Herkunft vergessen
Die Hoffnung, das Haff, fruchtwasservoll?
Ausgeburt, nun trinkst du die Lache
                              Flugbenzin
Auf dem Airport Cape Town. Ich zeige dir

Einen Platz für Hochzeiten, entlegen, verhüllt
Von der Decke der Dünen, Salz und Gras
An der Mündung des Touws River, Eden-Distrikt
Wo sich die Meere mischen und alle Wesen
Von der Gischt
                    beleckt
                              bis zum mineralischen Grund.
O Vielzahl, Vielgestalt, die Wildnis der Ganzheit
Keiner Gewißheit gehörig, "ungestüm"
Kein Gesetz lehrt sie überleben
Und ich wittre wieder die Gier
Gemeinsamkeit,
                    das Notwendige, ohne Zwang
Unbändige Freiheit.

Volker Braun, *Wilderness*, Warmbronn: Verlag Ulrich Keicher, 2014, written in Spring 2012, first published in SINN UND FORM 4/2013.

Wilderness

Exiting the mother-womb, stool-belathered
You know how sensational are thundering blood
The throbbing of the dark lagoon, the secretive fern
Of this shoal-bar, thrilled sensate. Nearer
                                                  to the heart
You can't get, accomplice in shameless lust
Fearfully held safe, in the uterus sea.

Expellee, naked
                          traumatised in the universe
Of your singularity: can you forget where you come from
The hope, the haff, brimming breaking waters?
Ex-spawn, now you're drinking the pooled
                                                  aviation fuel
At Cape Town Airport. I'll show you

A place for weddings, remote, cloaked
By the blanket of the dunes, salt and grass
At the mouth of the Touws River, Eden District
Where the oceans mingle and all the beings
That the spray
                    licks
                              down to the mineral bed.
O multiplicity, protean diversity, the wilderness of the whole
No certitude obeying, "impetuous"
No law instructs this to survive
And I'm scenting again the craving
Commonality,
                    the necessary, without compulsion
Boundless freedom

Translated by Tom Cheesman,
October 2014.

Running boy. Hand-mixed oil on canvas.

'In Wales they measure men from the neck up'

CHÉ OSMOND

Growing up I heard Ozi say this a lot! Whilst he may not have been the tallest around, he often cast the biggest shadow; he still does. Notice how I didn't say 'Dad', it was always, and still is, Ozi.

While Dyffryn Farm was my first home that I can recall, and was great, Bryn Celyn was really the one that holds most of the memories. Probably because I did most of my growing up there and my schooling. The farm was also far from school at Whitland where we were driven to and from daily as this was the nearest Welsh school – by default we should not have gone there but Ozi wanted us (including my brother Luke) to be schooled in and speak Welsh – and in the end it worked.

My memory is not great, school was tough and exams even tougher – they were not my forte. I was never forced into them at home, in fact probably the opposite, and maybe this was not ideal but that's how we were brought up. For many of my friends their parents were quite the opposite, and revision was mandatory. Not so in the Osmond house. Consequently my school days whilst being great, really great, were perhaps not quite as successful from an academic perspective as they should have been. Living where we did was also detrimental as I enjoyed working on the local farms enormously at every opportunity – and for this I was rewarded with money, memories, and the odd scar! Having the name Ché didn't make school any easier, being put into Welsh schools (see above) but from an English-speaking house, I might as well have been called Sue – in fact that would probably have been easier!

Looking back I can see how lucky we really were. At times it did not seem so, and was not always easy. Money was short, we didn't get the latest stuff, the next craze sweeping the school, what everyone else had. Fortunately it was much easier than it is today; computer games were only starting to become available and bikes were still the main weapon of choice where we grew up. We also had vast expanses of Pembrokeshire countryside to roam and explore, build bridges, dam the rivers, set up camp and defend the castle. Ozi taking us to collect logs, reluctantly at first until we could have a go with the saw, and better still the axe, and the day when I carried the biggest log back to the house and not Ozi. Fond memories of using a bonnet from a VW Beetle as a sledge in the winter, and ice burns to prove it! It wasn't so bad living in the shadow.

My memory (remember the exam troubles!) cannot recall all of the things that happened, there are also too many. But it does a great job of remembering faces, if not names, places, and events. And we saw many faces during our childhood that were part of our lives and helped forge our character and future. Our house was informal, always a fairly open-door home, and people seemed to come and go freely and often. And for most of our childhood it was a happy home. We (I include my brother Luke in all of this) spent quite a bit of time in various hostelries around Narberth, notably the Dingle and Angel Inn. The house in Lampeter Velfrey occupied by Vena Morris was a great place for two young boys to play and explore. On the farm, Colwyn James at Llwyn Celyn (just down the road from Bryn Celyn) played a huge part – and introduced us to 'home brew' made in an old upright washing machine. He would always stop outside our house to talk with Ozi (usually blocking the road then both being mindful of anyone trying to get past!) and both relished the conversation, sometimes just for a minute, sometimes for hours, often unfinished, but significantly both had time for one another. All of these people deserve, and possess their own stories, but were brought into our

160

New Orleans (Sitting Figure).
Hand-mixed oil on canvas
62cm x 62cm

lives through Ozi as they wanted to be part of his.

When Ozi and my mother, Lynda, parted company there was a fairly lengthy dark period – I did not see or even talk to Ozi for quite some time. No relationship break-up is easy or pleasant (for many affected parties), but time is a healer and eventually father and sons were reunited and another chapter began. By then I had pretty much flown the nest and started to forge my own life – not easy, having grown up in a shadow. This is also when Ozi asked our permission to marry Hilary – by then we were only too pleased to give permission, strange as it may seem to have been asked, but Ozi genuinely wanted this and be sure that we were happy and willing for this to happen.

As Luke and I continued with our lives and relationships to Kim and Josie respectively, the Osmond gene began another round. Though both these fine ladies are not of Welsh descent, and none of us now reside in Wales, all have been welcomed into the Osmond fraternity with open arms and warm hearts. When Gwion arrived, being Ozi's first grandchild, and a grandson at that, it brought a new lease of life and energy, and focus into Ozi's life and work. Gwion was followed by Osian (so far all from Luke) and the family continued to grow. In November 2001 at last I made my mark and Macsen arrived like a cannon ball (literally!) in the delivery suite of the University Hospital of Wales, Cardiff – and he continues to enter houses, rooms, and conversations in the same way! And Ozi, not wishing to miss out, was quick on the scene to witness the newest Osmond into the world. Last to arrive was Aled, destined to be the smallest of the grandchildren, but just like Ozi, he always seems to cast a bigger shadow. These cousins have an incredible bond with each other and always want to go down to Llansteffan and spend time with Tadcu, a name that Ozi

has been so fond to hear. And furthermore, all of these grandsons boast strong Welsh names, perhaps unsurprising, with which to take the Osmond name forward. But will any of them cast such a big shadow as Tadcu?

Living in the shadow

Where to begin, where the story starts
Those memories, etched in our hearts.
Of growing up, of growing strong
Family first, but friends all along.
His shadow cast, for all to see
An audience where he likes to be.
Textbook father, maybe not
But colourful life is what we got.
Quiet house, not even at night
Happenings, a daily sight.
But slow down now, hard astern
Take stock where we are, let the candle burn.
The shadow may fade, the voice may soften
But the memories, never be forgotten.

Ché Osmond – eldest son, patient, broad shoulders, thick skin, lived in the shadow.

A man's colours

MACSEN OSMOND

A man's colours

How to start there's so much to say
Let the red fish swim in the blue sea
Let the green birds sing in the yellow sky
The colours the passion all on one page
The art that sold a thousand pieces, the strength
And willpower to carry on, the one man
That cancer could never defeat and that
man's name is Osi Rhys Osmond
My Tadcu, a hero amongst men, an artist among
singers, let his soul, passion, strength and willpower
live on forever.

Macsen Osmond – grandson, rugby player, Emperor.[1]

Cwymp/The Fall.
Hand-mixed oil on canvas

1. A reference to the legend of Macsen Wledig in the
   Mabinogion who became Emperor of Rome, Magnus
   Maximus 383-388 AD

Cousins
COLIN BREWSTER

I am one year older than Osi, so really cannot remember a time when he was not a part of my life. As cousins we crisscrossed the Bristol Channel regularly to visit each other during our pre-teen years. Many times when we slept in his home my brother and I would come across Osi's many drawings, sketches and paintings. I visited Osi's studio at Newport College of Art, where of course he knew everyone.

Marchog. 1998. Watercolour. 8"x8"

He has a 'force of nature' personality and commandeers every room he is in. No shrinking violet he. This quality has made him who he is today, still making ripples in the art world and in political thinking. You ignore Osi at your peril. Surprisingly for me, considering this strong personality, and volcanic presence, his watercolours are very gentle, impressionistic and considered. The other more masculine side of his work, is well represented in his wonderful drawings of the south Wales coalmines. These drawings and paintings combined with collage to include his beloved parents and family were shown at a sellout exhibition at the Rhondda Heritage Centre. Osi gave my wife and I a personal watercolour as a wedding present in 1978, and now I wish I had purchased one from the coalmine series. I love these drawings, they are among my personal favourites.

Many people will have heard and watched his numerous radio and television appearances where he has mastered another medium, employing his mellifluous Welsh voice with its poetry and cadences. Returning from holiday in September, it was Osi's voice discussing philosophy on Radio 4 that seemed to welcome us back home.

My early working life took a very different path to Osi's. Engineering and Town Planning were professions I turned to as outlets for my abiding interest in drawing. While my drawing skills are very inferior to Osi's, it must have been his influence that encouraged me to apply at the age of twenty-four to the West of England College of Art to study graphic design. Here, after previously feeling no empathy with Engineering and Town Planning, I finally found true happiness in my career, and I have Osi to thank for his (possibly unconscious) influence.

MVR GORLLEWIN CAERSALEM   WESTERN WALL JERUSALEM   GORFFENHAF 85

West Wall Jerusalem, page from sketchbook. 1985. Watercolour

Arwr

BEN DRESSEL

Saint Louis Missouri. January 2015

Wales is dense matter. Its physical body and spiritual soul forged and compressed by the weight of time and history. Inhabited long before Homer, Wales has its own heroic traditions with many legends and tales yet to be discovered by Hollywood or a savvy publisher. Like the white dwarf remains of an ancient star, Wales's gravitational force seems infinite and powerful beyond the scope of normal imagination. Not everyone in Wales meditates on the 'Matter of Wales' but there are those who've made it their passion, obsession, life's purpose. Osi Osmond is one of those unsung heroes (*Arwr* in Welsh).

During the 90s I was an ex-pat Yank living in west Wales charged with the task of coordinating the cultural education of visiting American university students. Wales, its culture, history, landscape and people served as a catalyst for a life-changing experience for each new group of students.

Living in a rural west Wales village was good preparation for the task. The late Tudor Bevan said of Llansteffan (in reference to *Under Milk Wood*), 'Life here is indeed stranger than fiction'. Like many Welsh villages it serves up an ample slice of humanity. Farmers, mechanics, civil servants, artists, expats and ex-cons all co-mingling in their own orbit around the core. Sitting peacefully on the tidal estuary of the river Towy, each tide seems to bring something to the place, sometimes taking on its return seaward journey. My first encounters with Osi took place when he floated in on an early 90s tide with his companion Hilary. Their marriage soon after in the village hall was a resplendent affair attended by some of Wales's finest sons and daughters. Myself, and many of the locals present, looking on in bemused fascination.

Before its sad demise to the omnipresent East-End landlord interlopers, I gradually got to know Osi in the venerable bar of the Sticks Hotel. His presence was formidable and I was drawn to his passion and intensity with the recognition that getting to know him might open new doors of perception to the Wales I was looking to for enlightenment. It was 'Cymraeg' that finally gave us a common language and a means to connect. We met weekly in the Tafarn Sticks for 'Noson Cymraeg' with our language mentor Carys Jones and anyone who wanted to practice their convers-ational Welsh. To this day Osi's commitment to learning and using the Welsh language as an adult is an inspiration. He would say, 'we are reclaiming the language one word at a time', a beautiful and poetic truth. Certainly my road to a new understanding of Wales started with the language; I feel Osi might say the same for his experience.

Wales affords accessibility like no other country. It can be crossed in an hour, circumnavigated in a day, with more landscape and history flashing past your window per square mile than probably any place on earth. It was this realization that lit the fire of my relationship with Osi as a teacher and fellow educator.

The 'Taith Gwladgarwyr' was conceived with our dear departed friend Nigel Jenkins. Four days touring Wales by coach, bringing as much of the country to a group of students as we dared. Nigel and Osi taking turns with the microphone, waxing lyrical on the history and praising the landscape rolling past the coach window. Social and historic commentary on a grand scale, delivered with a beautiful and sincere desire to share the secret wonders that unfolded for all of us on those trips.

Each tour we invited other guests, foreign and native, to experience the country in whirlwind fashion. I still find it hard to believe how

166

Coal leaving (detail). 2013. Oil on canvas

little travelling the Welsh do in their own country. North to South, East to West, I've gotten to know it intimately. There's a map in my mind, three dimensions, a synoptic chart. It was Osi who opened the door to the labyrinth. Great minds don't necessarily think alike but rather forge new ways of thinking for the rest of us to follow. I don't pretend to offer much in the way of intellectual fodder for the relationship I fostered with Osi but one of my talent is recognizing greatness in others and singing their praises.

When you're down in life, opportunities are easily missed, overshot by the momentum of the pity bus. It was the sudden separation from my wife that opened the door to a much deeper relationship to Osi and Hilary as compassionate surrogate parents. Invited to one 'mini weekend' Wednesday night supper at their table, I never left, refusing to miss the opportunity afforded. The warmth, hospitality and vitality of intellect and conversation that flowed from their hearth changed the course of my life. I sometimes feel one of my life's best decisions was inviting myself back to dinner at the Osmonds' and watching and learning from two people who know how to love and care for each other, in their own special ways. Osi the man is no different to the rest of us. In order to succeed and prosper we require a strong

168

Machlud Gorau Erioed/Best Sunset Ever (detail). **2009**. Watercolour. 16″x12″

companion to provide balance and bring a certain amount of magic to the table each day. Hilary Osmond is a special woman in her own right and Osi would not be complete without their especially rare breed of love affair. Being a guest in their home taught me the meaning of hospitality, warmth and what fulfillment with another human being really looks like. I know of no other home that sets the soul at ease as theirs. It's a real home, a four-walled manifestation of a life well lived. If I'm successful as a family man now, it's certainly a credit to their 'parenting' and generous wisdom through some of the darker times of my life.

In 2009 my not-yet wife and I made her first trip to Wales. More than anything I wanted Elizabeth to meet my surrogate family and adopted home. On exiting Carmarthen station there was no Osi in sight so I trundled across the car park to the taxi office leaving Liz outside. In her words:

> I locked eyes with a dark haired swashbuckler a ways down the street and we stood for a moment, regarding each other, dared not break his gaze knowing he would sense weakness. 'You must be Liz, croeso cariad', which he followed with a kiss on my cheek and firm hug. It felt like coming home.

Two years later we returned as parents with our 4-month-old twins little Osi and Genevieve. News of Osi's illness had forced a premature Atlantic crossing for the babies. It was imperative for the two Osis to meet. I hadn't planned on a rushed introduction or the possibility of the two not getting to know one another on a more prolonged basis. There are moments of shock and realization that cut the human condition to the quick. We're not a family prone to religious sentiment but a chilly October morning at Saint Anthony's well in Llansteffan, Osi and Hil baptizing our children in

their own Celtic tradition meant more to us than a lifetime of Easter Sundays. New life, new promise, connecting generations and souls in this place, as has been the case for millennia.

Little Osi may not remember meeting his namesake but the stories and legends will ring loud in our home. For this is the stuff that feeds the human condition, keeps us grounded in purpose and motivated to seek the extraordinary in the ordinary. Wales owes a debt of gratitude to Osi Osmond.

He has wrestled the demons of cultural oppression and stands firm in his convictions and love of country. My debt to Osi can only be paid with the fortitude to embrace life and proceed with optimism, enthusiasm and a child's eye for exploration.

I have heroes in my chosen passions of surfing and climbing. Laird Hamilton, Jerry Lopez, George Mallory, Henry Tillman, Barry Blanchard, Steve House, Vince Anderson. These are men true to their convictions and commitment to their paths in life. These are real heroes to me, but none more than my friend and mentor Osi Osmond. The Bardic tradition says, 'Let the poets of the people judge the one's of courage'. Osi's inclusion in the Gorsedd for his contribution to the arts in Wales is well deserved and I'm sure a source of pride for him. Were it up to me, there would be a category within the Gorsedd for 'patriots'; men and women whose commitment to the culture and country of Wales goes beyond the point of citizens and into the realm of servants. He is a Welsh Hero, a modern-day patriot, gladiator for a Wales that doesn't roll over. Spokesman for a culture that refuses to go away despite the thousand years beat down. The country needs and deserves successes like Osi. Coal miner's son, Wales's son but always a treasured father to me.

Soldiers. Series of oil paintings on canvas

Soldiers. Series of oil paintings on canvas

Soldiers.
Series of oil paintings
on canvas

173

The Reaper.
Hand-mixed oil on canvas

The thread of friendship

MEGAN CROFTON

Probably my first encounter with the young Master Osmond was at his junior school, I was there for a day to take my eleven plus examination. I'm not clear of conversations, or great happenings of that day, but remembered all the same.

My hometown was Risca; Osi lived just a few miles away in a small village called Wattsville. We were brought up in the environment of industrial south Wales. It seems to me that we have always been friends and we shared a deep love of our landscape, and hills and the mountains. With their great majestic beauty, the changing colours, the mists and moods of the seasons. Their influences were so inspirational to our lives and art. As children we were given so much freedom to roam and explore, climb trees and quarries, and were allowed to run wild on our mountains.

Risca had two foundries, a small steelworks, two brickworks, one firebrick, the other house brick, and two quarries. The coal-black river Ebbw threaded its way through the town. There were an incredible number of pubs, a well-attended Palace Cinema, shops, an abundance of farms, and the Great Western Railway. Risca Pit was at the edge of Wattsville, family members, and neighbours worked there, the majority of men were employed in the collieries, including Osi's father.

The many chapels were full of beautiful voices, male and female singing in harmony, and all terrified of the fire and brimstone sermons. The pubs and swings in the park were locked up on Sundays, officially chapel and the Bible were the only things acceptable for Sundays. Though happily, the Demon Drink lectures, and all that Pledge signing by all of us children didn't seem to have any long-lasting effect on most of us!

As a small close community bound together and linked by its dominant mining presence, everyone seemed to know everyone else, and Osi and I probably met many times over the years. Wattsville was only a few miles from Risca, and though you wouldn't exactly describe Risca as a town of 'bright lights', with its shops and industries and schools, it offered a little more than the village of Wattsville. Big-city Cardiff and Newport were not too far away.

Risca had an outdoor seasonal swimming pool. It was well used not only for swimming, but also as a social meeting place by the local young people. Keen swimmers Osi and I used it regularly in our teenage years. His school was also in Risca. Our paths must have crossed so many times but I do recall one particular occasion, chatting with him on the corner of my street, in school uniform, tie askew, of course, charming and looking quite handsome and making quite an impression!

Risca also had a quaint tradition of a 'Parade' on a Sunday evening after chapel; the young people, girls dressed up, Sunday best, boys too, came to walk up and down between the two Italian cafes. A lot of banter; courtships begun and ended! The evening drawing to a close with hot steamed pies in the cafe, accompanied by the Everly Brothers on the jukebox. Rock and Roll came to the valleys, dancing was the scene. It was so exciting and we all danced like whirlwinds, and attended dance halls up through the valleys.

Newport College of Art was then a small but excellent school of Arts and Crafts. I had been studying there for about three years, when Osi began. The college always made a big effort for Rag Week, collecting funds for local charities, and generally having a mad time. Those were the days of medical students and art

Mourning Woman. Oil on canvas

Pool-side. Hand-mixed oil on canvas

students being asked to pay more for motor insurance! However, one year some of our male students, fired up by enthusiasm and a good few pints, decided to take some of the classical figures from the corridors of the college to set them on top of the dome of the college building. The police and the press were in pursuit, a great local scandal ensued, and a great deal of laughter too; not so much a failure, nor a surprise, but caught out!

The good Governors decided to suspend the culprits from college. Pleading to our Principal to have them reinstated, in particular on behalf of my dear friend and fellow student Tom Wall, I became, in a somewhat longer story, involved with fellow student (also suspended) Jack Crofton. Eventually they were all allowed to come back to college.

They were very talented students. Jack was studying sculpture with fellow student and childhood friend 'Otto' (Peter) Davidson. Osi, Jack, Tom, Otto and myself, became lifelong friends. Jack and I eventually married. Jack, still at college, continued his friendship with Osi, and as a frequent visitor Osi also sometimes did some babysitting for us, as did his sister Lesley. He remembers our son Justin regularly manouvering his cot around the bedroom, and on one occasion the leg of the cot coming through the ceiling into the lounge.

The social life of the college was mainly meeting up in the pubs, having a great time, working hard at college, Saturday night dances, cinema, and rugby. The local publicans did very well out of the student population. Of course Osi and Jack were loyal customers, and they often got themselves involved in many 'adventures'. Newport was not well known for its pacifist attitudes, more 'fists first'. Often both came back after an evening out to

our house rather worse for wear, battered and bruised! Osi used to worry so much that his nose would be permanently damaged, with his good looks lost forever! He was a charming young man, emotional, full of confidence and never stopped talking, which often got him into trouble.

He and Jack spent many hours drawing and sketching around the quarries in Risca; some very good work came from it. Otto would often visit on Sundays to read the paper and then off home again. Osi and others started a studio in Newport; he was then already producing brilliant work.

He was, and is, such an extraordinary personality, kind, passionate, knowledgeable, a minefield of information about nature, birds, literature and art. Most of all, when he was 'on form' he would keep us entertained and in stitches of laughter for hours. What a great sense of humour. Teacher, lecturer, artist writer, broadcaster; it has always been difficult to keep up with him.

Jack and I moved to London in the early sixties, with our two small boys Michael and Justin. Jack wanted to study the bronze lost wax founding technique to cast his own work into bronze. We eventually started a small bronze foundry in Greenwich.

Osi often visited, they extended their adventures there, at a much bigger playing field, Twickenham, of course! On one famous trip to the Big Match, England versus Wales, the match ended, the now very merry group of chaps including Jack's brother Noel, Osi leading them out, found a short cut and fell into a quagmire of mud. Seeing the mini van, he got in and cleaned himself up on the rugs, until Jack called him and explained it wasn't his van. It developed further into farce. Jack, probably erratically, drove over a hump-back bridge, was stopped by the police and he ran off; they breathalysed Osi, who was told that he was over the limit. He explained that he wasn't the driver nor could he drive; the police were not happy. Jack came back, was also breathalysed but the test miraculously was clear. Their journey home was wild and exciting (for some) but amazingly they came back in one piece. Entering our first-floor flat, and in spite of having a quite adequately sized front door, they came in by the novel method of climbing up the drainpipe and in through the window. Mad bunch of Welsh and Irish men. For people now horrified by the 'apparently' excessive drinking habits of those ancient times, they were the days when on announcing you were leaving, it was the norm to have a traditional 'one for the road' forced on you! We survived.

So many memories, so many adventures, such a lot of time has passed. All through the years we have kept in touch off and on, a long and valued friendship. I have many paintings by Osi, and enjoy them very much. Some he generously gave as presents. He has also kept in touch with my sons, attending their weddings, made speeches, he really is part of our family and we are very fond of him. He entertained them during his stays in London when they were teenagers, lots of laughter and fun.

Osi has had very successful exhibitions across the years. More recently an exhibition that was so impressive, shown at the Rhondda Mining Heritage Centre, was a tribute to Wattsville. A very large exhibition and a huge amount of work, capturing the essence of the landscape and industrial life of Wattsville, its history and people. Of course the mountains, his detailed drawings reading as a visual image of his life, family, and love of his hometown and the area he lived in. Fantastic work.

I remember recently telling Osi that a friend of mine had bought a house in the foothills of the Himalayas. Osi jokingly compared my old street in Risca, as being at the foothills of Twm Barlwm mountain, I liked that!

Sadly, a year ago, Jack died, which is why I have brought him into the story, as I am sure Jack would have contributed to this book, possibly with many more 'encounters', and probably more that I knew about! We followed Jack's wishes and his funeral and burial were held in Newport; he was buried in a grave close to Otto's. At the funeral Osi gave a great and beautiful eulogy, tears and laughter, witty, funny, wordy, brilliant. It meant such a lot to myself, Michael and Justin and the whole family, and indeed the friends who were in attendance. He was far from well himself, and at that time suffering the effects of chemotherapy, but it was an outstanding tribute to Jack and their long friendship. It was so very much appreciated by us all.

He is unstoppable, in spite of his illness. He and Hilary are travelling frequently, visiting galleries in Britain and abroad, and entertaining friends and family, his life so full of energy and enthusiasm.

The thread of friendship still strong over these many years....

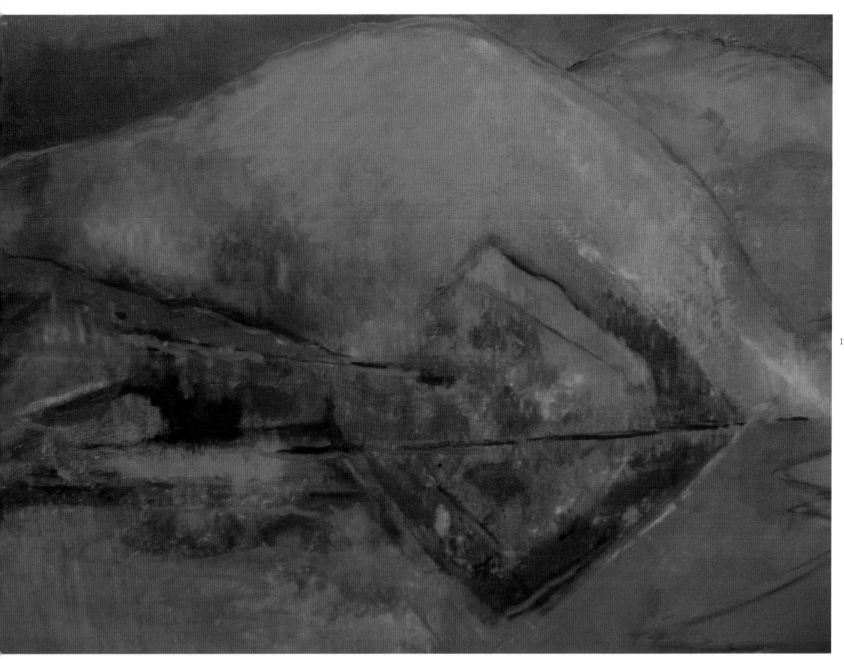

Landscape. Oil on canvas

My brother
LESLEY DAVIES

When I was born, Donald, as he was christened even though he prefers to be called Osi, was 5 years old. We lived in Wattsville at 21 Islwyn Road, in one room, sharing the kitchen and outside toilet with the owners, an elderly couple who owned the house, Mr and Mrs Parry. Two years later in 1949, when our mother was expecting her third child, we moved into 57 Islwyn Road; we still had to share, this time with a young couple, but only for about a year or so and it was a slightly bigger house. No. 57 remained our family home until Mam died a few years ago in 2011.

Dad worked in Nine Mile Point Colliery which was just a mile up the road, along with our grandfather. Wattsville was a typical mining village with the majority of the men working either in Nine Mile Point or Risca Colliery which was just at the end of our street. It was a close-knit, friendly community where everyone knew each other.

As a family of five living on a miner's wage there wasn't very much money about. We didn't have many material things but our home was filled with love, we always ate well, we were always warm and felt secure in our parents' love.

Dad and Grampa were deacons in the local Baptist chapel so we were all there three times on a Sunday. Mam always had all the time in the world for us, she showed us how to make things out of paper and cardboard when we very young and we all loved drawing and painting. She also taught all of us to read and write before we actually started school. Books were always important at home and we all loved them. Mam and Dad used the Family Allowance money to buy us a set of 'Arthur Mee's Children's Encyclopedias' on hire purchase, they were great and helped us a lot when we had homework to do.

One of Don's most treasured books when he was a youngster was *The Observer Book of Birds*, he loved nature, still does and soon learned everything he could about birds from this book.

We were surrounded by mountains and woods, it was a wonderful playground for us. We even played on top of the pit when we could get away with it. He had his 'gang' of friends he was always out with; being a girl and younger I was excluded, but he often came back from their adventures with 'gifts' for me – a shed snake's skin, a sheep's skull, injured, flea-infested bats and hedgehogs. I was so lucky!

They were carefree times, days spent looking for birds' nests, swimming in the local reservoir (that's where most of the boys learned to swim), playing cowboys and indians among the ferns and woods, building camps, running through the long yellow grass on top of Mynydd y Lan and picking whinberries and blackberries.

Don passed the eleven plus exam and then went to Pontywaun Grammar School in Risca. He was quite good at sport and always took part in the annual sports day event, but it was art that soon became his favourite subject. He always enjoyed making something for the annual school St. David's Day Eisteddfod. He got on really well with his art teacher, Ms Matthias who later encouraged him to go to art college. Don also loved singing, he had a boy soprano voice which then changed as he got older to tenor. In his late teens he sang for a while with a local rock-and-roll band, the girls loved him! When he was young he also sang in the local chapel anniversaries.

Tragedy struck our family three weeks before Christmas in 1957 when our younger sister, Gail was killed in a road accident on her way home from school. She was nearly eight years old. I will never forget that Christmas and the sadness and gloom that hung over our once happy family for such a long time afterwards. We were always close but I think this dreadful experience brought us even closer and Don seemed quite protective towards me as I grew into a teenager and always looked out for me. Two years after Gail's death our younger brother Nathan was born; we all doted on him after losing Gail.

After finishing his GCE O levels, Don took his place at Newport College of Art, and our home became open house for all his new art college friends, Mam especially loved having a houseful of young people. Don always had plenty of girlfriends – he was and still is, for his age – good looking! Eventually he settled down and married. Ché, his first son was born and after a spell working as an art teacher in Hartridge High School in Newport he moved to a new post in Narberth, Pembrokeshire to teach. In those days Pembrokeshire seemed to me to be a long way away and I was afraid we might lose touch with each other, but I needn't have worried because Don has always been very good at staying in touch with family and friends and we phoned and saw each other regularly. Luke his second son was born a couple of years later in Pembrokeshire. My own daughters, Rhiannon and Albany, loved spending a couple of weeks with their cousins in the summer holidays down at Bryncelyn and Don would take them on walks and picnics and swimming trips all around the Pembrokeshire Coast.

As an artist he was progressing and had his first proper exhibition at the Chapter Arts Centre in Cardiff. It was a great success and the first of many exhibitions he has held. Over the following years he travelled extensively; painting, making television programmes and writing. Like Mam and Dad I followed his progress with pride, watching him develop and change his style of painting over the years. I've noticed in some of his work over the last five or six years the appearance of the birds, the hawks that he loved so much as a young boy.

He has always been passionate about nature, the environment, Wales and the Welsh language and culture and I know he was so pleased to be admitted to the Gorsedd. Mam was thrilled that her son was now a Welsh bard!

I was devastated in 2012, along with all the family, when Don was diagnosed with terminal cancer. He told me at the time not to be sad and that he was going to make the most of the time he had left, which was supposedly weeks or a couple of months at the most.

He has accomplished so much since then, it's amazing really. He's continued painting, writing, doing some television and radio programmes, going to exhibitions in this country and Europe. All this has been done while undergoing extensive treatments for the cancer, radiotherapy and three lots of chemotherapy, being in a great deal of discomfort at times. He stays so positive and is determined to carry on having a full, interesting and stimulating life for as long as possible. His doctors are amazed at the way he has handled and reacted to his treatment. He has so much more to do and to give and I know that's what he'll do for as long as he can.

Throughout my life Don has always loved, supported and encouraged me in everything. No one could have a better brother.

Themes 5

Beverley Oosthuizen-Jones
John Barnie
Menna Elfyn
Richard Pawelko and
Mary Simmonds
Bethan John
Mererid Hopwood

Women at the well.
1997. Oil on canvas. 72" x 60"

Osi Osmond and South Sudan

BEVERLEY OOSTHUIZEN-JONES

Osi is occasionally seen wearing an elegant timepiece, acquired during the period when he travelled in Southern Sudan to prepare an artistic report on the region. Still ten years away from the Comprehensive Peace Agreement in 2005 which brought together for peace negotiations weary fighters from all sides of the thirty-year civil war, the country that Osi saw, drew and painted was one in which time had virtually stood still for centuries. Osi's watch also stands forever at 4 o'clock, the strap and face shaped and etched out of a flattened brass bullet. Yet, so convincing is it, at least one person has asked him 'How does it work?' Osi's reply is typical: 'We're not clever enough in the Europe to produce timepieces like this.'

Osi's companions for the journey into the equatorial basin of the White Nile were a very large leather-bound book of sketch and water-colour paper, and a South Sudanese artist called Samuel Bullen Ajak Alier. From this companionship emerged the visual story of a land which the world had forgotten, still marked by the scars of slavery and exploitation, and still being marked by internecine conflict over land, oil, water and identity. Over the months that followed his journey – on the top of trucks, hiking through swamps, skirting sunflower fields and passing the long-horned cattle which graze the region – Osi produced enough paintings for an exhibition in Narbeth. He spoke in churches up and down Wales and even shared with the Queen one of his own Southern Sudan postcards.[1]

South Sudanese people often quote Isaiah 18 to describe their deeply beautiful and beleaguered country:

> Woe to the land shadowing with wings, which is beyond the rivers of Ethiopia: that sendeth ambassadors by the sea,

even in vessels of bulrushes upon the waters, saying, Go, ye swift messengers to a nation scattered and peeled, to a people terrible from their beginning hitherto; a nation meted out and trodden down, whose land the rivers have spoiled![2]

I am sitting now, looking at the three paintings from Osi's South Sudan series which adorn our living room in Oxford: a woman walks purposely across a multi-coloured landscape, her long, red-dark limbs propel her; a group of women, coloured robes drawn across one shoulder, hold hands and dance, bright arm bracelets standing out against the deep purple black of their skin; in another, a reedy girl in red stands still in the centre of the picture while blue-black boys fall away from her. Osi understood that there are many colours for black in Southern Sudan. He also understood that the heart of the country is its women – the glue which may hold just enough of this fractured society together to give the men time to learn less violent ways of being warriors.

And Samuel? His country of South Sudan was born in 2011 – but the underlying tensions that fuelled the civil war were not addressed before or after the Independence referendum. By December 2013, the tensions erupted into a new civil war – this time within the state that had been created by the previous war. Samuel now produces illustrations for the Mennonite Central Committee religious texts. It is safer.

1. Osi's visit was sponsored by Christian Aid, and was supported by Christian Aid Wales.
2. King James Bible

The things of men/Pethau dynion. 1997. Oil on canvas. 16" x 12"
Private collection

186

The Red Beret/Y Beret Coch. 1997. Oil on canvas. 48″ x 28″

Planet essays

JOHN BARNIE

When I joined its editorial team on the re-launch of *Planet* in 1985, it is fair to say that I knew very little about Welsh visual art. Working on a cultural magazine, though, is an education in itself, and it rapidly became clear to us that the re-launch coincided with a particularly vibrant and creative phase in visual art, which *Planet* needed to reflect. So began a policy of featuring an article in every issue devoted to the work of a particular artist, artistic trend, or exhibition review, with artwork displayed on the magazine's full colour covers.

To do this we needed to assemble a team of art critics and historians we could rely on and in this we were lucky, because, as is usually the case with any surge in creativity in the arts, a number of talented people were to hand with ideas, and with a sense of excitement at what was going on, which we were able tap into. Peter Lord, Iwan Bala, Shelagh Hourahane, Peter Wakelin, among others, became regular contributors, and not least among them was Ozi Rhys Osmond (the Cymricisation to 'Osi' came later).

One of Osi's first contributions, 'Cultural Alzheimer's: Memory and Society in Post-Industrial Wales' (No.137, 1999), set the tone for the essays to come, being typical in his concern for the layered structure of society and culture, and the importance of having an awareness of the past in order to understand and engage with the present. Drawing a parallel between his miner-father's descent into Alzheimer's, which caused him to lose his sense of the past and so of his very identity, with the Valleys after the destruction of the mining industry in the 1980s, Osi saw signs everywhere 'that something fundamental was happening – young people gathered listlessly, the empty and run-down houses made the street look like a mouthful of bad teeth, and along the roadside there were cars without wheels.'

What was replacing the industrial past and its communities, he noted, was something fake and contrived, the product of the tourist and heritage industry:

> To travel in Wales today is to travel in a strange land. We are now the country of the brown sign, where every house with more than four bedrooms is a residential home, where the heritage centre is overlooked by the golf course, fantasy farming is an exotic experience, wind turbines pierce the landscape like picadors' pikes, and the evidence of our past is rapidly removed to improve our present.

This is where the arts come in, for:

> If the question of cultural Alzheimer's is relevant, it might mean that where no memory exists we may need to construct one. Now that the physical evidence of our past is disappearing, our present, like that of the Alzheimer's victim, is one of confused distress. It seems the visually-supported memory is vital to the emotional and psychic health of the individual and of the community.

It is a problem, of course, which confronts all minority cultures – as well as some that are not so small – and Osi returned to this theme a number of times and in different ways, especially when he reported back from his travels. In 'The Shadow in the Woods: America and Hallowe'en' (No.140, 2000), for example, he experiences Halowe'en in New York and New England, seeing behind the talismanic display of pumpkin-headed monsters on porches a palimpsest of the Native American tribes who the early settlers largely displaced. A visit to northern Australia produces 'Aeroplane Dreamtime' (No.187, 2008) in which he explores the

The Red Cibl/Y Cibl Coch. Oil on canvas 72"x60"

world of Aboriginal art and its intimate relation to the land and to the history and identity of the people. In each case, Wales and its sense of identity through history, and the expression of that identity through art, are the implied touchstones.

This is present in a more direct way in his review of an exhibition of miner-artists (No. 141, 2000), and in the essay 'Narrow Skies and Tilting Perspectives: The Art of the Valleys' (No.199, 2010) in which Osi discusses the ways in which artists from the Valleys have reflected the region and the industrial and social changes it has undergone in the past half century.

Osi is continually on the lookout for visual signs and what they say about our culture and one of my favourite essays is 'What Does Your Bus Say?' (No.149, 2001), an extended reflection on the iconography of bus liveries and what they tell us both about the companies that run them and the culture they reflect. He observes that:

> Continental coaches, generally look low-key, wealthy and serious, especially the German ones, often with those mystery-making, smoked-glass windows giving off an air of opulence and private indulgence. While French coaches are chic and the Spanish flamboyant, the former Eastern Bloc coaches remain utilitarian, up-ended tower blocks on wheels. Meanwhile, here at home, our Welsh coaches are engaged in a spectacular cultural crusade, entirely of their owners' creation... Our coaches are cultural touchstones, evidence of a subconscious conspiracy, an unspoken agreement on what constitutes appropriate appearance.

And when you look at the accompanying photographs from Osi's collection – at Johns Travel, Nantyglo, whose buses have a defiant 'CYMRU AM BYTH' above the company's name; at Cerbydau Cenarth from near Castell Newydd Emlyn, who proudly offer 'TEITHIO MOETHUS' – you realise that he is right and that you had just not picked up on the signs in quite the way Osi did, even though you see some of them every day.

The same socially acute observer is evident in 'Walking on China: The Global Trade in Stone' (No.183, 2007) in which he reflects on the ways in which globalisation is affecting even such basic aspects of our built environment as the stone we use in our houses and garden walls and paths. Local difference is being eroded; homogeneity and dull uniformity are the result. In a way that is typical for Osi, however, the essay ends not on a note of pessimism but one of challenge:

> The earth is indeed moving. However, in these confusing times of geological promiscuity, don't throw yourself off a high rock in discomfiture, examine your decorative stone, see to it that your pathways and patios are made of the right stuff, and ask yourselves that critical question, how green is my gravel?

Osi also engaged with contemporary art and twice reported for *Planet* from the Venice Biennale (No.185, 2007; No.195, 2009), as well as writing an insightful review of an Alfred Sisley exhibition (No.191, 2008) and profiles of the life and work of John Selway (No.147, 2001) and Tim Davies (No.154, 2002). Reviewing contemporary art, some of Osi's best criticism is delivered from behind the stalking horse of his wit. In 'The View from London' (No.144, 2000-01), a review of The British Arts Show 5, he observes that:

Even Tracey Emin's old boyfriend, Billy Childish, has been let into the temple after a decade of wailing from the sidelines and his wall-poem would have stopped you in your tracks, chiefly because of his policy of spelling by creative lunge. Published in 1999, but actually written in 1983, it seemed to be outside the remit of this project, looked like homework handed in late, and was included, as much of the other work shown, for seemingly unrelated reasons. It did, however, establish an under-the-desk lid humour, which seemed to have exercised the energies of many of the newer artists in the exhibition.

Osi, of course, is himself an accomplished painter, and although his publications in *Planet* exhibit an interest in all kinds of visual art, his essays on painting and painters are among his main concerns. One of his finest contributions is 'Painting Our Times' (No.174, 2005-06), a defence of painting in an age of unimaginative installation art and artists' videos (most of which would fail to get the maker into Film School), which is at the same time a celebration of the renewed vigour of the painterly tradition in contemporary Wales.

The essay opens with a typically sharp piece of social observation:

> The discrete epiphanies of our post-modern world and its meanings can arrive at the most unexpected times. Gentlemen's underwear these days carries the maker's name in small letter letters inside at the back, as clothing almost always did, but now the much more important designer's name and logo are often displayed boldly at the front in even larger letters, sending out a vital but sometimes confusing signal to the wearer and all who may

Photo: Iwan Bala

come into close contact with him. It is a perfect illustration of the complexities of contemporary cultural provision in which it is easy to get things back to front and even, on occasions, inside out.

There follows an inquiry into the state of contemporary art and the ways in which painting has been marginalised, scorned even, in the rush of adulation for the Young British Artists and their confrères, and the multi-million art dealing scene which payrolls it and lives off it. The essay ends on a suitably defiant note:

Painting is as viable and as important as any of the newer visual arts languages, it needs to be reconsidered in the light of its recent persecution and neglect. We have painting here [in Wales] as good as any in the world and by some strange quirk of curatorial fate this year's Artes Mundi award has one of our finest painters, Sue Williams, on the short list.

'Sometimes', Osi concludes with a nod to those designer underpants, 'things have to be back to front to make any sense at all.'

Auspicious

MENNA ELFYN

I'm writing this in my cell of a study and above me are two watercolours by Osi, one a magnificent, bold view of Llansteffan, the other a paler, yet just as powerful a painting of the river Tywi. Both signify to me the features I associate with Osi, that of a *cawr* (giant) who would be on the hill of Llansteffan and also the exquisite quietude of the river Tywi. Contemplation and the need to be vocal and bear witness seem to me to be the two sides of Osi's personality, which have endeared him to all who know and admire him.

I remember meeting Osi for the first time in Brawdy, Pembrokeshire at a protest rally against the American base there. It was the nineteen eighties, and it was at the height of the CND campaigns against missiles being stored there. I doubt he would have remembered me at the rally where he spoke with such passion and conviction, though Nigel Jenkins and I also read poems to conclude the procession and proclamations. I can't remember exactly what he said, but I remember the way he said it and he seemed to me to be a man who could persuade even the faint-hearted to join a revolution. Later, when there was talk of the Welsh Assembly needing good politicians, I remember asking Nigel whether or not we should urge Osi to stand. That was not to be of course and, let's face it, he would have been a terrible politician. Instead, he became a vocal advocate and activist for culture and the arts. Politics after all, as noted by Philip Roth, is the great generaliser, whereas art deals with the particular. His need, his *raison d'être* was that of being free to paint, to be creative and to inspire others.

He was also an excellent mentor of other artists. As an inspirer, in his teaching of art in Carmarthen and later in Swansea, he was able to instil in the students a great sense of purpose and pride in their accomplishments. He wrote essays on art, made excellent television programmes for S4C, which I relished. His programmes were always interlaced with knowledge and opinion but also sprinkled with a wry sense of humour. I once invited him to teach on my Masters programme in Creative Writing at the University of Wales Trinity Saint David in Carmarthen, and he arrived brandishing a new laptop on which he hoped to display some of his artworks to the students. Unfortunately, he couldn't get it to work and so he quickly dismissed the laptop and talked for two hours breathlessly on art, without a single note in front of him. We were all enthralled as he gave us a thrilling account of art through the ages, concentrating in the final hour on Welsh art in particular. Many students commented afterwards that they had been hooked and almost wanted to change course to study art – such was his ability to mesmerise his audience.

Two other encounters come to mind. The first is the annual art auction at the Queen's Hall in Narberth, which he has presided over for many years, once again giving a helping hand to the wonderful Lynne Crompton who manages to run the Gallery by paying the rent from the proceeds of the auction. Every year, listening to Osi's comments on the art works on sale is a revelation as he infuses his deep knowledge of art along with pertinent anecdotes of his own. It's a lovely event with Osi as chief auctioneer. And the audience receive profundity and hilarity in equal measures.

The second occasion was when I bumped into him at Milan airport. I was on my way back from reading in Olbia and somewhere I hear a voice speaking in Welsh. Then Osi and Hilary passed by. They were returning from the opera in Milan, a treat for Hilary's birthday. Needless to say, I was glad of their company on the flight home as we chatted merrily at the back of the plane.

Osi is, in my mind, a unique artist, friend, *Cymro*, and such a necessary citizen of Wales. And when he was diagnosed with cancer, his first utterance to me at another event was that he was a *brwydrwr*– a fighter. A few months after that, he spoke of his condition on *Heno* and inspired me to write him a poem called 'Auspicious'. Sampurna Chattarji, the Indian poet once said that you can't do anything in India without the word 'auspicious' being bandied about and so I conclude with the poem I wrote to him, knowing that we all live wishing for favourable times. '*Addawol*' has such a strong meaning also in Welsh and can also mean '*llewyrchus*' as in prosperous. '*Aruchel*' is another word in Welsh that is a close relation, meaning not only 'high' but 'on high'. And isn't that what we do when we admire someone like Osi, feel a sense of gratitude? Awe-inspiring. Auspicious.

Y Cibl Coch 2/The Red Cibl 2.
Oil on Canvas

Auspicious

(*I Osi ar ôl ei weld ar* '**Heno**', 24.6.13)

'Addawol' meddir
Yw'r gair mawr
A glywir yn yr India,
O flaen unrhyw achlysur—
'Mae'r awr yn addawol'
Hyn a ddywedir,
Heb iddynt wybod
Beth a ddaw, nac ystyr
Y gair hynod o hudol.

Bodlon ydym wedyn
Gyda'r sylw
Sy'n ein sobri,
'yr awr sy'n ffafriol'
Meddir, 'llewyrched ei oleuni'
Bydd, fe rydd ffydd
I ni am ryw hyd
Bod modd i esgyrn
Esgyn (ac ymestyn)
Uwchlaw meidroldeb.

A dyma'r awr
Anfonaf i ti ar ddalen,
Latai i Gymro pybyr
Gyfarchiad sy'n gweddu
(ynghyd â'i weddi)
Namaste – fy nwylo
Ynghyd, cledrau'n cyffwrdd,
Bysedd wrth y frest

A bydded dy ewyllys hefyd
A'th ateb anhyglyw
Yn un 'addawol'.

Menna Elfyn

193

Valleys Scene (Pylons and Wind Turbine). Watercolour on paper

Osi: World of Colour
RICHARD PAWELKO AND MARY SIMMONDS

In 2004 we came up with the idea for a new television series on painting of Wales, one in which we would concentrate on seascapes to start with. Each programme would feature a well-known painting from art history by Turner, Sisley, Lowry and others. The location of the great work would be filmed and two contemporary painters would then offer their take on the scene. We would see the changes wrought by time, industry or architectural development. Or would we? In some cases little had changed which made the project that much more interesting. How would our contemporary painters approach these challenges and not fail by comparison? Indeed would they want to use paint? After all multi-media is a given in today's art scene. We knew that we wanted a painter/presenter to guide us through the programmes. One who could talk knowledgably and engagingly about the 'greats' and who could also interact meaningfully with today's practising artists.

We had heard about Osi from friends and colleagues and had seen him from afar but we had no previous experience of working with him so a screen test was arranged. S4C needed convincing that we had the right candidate. One sunny day we pitched up in Llansteffan with our own camera and took Osi down to his local beach. We went through a number of landscape descriptions and pieces to camera with the Tywi estuary as a backdrop. Osi looked a little piratical in his black leathers, dark hair and beard and the camera loved him. He seemed at his best when he described what he saw and told us how he could capture the light and colour as a painter. The historical stuff would come later after the usual research and picture selections. S4C liked what they saw.
In the end we made two *Byd o Liw* (World of Colour) series, one on seascapes and another on castles as depicted by well-known and not so well-known artists. We went on to deliver 'one-off'

programmes on the Art of Christmas and the Art of the First World War featuring French, British and German artists, which were distributed internationally. Osi made every one of these films a special experience.

He was often at his best when talking to fellow artists about inspiration and technique. Each one of them from the students to the professionals felt at ease with him in very pressured circumstances, and that comes over in the programmes. His passion for his subject and his genuine warmth encouraged contributions that were generous and illuminating. The package was a strong one and Osi was a strong personality – as was the director – but mutual respect and affection was the order of the day. Filming can be a tense affair. Constraints of time, weather, access, budget and schedules can and do add stress to programme making.

The programmes would not have had the go-ahead if the Commissioning Editor, Lowri Gwilym, had not supported us. She was instrumental in our putting Osi on screen and Osi filled it with warmth and his own depictions of what he saw. His abilities as a lecturer and mentor shone through. We would all have wanted Osi as our teacher.

Most of all we enjoyed being with him. Whether it was listening to him talk about beauty, encouraging us to view Al Jazeera, the Arabic Channel, listening to his order of coffee at breakfast, tuning in to his review of Welsh history and culture or hearing him declare his love for Hilary. It was all a pleasure and our only regret was that we did not spend more time with him.

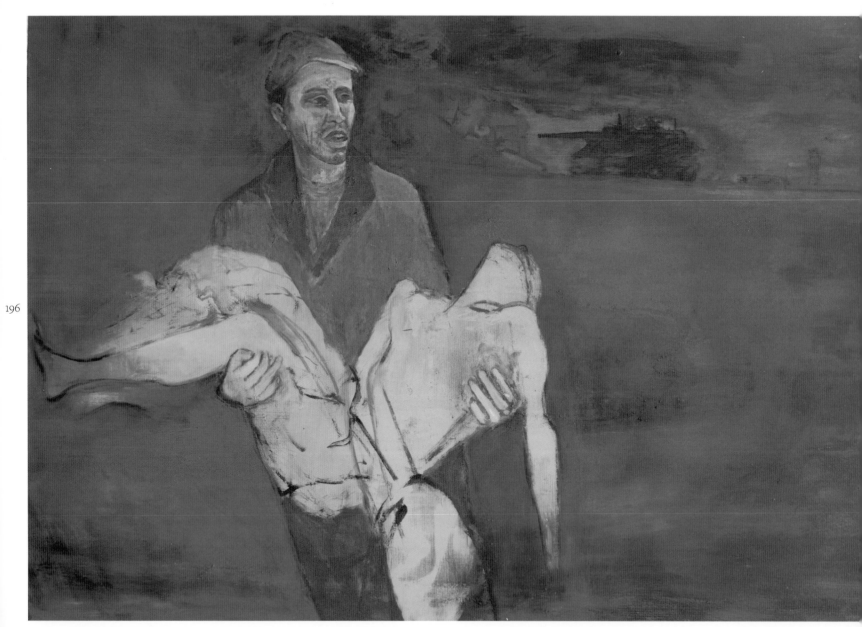

Aftermath. Mixed media

Living in interesting times
BETHAN JOHN

'Gaza cannot and must not be allowed to remain a prison camp.' Cameron's recent statement in Turkey has been seen as a dramatic assertion – further than any British minister had gone before in their assessment of the situation.

The BBC cited it as an example of Cameron's refreshing candour, stating:

> David Cameron often pitches himself as a realist, a pragmatic politician more interested in solving problems than being hitched to ideology [...] He prides himself on being straight with people – refreshing, perhaps, for a Westminster politician.

Yet however refreshing you may find this, it is little more than empty words with no policy to support the people of Gaza who have suffered devastating crimes against humanity – I suspect they would find his 'refreshing' words less than reassuring. The invasion of Gaza at the end of 2008 sent shockwaves throughout the world, not least because of devastating number of civilian casualties. The media bombarded us with graphic images of the victims; for many of us these images have been carved into our consciousness and continue to haunt us.

Bringing the conflict home
A year later and the artist Osi Osmond brought the horrors of the conflict quite literally onto my doorstep, in an exhibition that questions our cultural acceptance of war and violence.

Osi and I live in a small coastal village in west Wales called Llansteffan; in his highly emotive exhibition there were three large drawings depicting terrifying, chaotic scenes of war on Llansteffan beach. 'When they started bombing Gaza I realised that the Gaza strip is about the same size as the coastline and water that I see from my garden in Llansteffan', explained Osi, 'so I was struck by the image of a million and a half people down there with bombs and rockets falling on them.' This vision was further reinforced by the constant sound of bombing and machine gunning, which drifts over the water to Llansteffan from the military base in Pembrey.

Over the years the fact that the Welsh coastline is being used for military practice is something that has gnawed away at Osi. He said: 'I wanted people to begin to understand that our coastline, as beautiful as it is, is used as an instrument of war.'

This really struck home for Osi a few summers ago when his three grandsons were on the beach playing in the water. 'There were bombs dropping behind them', said Osi. 'They didn't take any notice but I was thinking, "God if we were in a different part of the world those bombs could be dropping on them – they'd be dead, they'd be in bits".'

Pacifist Osi, who has travelled extensively throughout the Middle East spending time in war-torn areas such as Palestine and Sudan, demonstrates that this cultural acceptance of violence and war is not only devastating for the victims but also for those carrying out the atrocities. One area of the exhibition, The Soldiers' Wall, depicts young men gripped by terror. 'Often soldiers go in to war looking gung-ho and heroic, and they end up terrified', said Osi. 'They become victims themselves, damaged through psychological trauma.'

Lying just around the corner from The Soldiers' Wall is the Dead

Helicopter (page from sketchbook). Graphite

Children's Wall. Osi said:

> When people discover that those six images are of dead children they are often disgusted, but we need to face that reality. We need to be more vigilant, to question what our culture, our society, and our politics are doing. The atrocities that are carried out in our name is something that people don't really think about, and they need to.

Osi is not only concerned about how our politics and culture affects other nations, but also how it curbs our own freedoms. Talking of the anti-terrorism laws Osi said:

> Our governments, along with the American and most European governments, are keen to instil fear within us. They want us to be afraid so they can get away with whatever they like. I'm as equally afraid of the governments reaction to terrorists, as I am of the terrorists themselves.

Evoking the Chinese curse, 'may you live in interesting times', Osi's work is a response to the very interesting times that we are living in.

Before the BBC state that any politician is 'more interested in solving problems than being hitched to ideology', maybe they should think a little harder about our cultural and political ideologies that accept war as a means of control.

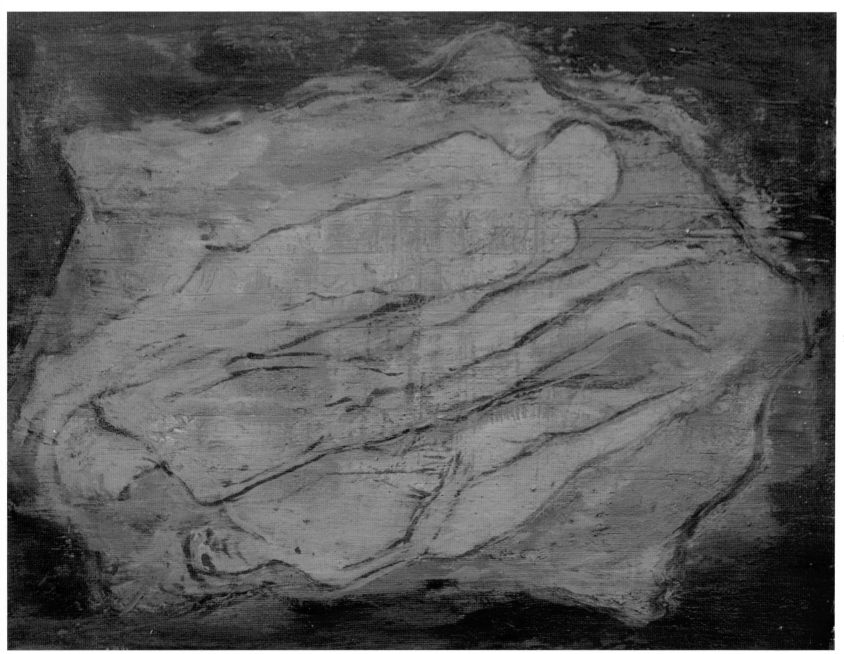

In evidence. Hand-mixed oil paint on canvas

'Mewn Heddwch'
MERERID HOPWOOD

Osi stands and glances around the room. Dark jeans, dark jacket, dark curly hair and dark blue-grey eyes made of light. He starts to speak, passing sentences from hand to hand, turning phrases around the fourth-finger ring on each – first the left, then the right. He punctuates the paragraphs by looking into his mind. Somewhere between the comma and the colon beat, we hear him sensing thoughts. Scanning the map of his mind, he searches for paths that might best deliver complexities to us, roads wide enough to carry the vast vehicles that contain them, trails narrow enough to dart directly into the listener's understanding. And every now and then with both hands, he gently moulds the air in front to give the carriage form and momentum.

Otherwise, he is still. Feet firm. Until he surrenders to the 'unreliability of words' (his expression), and turns to the painting, leading us into a divided day on a divided page, to the split between the sea and the land. The sun is setting off-centre, ready to rise elsewhere, and slightly to the left of the line in the leaf, the hawk hovers. From the twilight a Chinook helicopter approaches. We can just make out the noise of its blades slicing the distant sky.

Osi explains that he has painted this Llansteffan-scape until it has painted him.

It's 2011 and we're gathered in the aptly named Mission Gallery, for he has something of the missionary zeal. Not the 'preachy-this-is-how-it-must-be' type, and not from the blinkered 'my-way-or-no-way' school, but an artist-teacher with passion all the same. Passion for life on earth – all of it. This, it seems, is what allows him to glimpse the meaning of our being here in its many manifestations, in all its different shapes, different sounds, different customs, different clothes. Above all, perhaps, its different colours. These differences are not threats, but rather threads, threads in the same fabric. For when Osi travels he returns amazed by the sights, yes, but more amazed by the people. In the fabric of his friendship we find the Germans, the Italians, the English, the Jews, the Palestinians, the Arabs, the Africans, the Australians ... From Wattsville, Sirhowy to the end of the world, all people are Osi's brothers and sisters.

The gathered in the gallery are members of Cymdeithas y Cymod, the Fellowship of Reconciliation, and it is mainly through this movement that I have come to know Osi. It's part of an international society of pacifists, and if 'reconciliation' is an unfashionably clunky word, it does at least remind us that this group places the emphasis on the practical. Achieving peace means finding common ground. This chimes well with Osi. It combines the ideal with the realistic. It recognises that people will disagree, fall out even, but ultimately, it knows that war is not the solution. There are always other, calmer roads to bring us back together again and to the state of harmony. Back. For this harmony is our state of origin.

We have come in a bus from Carmarthen to Swansea, a fellowship of admirers, no less eager to see the artist's work than to hear his words, as he takes us for a walk to the top of the cliff to look down on the Carmarthenshire beach that is so familiar to us, and lets us see it anew. He has called the exhibition *The Hawk and the Helicopter* and in each frame he has drawn our divided selves, brushing colour onto and into the confusion of the human condition. He knows, as deep as day, as deep as darkness, the harmony that can unite humanity. Yet he recognises the easy hate that can so swiftly disrupt it, the hurt that discord brings.

Manafon (detail). 2012. Watercolour and collage.

Cymdeithas y Cymod protest on Epynt military training range. 2011
Photo: Marian Delyth

In our Carmarthen branch of Cymdeithas y Cymod we have learnt so much from Osi. 'We must take a stand *against*!' some of us have cried, only to hear Osi, wise, impassioned and determined suggesting: 'Let's make a stand *for* ... instead!' And so we have called people to work for remembering the darkness of war, to work *for* achieving the light of peace. And whatever the occasion, from lonely congregations on the back-roads of west Wales, to busier placard-bearing events in Cardiff Bay, there in the rain, in the sun, will be Osi and Hilary – solid, inspirational in their support.

It is Osi's enormous banner that we unfurl on Epynt when we commemorate the community hounded from their homes to make way for an army training camp, a camp that is complete with an imitation central-European village. On six feet of canvas, Osi has drawn the fields and beaches and towns, the mountains and skies of Wales that have been handed over to the business of practicing warfare.

It is Osi who worked with the expert craftsmen of the National Library to create the beautiful Llyfr Gwyn, a testament of peace from the people of Wales to the people of the world. A champion of the cause for curing what he once diagnosed as 'cultural Alzheimer's', Osi treasures the memory held in the Black Book of Carmarthen, the nation's oldest extant book. The new White Book, by association, places itself in this tradition, only this time the words project not to the past but to the future. They are the names of people who have signed up to 'work for peace in the world'. Welsh names from the Welsh branch of the family like John James, Emyr Williams, Margaret Davies, and other names from other branches – family members from further afield who have stopped by to visit us, people like Desmond Tutu.

Earlier this summer, I called to see Osi and Hilary. I had a book with me. I wanted to discuss with them the title of one of its sections – the intriguing Welsh word '*trigo*'. It means both to live and to die; an unusual verb that makes perfect sense. There followed a long discussion.

It got us contemplating other beautifully curious words. Words like '*tangnefedd*'. Now there's a good one. Hard to convey in another language. Look it up and you'll find 'peace'. Yet we have 'heddwch' that does for that. Perhaps '*tangnefedd*', I think we agreed, is the serenity you can find when you're sufficiently at peace with yourself to enable you to feel at peace with others.

Out the back, in the garden in Llansteffan, that is as full of practical fruit and veg as it is of fantastic archways and corners, I could almost fancy that we were within touching distance of '*tangnefedd*'.

Like Waldo Williams, Osi knows that we – all of us – stem from one root, and knows that at the root of life – all of it – there is no decay, no withering, no paralysis. Each of our stories is part of the same story, an ongoing narrative. He finds that, on the cusp between yesterday and tomorrow, our life in our particular today is our brief eternity. '*Gobaith yr yrfa faith ar y drofa fer.*'[1] What we make of it lasts not just for us, but for others. It shades the sky a deeper blue .

Later that summer, at the National Eisteddfod in Llanelli, I thought of the afternoon in the garden (I normally see Osi at the Eisteddfod as we both get robed for the Gorsedd y Beirdd ceremonies). When we chanted '*Heddwch*', echoing the centuries' old plea first cried out by the radical, creative Iolo Morganwg, it

Robed for the Gorsedd y
Beirdd ceremony 2013
Photo: Marian Delyth

was good to know that Osi's voice was there. It's always good to know this.

And as I try to shuttle these syllables and weave them into words to say something about this '*bardd-arlunydd*', this poet-artist, I wish I could draw. If I could, I would start by tracing the flight of the dove that came from Osi's hand onto the opening page of the Llyfr Gwyn, then the hope he painted in the eyes of the woman who watches the bird as her sight reaches for peace, and then the figure of the man, who bends down to let his redundant sword turn red with rust on the earth from which he has coaxed the olive branch to grow.

For some time now, Osi has been signing off with '*mewn heddwch*' – 'in peace'. That's probably a good place to end all encounters.

1. 'Glasach ei glas oherwydd hon' – Geneth Ifanc, t 14 *Dail Pren*, Waldo Williams, Gwasg Gomer 2014 arg. 2010.

Osi 1964, Newport School of Art

On tour

Osi for Plaid. Photo: Iwan Bala

The allotment

The studio. Photo: Luned Aaron

The kitchen table. Photo: Siân Lewis

'Y Lle Celf', National Eisteddfod of Wales, 2010.
Photo: Marian Delyth

Osi Rhys Osmond: educator, creator, thinker, friend.

AN INTERVIEW WITH
ANN OOSTHUIZEN

My son, who has lived in Sierra Leone, gives this advice to travellers: when you get to a village, greet the Chief, 'For my children and grandchildren.' Osi has most definitely always been the Chief. I believe that he is this for many people who know him – family, friends, colleagues, ex-students, neighbours, even acquaintances. These interviews are an attempt to give the reader a chance to experience something of the man and I hope those who know him will be reminded of other conversations. Anyone who has heard him rant over the Sunday papers, or who has been given a lift in his car, will know that with Osi you have to expect the bad with the good, but sometimes, when you talk with him or look at his paintings or hear him speak in public, it is as if he has punched a hole in the ordinary fabric of our lives to give us a glimpse of the sublime.

First day at school

On my first day at school we were already living in Wattsville, Number 21 Islwyn Road. My parents had a bedroom, but as for the rest we lived in one room, which I slept in. We didn't have any cooking facilities in that room. We had to walk through the house to the back kitchen to cook on other people's kit. That was very common in the valleys in those days after the war. The school was behind the house so when I was told I was going to school, I accepted it as I accepted a lot of things, but I lived in a very private world – I had a very strongly developed interior world and I could accept all these outside challenges without any trouble, it didn't worry me. But I always thought they were an intrusion as I felt that my life, as I experienced it, was a very complete thing. I lived in a kind of vertical world. The school was built into the side of the mountain, terraced, so it was a big climb to get there up these little narrow steps and through a great big iron gate and across a big tarmac. I was quite perplexed that we had to queue up to go in as if it was something that was that wonderful. The experience of the day at school was fine. We were allowed to draw on blackboards that were child height and all the way along the side of one wall. There were various coloured chalks and in the moments when we had finished our work, we were allowed to draw on these blackboards, as we wanted. I was taken with this. All the boys drew aeroplanes and war and all the girls drew heads or homes. One girl in particular drew a head that was shaped like a banana. When the bell went at eleven o'clock, I thought that was the end of it. We all charged into the playground like dervishes, and I went out through the gates, and then forgot to go home. I went for a walk up the mountain, and then got lost in my imagination, looking down at the village and the whole world.

It wasn't until 3.30pm, when I should have been at home, that they realised I was missing. A search party was sent out. There was a hue and cry so I answered to their calls. I wasn't far away and I was brought back down and sort of admonished by the authorities, the teacher in the school. My mother understood, she was a bit forgiving, but the next day it was arranged that a very powerfully built girl called Avril, who lived a few doors down, was engaged to accompany me to school and make sure I didn't escape!

Childhood in Wattsville

Growing up in Wattsville was fascinating, wonderful, extraordinary, brilliant. We lived in a very narrow belt of industrial development around a river, a railway and a road, which led to the colliery. Everything that was built was a compromise with the terrain and that created a very higgledy-piggledy upside down world, which gave a sort of tilting perspective. Almost any step you took presented a different view. So you had this kind of verticality, and then this sudden drop and turning view, so it was very exciting. There was one colliery at the top of the village, and one at the bottom. They weren't silent things; they were noisy because they breathed. They had a ventilation system that went ooo-aaa-ooo-aaa that was constant over twenty-four hours. The colliery breathed so the air moved. There were two shafts for the ventilation system and the air was pumped in and out. There were great fans in the colliery. So the valley was like a living thing, it was like bestriding a massive monster, a great animal, a Leviathan. It was almost like the breathing tubes of a whale, I suppose, and we were on the whale's back. Because it was a narrow industrial development, the rest of it was all wild mountainside or coal tip. What it was, was an unregulated terrain, unfenced and unordered so that you had complete freedom of space and perspective, which allowed your imagination freedom as well. You never felt that you were tied down, caught or trapped. You always felt you could go on forever into a kind of eternity of adventures, always skyward, towards the light.

There was always something moving. Although they didn't cut coal at night, the colliery workings were continuous. There were always trams moving and trains moving and the trains went up and down the main line. They were small lines, narrow gauge, on which the colliery vehicles travelled, with coal, with pit props, with the waste from the colliery, which went up the mountain on this great hawser with buckets, up a thousand feet, to dump the waste at the top, on the mountain. There were ubiquitous sheep, and there were dogs everywhere and there were children everywhere. Every child belonged to everybody. You had your parents of course, but you still belonged to everybody. You were constantly touched in an affectionate way – your hair was ruffled, not in a threatening way, but in a very caring way. So if you were doing something really stupid, there was always someone to tell you not to do it. If we played around the colliery, as we were quite welcome to do, we could walk in and out of the colliery – there was no fence around it. The men who were working there knew us. You were always referred to by your father's name. They wouldn't know your name necessarily, but you'd be Malcolm's boy or Johnnie's boy or Dai's boy. I was Malcolm's boy or Young Malcolm. It was a fabulous, wonderful culture to be brought up in. And there were dogs everywhere, and they also belonged to everybody. The interesting thing about the dogs was that they had surnames, Fido Pearson, Bruce Gregory or Hugo Lewis.

Grammar School

It was a huge effort of my parents to send me to the grammar school. My father was one of five children, my mother one of seven. Both had lost their mother pretty early on in life. They'd both gone to the grammar school. They were the only ones in their families who had gone to the grammar school, but they each had to leave at fifteen due to domestic circumstances. My father went to work in the pit, my mother initially looked after her father and then she was sent to London to work as a nanny or a maid, domestic service. So they were determined that I and their other children would go to the grammar school and that I wouldn't go down the colliery, although I had a great urge to go down the colliery – it seemed like the life real men led. I didn't know a man in the village who didn't work in the colliery. There were one or two men who didn't, but they always seemed to me to be less than men, somewhat. But at home the emphasis was on passing the eleven-plus and it was always held over me that if I didn't go to the grammar school, I'd have to go down the colliery. I didn't feel special, but I did feel different because there wasn't another boy in the village who had passed the eleven-plus. Certainly there wasn't another boy from Wattsville in the grammar school in my year. There was a boy in form six, the son of the man who ran The Co-op, Ken, who went on to become a doctor, I think. There was no one else, and nobody below me, until I left.

Recently my headmaster came to a couple of exhibitions of mine. His daughter bought him a painting, it was a big drawing of the old Risca Colliery and he donated it to the library in Risca. When I was at school I was difficult, not because I was malicious or malevolent, but because I was daydreaming and in my own world, like in a cocoon of some kind. But I was an extrovert. That was the other thing. I laughed a lot. I was always sociable, but I lived in a private world. I didn't count other people's praise as valuable, necessarily. I made my own judgements about what I was doing, which was a bit difficult for them to understand. I couldn't see much value in the school system. It seemed to me to be an intrusion into what was otherwise a very interesting life. I would gaze out of the window when we were talking about the Romans. I'd imagine them coming across the mountain. What the school gave me was a sense of injustice in the world. In Wales we seemed to be the victims of invasions, incursions, assaults, attacks, and all our wealth went down the valley, down the river, out, away from us. We had nothing in out village except somewhere to live and somewhere to be buried and that was it. And of course we had two massive places to work. I thought that as a child.

When I saw television for the first time, there were these serials. I couldn't understand why nobody ever went to work. That's one of the things that stuck in my mind. I thought; what kind of world do these people live in? My mother, being a nanny, had been given a lot of books, particularly by these two doctors in Harley Street for whom she had worked for a number of years and looked after their two daughters. In fact my younger sister was named after them, Gail and Priscilla. They'd given my mother their books: *Christopher Robin*, *Tom Brown's School Days*, English books about English families and in them nobody went to work. I thought; this is weird. How can they do it? Where does the money come from?' The money in our house came in on a Friday in a brown envelope and it was in notes with some change as well. It was put on the table and shared out. So much for this, so much for that, so much for my father's needs, which were many, but small, so much for us, and it never lasted until the following Friday. It had always run out by the Wednesday. There was never any money in the house between Wednesday afternoon and Friday afternoon. If anything was necessary or needed, you just couldn't have it. So if I lost my pen at school, which I did frequently, or needed anything else, it wasn't possible. I couldn't have it.

My headmaster told me that they had considered sending me to The Slade School of Art. I was quite young, fifteen, sixteen. They seemed to have decided that I wouldn't cope socially. I didn't find out about this until fifty-seven years later. Fifty-seven years ago they had this discussion at school because they wanted to find something for me to do. I wasn't university material because I wasn't going to pass all the academic exams, but I had something about me. The headmaster said to me; 'You were the most peculiar and interesting child I ever taught. We always knew you had something about you. We just couldn't work out what it was, so we thought The Slade because you could draw.' So they had this meeting and they said, 'Oh, send him to The Slade.' But as the time came closer they decided against it because they thought that I might be socially overawed by all those sophisticated young people who would be going to The Slade. But, of course, anybody who knows me knows that wouldn't have been the case at all. I would have thrived. Be that as it may, I'm not sad. My life would have been completely different and I know my life and I would hate to have had a life that I didn't know, even in my imagination, so that I'd be like a stranger in my own world. What is is. It's always been my philosophy that what we're in is what we're in – get on with that. Although I was a daydreamer and wished for all sorts of things, I had this other grasp of

reality. I'm a pragmatic optimist, so I'm willing to dream, willing to desire, but I do know where I am. I do realise the reality of the situation I'm in. That doesn't mean I don't want to change it or anything, but those two things have gone side by side, always. Since I've been ill, that attitude has been a huge comfort to me. Other people are a bit baffled by my optimism, but at the same time I'm very pragmatic. I'll say, 'Remember when you bury me, Hil, treat so-and-so like one of the family.' Other people will say, 'How can you say that?' But I can say that because it is a reality that is going to happen, therefore we have to accept it – we can't wish it away. The Slade would have been great. Of course it would have been great. The headmaster was puzzled. To be honest, school was a huge disappointment to me because I had been led to believe that it would be about revealing the truth in life and that it would be an extraordinary experience, and it just didn't feel like that.

Newport College of Art
The constant phrase my father used was, 'What are we going to do with the boy?' His other two children were girls. It was a dilemma for my father and it was a dilemma for the school. So eventually I went to the local art college in Newport. That was the line of least resistance.

At the art school, we did two years basic and then two years International Art and Design. I was told to apply for The Royal College of Art. I did it for two years running. You'd send up a folder of your work – drawings and paintings etc, and if they liked you they'd call you in for an interview. That was the examination system. We were expected to paint very nitty-gritty, dark, working class social realism and because I came from south Wales, they couldn't understand why I didn't paint miners. I didn't paint miners because they were part of my life. I wanted to paint the experience of being in that place, which was in a sense a wonderful natural landscape with these beautiful mountains all around us. So I didn't see all the dirt and the filth and the muck and the coal dust. I saw the beauty of nature and the ferns and these huge expanses of red and orange and green. They were like Rothkos, those mountains, a thousand feet rising up behind the house. Not a tree on the one behind the house. A thousand feet of just one colour, more or less. The famous Ruskin Speer came in late to the interview. He had a bit of a limp. He said, 'You are from Wales. Where are the *miners*, young man? Where are the *miners*?' I said, 'Well, there's more to Wales than miners, you know.' I don't think I endeared myself to him, so I didn't get in. I continued at Newport and then I started teaching. I didn't go to London to study, and I'm glad because, as I said, my life would have been an unknown. I wouldn't be sitting here now.

Our group of students in the college all became well known in a narrow pool. The college was considered one of the best art schools in Britain. It had a tradition of very closely observed drawing, documentary drawing of an extraordinary quality. That was the bedrock of the teaching. We studied perspective, anatomy, and the history of costume. The old system was on its last legs – it was going by then. Before I finished they introduced the new system, the Diploma in Art and Design, but I was still in the fag end of the old system, which was very much based on the three elements of composition. So you had to paint 'A rainy day at the bus stop', 'Down at the Butcher's', 'Hanging out the washing' and every painting had to have at least three figures in it, and you had to bear in mind composition, perspective and all this other stuff. We knew at

the end of three years we'd have an examination in this kind of painting. So, as long as you could do it, in your own time you could do whatever you liked. People were painting huge abstract paintings, all sorts of things, trying to follow the latest trends, difficult as that was in Newport. There was no question about not having a grant because the grant came every year from Gwent Council. They were very generous. I used to have a hundred pounds a term and I used to go down to the Co-operative in Cross Keys and cash the cheque in ten-shilling notes. So I'd have two hundred ten shilling notes and I used to stuff them in my drawer and take one out every day – and on special occasions two or three!

I shared a flat with other students among them Otto, Alan Osborne, Bryan Jones. It was in a huge house in a Victorian terrace. It was absolutely freezing cold – we slept in our coats! The landlady was called Miss Huxtable. I can see her now. She was very frail and it took her all day to get a few buckets of coal up from the coal cellar. But she always had a runny nose. So with her runny nose and her tendency to wipe her nose with the back of her hand, by the end of the day her face would be a black, shiny, crisp carapace, almost like some kind of insect.

I left Art School in 1965, so I missed the upheavals of 1968. I'd been brought up with the concept that we'd been badly treated in Wales because the story of our history was one of invasion. We learned about Synchronistic Time. From the time of the Beaker People, there were always people from the east who were threatening us. In my time it was the English. So, as students, we tended to go east like on a revenge mission. So it was like a Viking raid on an unsuspecting settlement because we went to London with a sense of class warfare. It wasn't political, but it was cultural. We were still the Beat generation. They'd led the way. It wasn't about changing the world; it was about making your world the world you wanted to be in. It wasn't about changing the world for anyone else. Selfish, in a sense, but that was the Beat philosophy. We were the blues generation – Charlie Parker, Big Bill Broonzy, Lead Belly, and Dinah Washington. These were our musical stars. I've no idea what London made of us, but they thought we were interesting and I always managed to find myself in interesting situations, talking with interesting people. I remember this girl saying, 'Oh, I say, is your father really a miner?' I remember saying, 'Yeah!' and she said, 'Oh, how basic!' I won't tell you what happened next!

Moving to Pembrokeshire

I stayed in Newport for about five years. By then I was married and had a child, Ché, and we were living above a butcher's shop in the docks in Newport, then we moved to a house in Risca, which we rented. I had two teaching jobs, which were permanent, but not full-time, so getting a mortgage was difficult. I didn't have any money and couldn't save any money, so we moved to west Wales where I found a job as head of Art in Narberth Secondary School.

The day I took the train for the interview, Porthcawl was the furthest west I'd ever been. We used to go to Coney Island beach there. So, going through Swansea and then onward was an absolute surprise. When the train left Kidweli, it came round the corner by St Ishmaels and there were two men in a field cutting hay with a scythe. I'll never forget that image because I thought, 'Where am I going? I'm going back in time, back in history.' My perception of time and history is an east/west one. The west is old, the east is new. East is intrusive, the west is inclusive and ancient and substantial and peaceful and formed. I suppose in a sense that's how the framework of my thinking has set around these parameters. Even now, because that's how my education was.

Narberth station is a mile away from the village. It's in a hollow and there was in those days a shop in the station and some terraced houses around it, so I thought Narberth station was Narberth. The headmaster met me and whisked me away to the school, which was on a crest about half a mile away, but that too was outside the town, on the east side of the town so I didn't see the town on my trip to Narberth. I could see the school and the great rolling view over the Pembrokeshire countryside. It was late May and they were desperate to appoint someone because the incumbent had left very suddenly – he'd become ill, I think. I was interviewed by the headmaster, who could appoint me or not in those days. He wasn't interested in my experience. He wasn't interested in anything very much. He said, 'What does your father do?' I said, 'Well, he works in the colliery.' He said, 'What else does he do?' So I said, 'He's a lay preacher.' With that he sat up and began to take an interest. The next question was, 'What denomination?' And I said, 'Baptist.' And he sat up even further and said, 'Thank you, Mr Osmond, that will be all. You'll be hearing from us.' I went back to the staff room as I was having a lift back to Carmarthen to catch the train with a man called Dai Williams, who was a Welsh patriot of a high order. In the meantime I sat in the staff room with a number of people, smoking and chatting. So they said, 'What did he ask you?' I replied, 'Well he didn't ask me very much. He wasn't interested in anything really. He asked me about my father who is a collier and a lay preacher. He asked what denomination and I said Baptist.' And they said, 'You've got the job!' I got home on the train that night and in the morning the letter arrived.

The interesting thing for me that day was that because we went on the back road rather than the main road from Narberth to Carmarthen, the whole way was plastered with Gwynfor Evans posters, Welsh Nationalists, Plaid Cymru. Well, up until then I'd been a stalwart of the Labour Party, I'd been out canvassing for them, I'd been a member. I disliked nationalism. I had viewed it as an inferior political philosophy, narrow-minded and exclusive, so it was my first encounter with fervid questions about Wales that I'd never asked myself before. It wasn't until I went to west Wales to teach that I began to think much more carefully about questions of Welsh culture and the language in particular. And it took me only a few months to ask for the papers for Plaid Cymru, which I joined as soon as I could, although much of Plaid Cymru in those days was a Welsh coterie and you weren't necessarily that welcome if you didn't speak Welsh. From that day on I vowed that I too would one day speak Welsh. It had been an ambition of mine for a long time and I'd wanted my children (I had one son, and soon I had two boys) I'd wanted them to speak Welsh.

Meic Stevens, who was at art school with me, spoke Welsh. I couldn't understand how he spoke Welsh because he was the same age as me. In our village, the people on both sides of us, neighbours, were Welsh speaking, but they were in their forties, fifties, sixties. They were adults, they were older. Their children didn't speak Welsh. No child spoke Welsh, only older

people. And I remember somebody saying that Meic Stevens spoke Welsh, and I said, 'He can't, he's too young', as if it was some mysterious misunderstanding. But I was determined, as soon as I met Meic Stevens that one day I would speak Welsh too. It took a long, long time, but eventually I got there. Those are the formative moments for my real embrace of Welshness and the Welsh language. Coming to Narberth, the shock, the change, and the sense of going into something old and substantial and valuable. It was a culture where people seemed to care for things in a different kind of way, even compared to the valleys there was a much more communitarian spirit. There was still a body of people who believed in a certain series of ideas and they were good ideas and I believe they lived in a very good way. It was something I embraced.

On Politics
In my private life politics had been a position, now it was an attitude. More than an attitude, it was an action. I stood for Pembrokeshire Council twice, and failed. Those political battles went on for twelve to fifteen years, but fighting in an election campaign, even in a hopeless cause, is nevertheless an exciting thing to be doing. Although I never got onto the Pembrokeshire Council, I did get onto the County Council in Carmarthenshire at a much later date. I did three years as a County Councillor, which was a very dispiriting experience. I didn't feel it was possible to make any change or to contribute to any worthwhile thing. My emphasis was on housing for local people – self-build – and there were a number of schemes across the country, which we could have embraced, but to get officers or fellow councillors interested in it seemed a lost cause. It was a bitter disappointment to me. There was no vision whatsoever. The County Council is supposed to be run

by the Councillors. The Executive is supposed to carry out the wishes of the Councillors. In Carmarthenshire, and most other councils, the Councillors carry out the wishes of the Executives. They make the decisions and the Councillors by and large rubber-stamp them. Young people were unable to purchase homes in Wales – it happened to me when I went to Narberth. It was difficult. You'd go to see a house and say, yes, you'd like to buy it and the next thing you knew was that somebody from Birmingham was coming with a bigger offer. And it was to be a holiday home, while mine was to be a family home. I remember the use of the word 'property'. Where I came from they didn't talk about 'property', they talked about houses or sheds or coalmines. Property seemed to be a strange word. To me it was tied to an in-built morality. It was about profiting at other people's expense. Property. It was about greed. And I saw this sudden growth of estate agents in the west. Estate agents used to be people who managed estates. It was a job, but these people were selling property and there was a property market and nobody talked about homes and this was something that has got to me all through the rest of my life. It's a conundrum. What's gone on in London particularly leaves me shocked and bewildered and puzzled why governments and other agencies can't do anything about it. We seem to be at the mercy of the moneymen and the idea that you can sell your house in England for twice as much as you need to buy a house in Wales.

All my life I've had this reputation of being aggressive and quarrelsome because I'm not happy suffering fools. I can be critical, and a lot of people have misinterpreted that as a sort of anxiety. I was quite aggressive as a young man – brawling and fighting as part of a tradition. When I got much older I realised I didn't have to be like that. People who don't know me well still think this and they're always shocked when they deal with me and do business with me – even today in The Arts Council people have said, 'I didn't realise you were so reasonable. You're a much nicer person than I thought you were.' My reputation of being outspoken and critical is misunderstood as an unpleasantness when it's not. I think society generally is too polite. It's not polite actually; it's very deceptive and sly. It cheats. At meetings there is a layer of duplicity over things.

On learning to speak Welsh
I was always aware of the Welsh language but when I went to Narberth I went to classes and I encouraged other people to try to help me. I never got very good at it although I did learn some vocabulary. I had the bricks, but I didn't have the cement. I didn't have the means of using the language. I had the nouns, but I had no idea how to get the verbs to work, so when I met Hilary all the learning I'd done, but forgotten (it was deep in there somewhere) came to the fore. We were deeply in love. One of the vows we made to ourselves was that when we had a home we would speak Welsh there, which we did. In the beginning our Welsh was limited to the kitchen and the bedroom, but eventually I got fluent enough that I could make TV and radio programmes and perform in Welsh. I'm still a learner, but I'm still a learner in everything. I never believed that speaking Welsh mattered, when I lived in the east, and most people don't believe it matters at all. We've never really properly come to terms with it. It's something we push to one side, wrongly I think, but it's partly to do with our media and our educational system that has split us as a people into those

who speak Welsh and those who don't. I think the Welsh are unaware of what their own country is. There's a huge ignorance about what Wales is and unless you speak Welsh you will remain ignorant in that sense. Welsh is a language of 'being'. This is my conclusion. When you come to a language almost, but not entirely as a stranger – certainly I can say that I was a stranger – it is like entering a new country, a new world, a new dynamic, a new philosophy. It was an extraordinary experience actually. It was like opening a door, stepping into this world with a few hesitant steps, and a bit further in, and there's still lots to do and further to go and further to explore. And gradually when you learn a language you become enchanted by it, especially if it is a poetic language, like Welsh. One of the things I discovered early on was that the verb to be, 'bod' in Welsh, was a continuous feature throughout various adjectives and adverbs and nouns. I discovered, I felt, that Welsh is a language of *being*, and when I considered English it seemed to be a language of *doing*. Now I think being has a great superiority over doing. English is the language of the busybody, Welsh is the language of the contemplative. For me, Welsh is such a private language. You make these discoveries about the language that someone who is a native speaker might not recognise. So you are privileged as an explorer sometimes to see the world that someone else inhabits in a way that they haven't noticed themselves. In a way it helped me to understand myself better because I'm a being person. I am an active person, no doubt about that, but my greatest joy is being. Getting up every morning and being Welsh was always problematic in a sense because what you were in your culture was always threatened. It wasn't like being a Norwegian or an Italian in the way you could get up and have an espresso and feel completely Italian, nothing to worry

about in the Italian business. Or being Norwegian, you could have your gravlax and not worry about being Norwegian. There is nothing to threaten it. But when you get up in the morning and you're Welsh, you go down for your cheese on toast and you know you are under threat. Your culture is never secure, it's unstable and you have a responsibility towards it. I think many people take their culture for granted, but in Wales we can't, it's always under threat from the east.

On love

My marriage to Hilary changed me. When you have true love and deep love you have faith in the other person, and you also have faith in yourself. You don't seek anything anywhere else and love is the only thing that is infinite in the world. I realised this quite early, but what clarified it for me was the financial crisis in 2008 when I got the impression that people thought that money could go on growing exponentially for ever and ever. Obviously it couldn't. And I began to think, what can? I couldn't think of anything other than love. Hate couldn't because hate would kill itself, destroy itself. Give it enough time and it will kill itself. But love, true love, is just never going to stop growing. That was one thing I learned that if you have love, you have more opportunity to be who you really are. Your fears and your doubts and your anxieties about yourself and your place in the world and your relation to other people subside in the face of love. Real love drives fear away, drives anxiety away. You have a greater chance to be who you are in a pure sense, so I am much more like I think I am or how I wanted to be because I am fulfilled as a person now in a way that I couldn't be before when there were other anxieties that prevented the development of this person. When you are giving so much to someone else, you are unconsciously growing yourself, not thinking about me, but thinking about her/him that allows you to blossom unselfconsciously.

Visiting Lourdes

My father was a very religious man. I am religious too, in a spiritual sense. My father's life was one of great disappointment, as well as grief with the loss of his daughter. He had been ambitious, with a clever, mathematical mind, but he could never fulfil himself. He left the colliery on several occasions to try to find better employment in England. He always went east to find betterment, but it never worked out. During the war he was in the aircraft factory in Bristol, but before the war was finished, he was sent back to the coalmines because the Ministry of Works decided he should be sent back. My mother and I were living a beautiful suburban life in a three-bedroomed house, and then he was sent back to the collieries. He travelled down every week and stayed with his father or his sister and came back every Friday. But it couldn't be sustained because after the war the wages in the collieries went down and there was no work in the aircraft factory, so we came back, like a group of refugees, in 1946. It was a huge disappointment to him. The world, as he understood it, had let him down. He'd crossed the river Severn so many times, like a dog with his tail between his legs. In 1946 we lived in one room and he took up the religion of his father and started going to chapel again. He'd been religious as a young man, and then he went away. As a young father (he was still in his thirties) he became religious again. I was born when he was twenty-five, so he was twenty-nine when we went back to Wattsville. He'd tried London. He'd tried everything. It didn't work. So he became religious and he got involved with the chapel and he grew and he grew and he grew, and it became his life and it became my mother's life,

although she hadn't been particularly religious before then.

One thing about my upbringing was that I wasn't embarrassed by religion. I did notice that people didn't want to talk about religion, or couldn't talk about it. If you have been brought up in a religious family, you do have a spiritual vocabulary. You've got a way of dealing with the world, which is not the material world. I think that was a blessing and I'm really grateful for that and I despair that young people now don't experience that. After being diagnosed as terminally ill, one of my very good friends took me to Lourdes. I was brought up a Baptist, so I am the polar opposite to a Catholic. I remember saying to him, 'But I don't believe,' and he said, 'I'll do the believing, you do the healing. That's your responsibility.' So we had a demarcation of labour! I found it one of the most moving experiences of my life. I went without any cynicism, completely open-minded in the hope that it would affect a cure. When I went to take the waters, I was in a wheelchair because I couldn't walk at the time, and the man who was helping me into the bath said to me, 'Are you a priest?' Perhaps because he thought I had a peculiar look about me. I said, 'No.' He held me down in the water and he said, 'Pray in your own language,' which I did. When I came out of the water he grasped me by both arms, grabbed my elbow and looked me right in the eyes and said, 'You are a good man.' I was absolutely shocked, astonished, moved and burst into tears, but the strange thing was that I'd gone to the pool in a wheelchair, but I pushed the wheel chair going away from the pool. I didn't even think about it. I didn't think to get back in it because somehow I now had the resources to propel the wheelchair and not to be propelled sitting in it. You get a sense of something working, but I didn't actually think about it at the time particularly.

216

Study for *Cyfarfod/The Meeting*. Oil on canvas. 51cm x 41cm   *Cyfarfod/The Meeting*. Mixed media on paper. 92cm x 140cm

Earlier we'd gone to Mass in this huge underground church where fifteen thousand people take Mass. My friend wanted to go. He didn't insist that I went, but I thought that I would. I remember going in a wheelchair and I was placed in a long line of people in wheelchairs. Hilary and I were separated. She was placed at the back with my friend and his wife and I was amongst all the people in wheelchairs. I was third from the end. I enjoyed the service, I really enjoy singing and services and the priest came along with the host, and I had been instructed to fold my arm across my chest and shake my head to show I wasn't a Catholic, which I did. The first three people had the host and then I did this, but the priest refused to accept the no. He nodded his head and pushed the host towards my mouth. I said no again, but he did it four times and in the end he caught me in an unguarded moment and it just went straight into my mouth! So I had the host, and he went on. The person next to me indicated no, and the priest accepted that and went on to the next one. I was baffled and asked my friend afterwards, 'What is the significance of this?' and he said, 'Well, if the priest thinks you are in a state of grace, he'll give you the host. You are supposed to have confession and go to Mass before you have the host (I had done neither), but he must have looked at you and thought that there was something about you that was a bit different.' It was very flattering and moving and I was grateful for the experience. So I had these three extraordinary moments in Lourdes and I felt I was in another world, on another plane. Two people who had never seen me, never met me, didn't know who I was, looked at me and saw something.

On being an artist

I've never earned a living solely as an artist. I didn't want to. I would hate to have to make paintings to live. It seemed to me that teaching was a very liberating thing. It meant that in my time I could do what I needed to do for myself, whereas other people who are dependent on making a living as an artist are forced to make things they don't want to make. I never did anything in the visual arts or anything else for that matter that I didn't want to do and that I didn't believe in passionately, whereas I've got a friend who makes his living by making things and very often he's frustrated because he's not making the things he really wants to be making and that's a compromise. I was brought up in a culture where there was no such thing as art – it didn't exist. I'd never been to an art gallery until I went to art school. I didn't even go to many when I was there because we were generally encouraged to find our resources within ourselves. It's a much better way of teaching than we have now. So the idea you could earn a living from art seemed absurd, but you could have a life in art, messing about, being bohemian. We were brought up with the mythologies of the Paris Left Bank, which is totally unrealistic, because most of the people who inhabited the Left Bank, artists, were people with some form of private income, no matter how small, and where I came from if you wanted to eat, you worked, and painting wasn't work, like poetry wasn't work.

I hope my painting has changed over the years, as I have changed, but it's still got lots of the same concerns. My interrogation of the world is something that happens every day. I'm concerned about the parts of the world where people are under pressure, where there's violence, where people are squeezed between powers, and I see their helplessness in the face of power. That sense of injustice has been with me since childhood. Growing up in the south Wales valleys, you want the world to be a better place and you know that it isn't. You would like to think that decent human beings are working for that end, but you realise before too long that there are too few of them to reach that end. Since I was ten years old, what appeared to be a dream of social justice, I hoped, as an idea, was coming, was growing. Now my grandchildren are ten and that isn't happening any more. It's going in the other direction.

On teaching life drawing

One of the things that fascinated me and of which I was very aware all the time I was teaching is that art could be more than imitation and could be a way of thinking that could be developed without necessarily using words. This is a very contentious idea, but before I left teaching in the school, which I did for fourteen years, I started teaching in the Carmarthenshire College of Technology and Art, part-time in the evenings. I used to go up to Carmarthen once or twice a week to teach life drawing or the history of art. When I began teaching full-time there, I began to develop a philosophy of teaching art that looked at life drawing as a means of what I used to call press-ups for the brain. I wasn't interested in reproductive qualities, or representation, I was, but it wasn't the overriding factor. The most important thing was the thinking you were engaged in as you examined the figure, because what you were doing was making a series of judgements and you were making marks. Now the mark couldn't possibly represent anything like human flesh, but it could represent its position in space – where it was – and it could represent it in relation to another mark in space. It wasn't a question of being imitative, it was a question of being analytical, thoughtful and philosophical, and what I found was that the more students put into that and the better they got at

it, the better their overall performance was. They became better at being who they were. So my overriding philosophy as a teacher was this idea that art wasn't an entertaining or diversionary activity, it wasn't something that could be used as a kind of escapism. It could be used in therapy, obviously, but that wasn't for me its overriding strength, its overriding beauty and its overriding quality was this ability it had to engage people in the world in which they lived. An opportunity for them to examine and interrogate that world by visual means and when they did it by visual means, they did it by other means as well.

Another way of teaching art

I was very anxious to free art of the word, because the description of something – the word – isn't the thing itself, and most people in Britain were brought up with a very, very limited thought process, so if I, which I did, remove my wedding ring and say to my students, 'What is this?' they would all say, 'It's a ring.' And I would say, 'Well, that's what it's called, but is that what it is?' And of course this would engage a philosophical debate, which would take some time. As we were living in a bilingual country, I was able to say, 'Well, that's what it's called in English, but what is it called in any other language?' And of course there would be quite number of students who spoke Welsh. So they'd be able to say '*modrwy*'. Now if you use the word 'ring' to describe this essentially metal cylinder, you will be led in certain directions and generally in English sound plays a huge part in thought, so ring goes to ding goes to bell goes to dong in English, but in Welsh a close word to '*modrwy*' is '*modryb*', which is auntie and auntie isn't anything like a ring. So in English you'll be going for a sound, while in Welsh you'll be going for a person and in

219

other languages you'll be on a different path. So when we were developing creative thinking, expanding ideas, it was important to rid the object, the thing, the idea, of its title, or its word, or its signifier, because you want to see it of its shape, a form, cylindrical. If you could then introduce notions of space and scale, you'd then ask what it reminds us of, in that sense, where does it lead us, and of course the clever ones would say, 'Well, if I put them all together I'd make a long tube, it might be my aorta, and if you made it tiny it would be a vein', and someone else would say, 'If you made it enormous it would be the universe', and someone else would say, 'A traffic roundabout, or an amphitheatre', so what began as a humble 'ring' if you remove the title, the signifier, the word, you can have a great visual adventure. And you can also conduct this adventure in diagrammatic form by drawing very freely and loosely and by introducing notions of scale, so if I draw this metal cylinder on a piece of paper, if I put an aeroplane next to it, it will take on a certain scale – if I draw a little aeroplane next to it – but if I put a Boeing 707 next to it, it will become bigger. And so on. So introducing this notion of scale in thinking, what other ways can you explore it? Well, you can chop it up, you can repeat it, you can talk about pattern and repetition, you can twist it, so this simple thing, which is a cylinder, a ring, can take you on an extraordinary journey. What I wanted was for the students to make those journeys with whatever object or thought or thing or experience or feeling that they encountered in their lives, and that too could be taken on this journey, this adventure to who knows where. It was Wittgenstein's theory I was expounding, without knowing it. It came to me a long time before I read him. The idea that words cannot express the reality of what they attempt to describe, which becomes a tyranny that interferes with our comprehension of the world.

On Friday afternoons, when the course for the week was coming to an end, they would be given a task to undertake for the weekend. One of the things I was interested in was not leading people, but driving them, and so I would open the gate and say, 'There's the field and you can go and graze in whichever part of it suits you.' Some people found that very difficult, some people found it liberating. Students would prefer to be led initially, but I was determined that they wouldn't be. So on the weekend the course was meant to be diagnostic – to see what was right with people, what was good with people, what they were about, whether they were naturally inclined to three dimensions, or to two dimensions, but most importantly to find their intention.

There was an artist called Marina Abromovic who wore clothes made from pieces of meat. So I used to ask the students, 'Well, is she a butcher, is she a fashion designer, or is she an artist?' They would reply, 'How do we know?' I'd say, 'What was her intention? Is she selling the steak? No. Is she selling it to wear? No. She's telling you to have a visual experience on confronting it. So that makes her a visual artist.' Now, traditionally people who did drawings of women with long necks would be propelled in the direction of fashion. There was no real pertinent question being asked about students and their abilities and certainly not about their intentions. If you like it, you do it. It was like going into a sweet shop. Do you want the dolly mixture or do you want the liquorice allsorts? I did it differently. I didn't make any division between fine art, graphic design, theatre design, three-dimensional design, ceramics. I didn't make any distinction. The students might make work from a simple idea that might be taken in any one of those directions. So every Friday I'd give them a task for the weekend, and it was in the days before Google so it was much better and much easier to do this, and I would say, ' No conferring. This is for you alone, because I don't want to know what other ideas other people are putting into your head.' I thought the English language was a very interesting language – the first language in the world to have crossword puzzles – because of its flexibilities and its absurdities and its cleverness. So, if I said to the students on a Friday afternoon, 'Jacket potato', they had to go away and react to this. Now some people would bake a potato or two and do a painting, some would write a short story, some would draw very carefully, with a pencil, a potato that had been baked, all the crinkles and the crunches, some would open it up, some would put some butter in, some would fill it up, some would make an illustrative response, some would make an expressive response, one student made a beautiful denim jacket for a potato. Somebody baked potatoes over the weekend, cut all the skin off, made a jacket and wore it on the Monday. All these were then photographed. So this was a way of saying, 'What are you about?' and it gave people an opportunity, especially the more creative, gave them an opportunity to really find themselves, really express themselves and it was the delight of English, the wonder of English, the extraordinary flexibility of English that allowed this to happen. It probably couldn't happen in most other languages. Because I could say things like, 'Washing up'. Somebody would draw a bowl of washing. Somebody would draw a draining board with various items on it. Somebody would draw a shoreline with flotsam and jetsam. Some would paint it. Somebody would make something from flotsam and jetsam. One student made the letters UP about eighteen inches high, beautifully made, three dimensional, thick, simple, non serif letters, painted them beautifully with a base, put a ladder

up against the U and had a tiny figure with a bucket washing UP. You see, English allows you to do this. So when you've done this business with the ring, that it is not what it is called, and you expand that into the visual language it represents, you and the students have these quite extraordinary adventures. The weekend task was assessed in a public, a very open assessment, where the whole group would be in one big room, with all the examples of what they'd brought in, what they'd done over the weekend, and fair play, in those days it was a much more comfortable economic climate in that they didn't necessarily have to work on the weekends in jobs in pubs and Macdonald's as they do now. They had time, and they sometimes made the most extraordinary things that you would never have thought possible, that you would never have dreamed of because you'd have sixty or seventy individual imaginations working on one simple source of inspiration, and off they'd go. It was a most rewarding experience. I couldn't wait to go to work on a Monday morning. Have you ever heard anything so ridiculous? The other staff couldn't understand it. And what was difficult was convincing other people that what we were doing was valuable because they kept saying, 'Is it fashion? Is it graphic art?' The answer was, 'We'll see what it is, when there's a body of it, when it has become an undeniable intention within that person, that this is the direction they are going in.' The other way of running this kind of foundation course, was to do it like a sampler, so you give them a 'fashion project' or 'an interior design project' and they'd do that, and if they liked it and did well, they'd choose that as their subject area and off they'd go to university. Well, that wasn't good enough, that wasn't a thorough enough analysis, a thorough enough diagnosis. So I thought, I resolved, that we would make it different. We would look at the abstracts and let's think about the abstracts, and let's talk about the intentions. It doesn't have to be labelled into cosy compartments of graphics, fine art – it's what it is. Like the rain, don't give it a name, just look at it and wonder.

Teaching at Swansea University

After I left the college, I carried on teaching history of art and life drawing at Swansea University, which was wonderful because I had finished at fifty-five in Carmarthen. I did about twelve years, and then the climate got too uncomfortable for me. There were too many changes in the management and they were losing their way at art schools. They were becoming enmeshed in the pathetic administrative service of tertiary education. The Government and the Welsh Office, which later became the Welsh Assembly weren't helping. There was a great urge to get everybody into college simply to lower the unemployment figures and so what we had eventually was that students were paying for what they were doing and in this way subsidising their own unemployment. They were borrowing money to be unemployed, but they were in a college, studying something. It's a very clever ruse, but somebody ought to expose it. I don't say that many of the courses weren't worth doing, but I think people are being misinformed about their likely outcomes, the cost to them, and the real purpose of the government. Anyway, when I went to Swansea the students were more urban. They didn't come from a very large catchment area and initially the course didn't have a great reputation.

When you have people coming from diverse backgrounds, you might have sixty to eighty people on a course. You are in a confined space. You have big rooms, but narrow entrances.

You might need to use a washbasin, but there'd only be one. What I found when I began teaching in colleges was that there'd be a hullabaloo. There'd be disorder; there'd be chaos and anarchy. There'd be almost a kind of violence, a pecking order, so I thought it would be a good idea if when we began the year, if we took one word as our motto, inspiration, key, so I'd come up with words. One of the most successful ones was 'Grace'. I used it more than once because I found it so successful. I could never talk about humility because the students would never accept it from me because they thought I was so conceited! I'd say, 'this will be the year of grace. Our grace. We'll learn to go into a room gently and quietly. We will say, "After you". We will move slowly, we will think sharply, but whatever we do, we will do the action with grace. We will be graceful and live in graceful harmony.' They loved it. They thought they'd learned a huge amount from that, never mind the drawing and the painting and the history of art and so on. Just the simple idea: we can conduct ourselves in a better way, in a more human and harmonious way. They loved it and sometimes they'd forget the word. They'd say, 'What was the word again?' and I'd say, 'Grace'. They just thought that was wonderful. We had an Iranian student once, a refugee from Iran. Swansea was becoming a centre for refugees. The Home Office was buying homes in some of the run-down council estates and Swansea was becoming a centre for refugees. They were, in a sense, imprisoned there, not allowed to leave. We had a student who came to the college who was a Muslim. She always wore a scarf and clothes that were modest. She had grace. The girls from Swansea were very often wild and uncouth and prone to drunkenness. Wednesday was the day the students went wild, went clubbing, and on a Thursday I had seminars. I remember in one seminar there were three or four of these young women, who had had a very wild night out, and they were sitting in the seminar and in the seminar was this Persian girl. One of them said to me, 'Why can't we all be like Aisha? Why can't we be like her?' They'd been out, probably on a sexual adventure with somebody they didn't know and couldn't remember. They were still sort of drunk in the morning, but sorrowfully sobering up, and they realised that Aisha had something they didn't have. But that idea of grace, furnishing a cohort of people with one word so that they become different people for a period of time, was a very useful thing to do.

On art and literature in Wales

While I was teaching at Carmarthen I developed another course at Lampeter University for students who were wishing to begin a university education, who were mature, but who hadn't got the necessary qualifications. So I worked on the access course there and developed a course on the history of art and visual language, visual language and the word. I worked on a sort of condensed history of art and then we looked at ways the word could be as powerful in the creation of images as the visual arts are and we had some very interesting results.

I was very interested in the way the visual arts in Wales seem to have been underdeveloped. Whatever people say, we haven't got a great history of picture making and image making. We made some and I would say that in most cases what we have made prove the point. In the mediaeval world, the stained glass and the carving of the rood screen, those are very beautiful and wonderful, but we didn't make two-dimensional moveable paintings. The people did link to the carving in wood when they called a poet a carpenter in song.

But poetry was considered the important art in Wales, not visual art. It was poetry that mattered. In those poems were extraordinary images and in some cases you could claim that the Welsh were the first conceptual artists because they didn't need the physical image, they could generate the image in their poetry and if you look at the Mabinogion, if you look at Taliesin and the great epic of Aneurin, you'll see so much imagery, it's extraordinary. There is one passage where they are boasting about the blueness of their swords and it goes on, 'Their screams shall echo in the heads of mothers.' This probably didn't happen at all – it is a verbal image, which generates a whole visual image.

The history of the twentieth century through art

Another course I developed was the history of the twentieth century through art. An American university asked me to develop a course for their students that were studying at Trinity College in Carmarthen. An American degree must have an art component, whatever you are studying. This comprised of fifteen three-hour classes with a paper at the end of it. So I devised a course. What I did was I looked at the nineteenth century first of all: at the American Civil War, the post-civil war renaissance and what kind of art was produced in America, and then we went on to the twentieth century, but I took it decade by decade. We looked at everything from art production, theatre, novels, music, poetry, science, exploration, ecology, innovation, politics, war, and conflict. We did everything. I'll give you an example. The American Civil War was a brutal war, but it was carried out in very strange ways because a lot of the supplies for the troops arrived by railway, but from there they went by ox-wagons or horse-drawn carriages to the front. The railways moved closer to the front, as close as they could, but they never got there. Photography played a huge part in people's response to the war and their feelings about it. Because photographs in those days were long exposures, the action could not be photographed. All that could be photographed was the tension before, the waiting, and the aftermath, where you would have a field of bloated bodies, because by the time the photographers got there, the bodies had started to bloat. It was an extraordinary, theatrical image that was produced.

In the Crimean War, they didn't publish the photographs of the wounded and the dead in the way they did in the American Civil War and what was interesting was that artists like Winslow Homer travelled as a young man for the New York newspapers, and they made drawings and they also made drawings from photographs because you couldn't print a photograph in a newspaper. So the photographs were taken, then they were put in theatrical shows in rooms where people would go to see them. And the photographs were also used as information to make drawings from, which would be published in the newspapers. The camera, which had only just been developed, was made by a cabinetmaker, a bellows maker, a lens grinder and a clock maker. The clock maker made the mechanical parts, the lens maker ground the lens, the bellows maker made the shutter and the cabinetmaker made the case. So you had these four crafts coming together to make this strange object, which nobody had ever seen before. No one knew what a camera was supposed to look like, so the camera looked like it had to look from its manufacture, in the sense that its making created its form. It was the same with the motorcar, the railway station, the train, things of modernity, they continued to look like that until the age of digitalisation, and there was no real reason why

they should. When they built the first railway station, all they needed was a cover. So what did they do? They built them like Greek temples or Renaissance churches because there was no alphabet, no vocabulary for that kind of form. This is one of the great dilemmas of modernism.

So we'd talk about this, the nineteenth century and the coming of modernism. And we also talked about after the American Civil War when the country was in a terrible state. The proportion of men injured or killed out of the total population was enormous. There's never been another war like it in the world. It was the most savage war, and sometimes it was trench war, sometimes mediaeval, sometimes families were split – it was a dreadful war, an incredibly vicious war, and there was a huge shortage of men after the war. You read that General Sherman at Appotomax allowed General Lee and his men to leave with their horses because they would need their horses for the spring ploughing. They had to do that otherwise the country would have been in a terrible state. But the other interesting thing about the American Civil War, if you look at what comes next, is in terms of cultural production and how that affected America. You had writers like Mark Twain and many of the novels that were written at that time were about children. They had to start again and the child was the hope of America. If you look at the American literature of that period – late 1860s, and well up to the 1890s, the child was the focus of the American imagination. And it was true of painting as well, like in Winslow Homer. The child or the young person symbolised hope, so that was a way of illustrating to these students how cultural affairs and political matters had a social output.

The students kept telling me that they had never had lectures like these. It was a huge help to them. People in our culture are unaware of why. They know how, but they don't know why and they tend to think that culture grows on trees, and it's not like that. Culture is a manufactured thing. And it is a hard thing to get your head around. Our educational system doesn't encourage this kind of thinking. It encourages acceptance and learning and craft and repetition of fact, so in a sense education is a series of quizzes and nobody is asking the question why. They're asking the questions: What? Where? I used to emphasise this with children. I used to say never worry about what you want to be, worry about who you want to be, and in the end the what will fall into place. So my ideas were contentious and somewhat difficult to understand, especially by careers officers and parents. But when you were teaching people who were now at university, you could introduce these ideas.

For example, the reason why the Americans were in Paris after the First World War was largely due to prohibition, because prohibition started in 1919. And you could say that the reason they had money was because from 1885 to 1905 was a period in America which we call the American Renaissance, when the country got itself back on its industrial footing and people became very, very rich, and the children of those very rich dynasties wanted to play. They couldn't play in New York or Chicago because it was all closed down and very dodgy, so they came to Europe. What followed from this was that jazz musicians, who had been playing in America, suddenly found themselves out of work – dance bands and so on – so they went on the ocean liners, because you travelled to Europe on an ocean liner. And they went to Germany. Hitler disliked black people and black music because he's seen them in bars and it

was not what he wanted. What he wanted was Wagner, not ragtime. And of course, with this African influence on European culture, you also had expressionism which was feeding off African so-called primitivism, which had been exposed in the great exhibitions of 1901 and later, and people brought back African artefacts which seemed to speak more powerfully about the human condition than the art of the Graeco-Roman classical tradition. Some people, Freud, Havelock Ellis and Jung, were unravelling these questions about the human mind and consciousness and sexuality and it seemed to most people, when they saw these objects, that they had a power, a sexuality that wasn't present in the cool marble of the Greeks. These things didn't happen by accident. They happened because of colonisation, they happened because of the great exhibitions and they happened because of prohibition, which ended in 1931. These were huge influences on European art and architecture.

The artist interrogates his world

I don't know if all these lectures and ideas affected my own work. My work was very much a reaction to my immediate environment, my place in it. It was also conditioned by what I saw on the screen – TV, newsreels, photographs and newspapers. I was very interested in the oppressed, the downtrodden, and the persecuted because they seemed to be in a violent, dramatic situation which in a sense was something I couldn't get out of my head. I found twentieth-century images bothered me and the only way I could deal with it was by re-creating them in my own way, by making paintings about the Israeli-Palestine conflict, the Vietnam War and the Congo. Those images were haunting images of humanity at its most bereft. I was aware of how and why these things happened, so

225

that kind of political awakening was always very strong, and as I developed this course it grew and grew, it rolled like a ball down the hill gathering things to it. So, what I found was that all my reading became based on these ideas about the twentieth century. Why does a railway station look like a railway station? Nobody ever thought to ask – there they are, that's a railway station. And once you've asked that question about a railway station, you can ask it about any damn thing in the world. What does he look like now? Why is he wearing those clothes? What about all the other clothes he could be wearing? It's about the choices people make. When we see all these refugees now, some are incredibly traditional. Coming in from Kurdistan into Italy, they look as if they come from two thousand years ago, others look as if they've just stepped off the pavement in Britain. The women generally look more traditional, and some of the older men, and when you look at them, you feel that the ones that have clung to their tradition are more dignified. They have a dignity about them because they are rooted in a huge history, whereas looking at the people in their tee shirts and Bermuda shorts and baseball caps, you feel, 'You've got something, but what are you losing?' These are interesting questions for us. I've always been like this. I asked the questions before I started teaching this course, but in teaching it, developing it, it certainly honed that sort of thinking so it did become part of my work.

My work became more verbal and more language-based as well. I developed these what I call graphic essays, where I do a big drawing and a map and particularly around here, where we have a military engaged in practising conflicts in places where there is an abundance of wild life – because the two things are quite contradictory. But it is the case that when the military

take over an area, wild life is pretty well off. It can flourish because, although there are bombs landing, nobody is making any direct interference, so birds and small animals can adapt to this in a way they can't adapt to the presence of ice-cream vans on a recreational scale. That is another interesting question, which would bear a lot of fruit, if it were examined. But I examined it in a more cautionary way than that in these drawings, where the contradictory forces of war and nature are seen in the same image. So I'd have what I call a concatenation of images and ideas: history and geology, poetry and geography, flora and fauna together with the military and the metallic, and pile them all up so that you had a drawing in which you could go for a walk. You could spend time, you could ponder and meditate and think and I call them graphic-psycho-geography, graphic essays, and that really came out of this course – that kind of awareness, and that kind of piling up of understandings and questions.

On art education in schools
I've written since I was young. I've always examined my world and I have my notes going back to the age of eighteen, not everything, but a great deal of it. When I was in art school I wrote a great deal, in Narberth I wrote. I was always interested in observational writing, documentation I call it, rather than expressive writing. I always thought the expressive would look after itself. Even if we were objective, subjectivity couldn't be denied and that was one of my teaching theories as well. Degas once said to Mallarme, 'I've got an idea for a poem.' Mallarme replied, 'You don't need ideas, you need words.' Degas was put down! But one of the curses of education now is the idea. It runs right through education and art education is in a disgraceful condition, it is appallingly disappointing.

Children are encouraged to follow the antics of various artists, generally from the period of Van Gogh. They can't go any earlier because it would be beyond most people – teachers anyway – to deal with anything earlier. Even in art school they are encouraged to imitate the ones who have been successful. The idea of success is measured by external factors, the market place, and that drives right the way through into education, and what is also worrying in education is the tick-box culture, is that every child is hopefully going to do very much the same sort of thing and there won't be too much difference between them. They'll all be of a type. There'll be a generic form of art, and it will be obvious. 'We've done Giacometti.' I've seen it in schools where classes of eleven year olds are making little imitations of Giacometti and everyone is very happy. The boxes are all ticked and we can all take one home and put it on the mantelpiece. And what does that tell us about their own imagination and their own development as spiritual and thinking people? It tells us nothing. It tells us what they can do as imitators. One thing about teaching imitation, copying as it is done nowadays, it's almost like in the Victorian times. It is a way of keeping people quiet and occupied, and by their lack of enquiry (which is a really important part of this education) the discouragement of real enquiry. They are very subdued as well, and they can also get a false sense of fulfilment and happiness because praise comes, and they are not too different from everyone else. They are living in a very safe world. I think it's absolutely disgusting. When I go into a school today, I'm shocked and appalled at what I see.

On reading and writing

When I began the course on the culture of the twentieth century, I really began to understand how important literature is, and how each art form reflects its cultural situation. So I began to look for books that could represent particular periods in the twentieth century. What do you need to read about the beginning of the twentieth century? What do you need to read about the 1920s, if you want to get an extra grasp or hold on this particular period? So I began to examine and look for a library of the key books for the twentieth century. Everyone recommended *The man with no qualities*, which I had bought years ago, completely by accident and I'd read and read, but never really completed. And of course there was James Joyce, Ulysses, and there was Proust, which I had poked my nose in, but never really read. So when I became ill, I realised that although life seems like the summer holidays, when you are a child you think it's still July, and suddenly you wake up and find it's the end of August. So I determined to read these books closely from cover to cover, which I have done in the last two years.

Poetry has always been important to me. I was thinking last night about the poets I'd read as a child, and it wasn't just the easy stuff. I hadn't just read *Hiawatha*. At Pontawen Grammar School we studied T. S. Eliot and Ezra Pound. I always thought poetry was a form of secular prayer. I'd sort of lost my belief in the idea of a heaven and a hell that was external to the experiences that we had while we were alive, and I believed that poetry was humanity's cry into the inchoate to try to make sense of it all. So I always believed that poetry was important, but I'd never attempted to write poetry. I'd made short selections of words put together, which I'd say to people, 'Well, they look like poetry from a distance, but they do not make poems.' My conceit isn't well honed enough to say I write poetry, but I write things which are like poetry.

Reading those three great books was a great thrill. I didn't find it difficult. I started off with *Ulysses* because I was told it was the most peculiar. I just thought it was wonderful. I really enjoyed it. It was not difficult. I've met so many people who say, 'Oh, Ulysses, I never really finished it', or 'I couldn't get started', but I just thought 'Well, why?' What interested me about these three books was that there was no story in a sense; there was no denouement in the end. 'Ah – that's how it was!' It was just a series of events, recollections and descriptions, which went on and then stopped. You didn't think 'Well, thank goodness for that!' So it wasn't like I had expected a novel to be – traditionally. 'Reader, I married him!' There was none of that. And I was doing my own writing at the time. I could never ever bring myself to write fiction that would come to a conclusion and have a plot and have a surprise, a twist. I couldn't bring myself to do it. I just wanted to carry on this non-stop description of experience. So reading those books was a great comfort in a sense because it gave me the justification that I didn't really feel I needed, but it made me feel that my efforts weren't so much in vain and could have value beyond myself, because initially I felt it doesn't matter, it only has to have a value as far as I'm concerned. Initially I do it for me and only me and if others are thrilled and delighted, so be it, and that's a blessing and a compliment, but it isn't the reason that you do it. I suppose that's something that goes right back to my childhood. I wasn't interested in praise from other people, like a performance indicator, so exams in school left me cold. I didn't care if I came out on top or in the middle, it didn't matter in the slightest and most people find that difficult to understand. I like praise. I like being praised. I like being told I'm good at things. I do like that, especially from people I

respect, but it isn't why I did it. It wasn't what I set out to do, so in my own writing I've just found reading those three great authors has been a huge help in coming to terms with my own problems, dilemmas.

I'm writing an 'auto-docu-com-fic-fan' with some comedic elements. I've patented this word. I'm well into this. I've written about 200,000 words, but it's non-stop and non-ending. Hilary reads it as it's written. I'm writing about Wattsville, the place where I was brought up in, spent my young life in, and the people and characters – the heroes and the legends, the giants, the oddities. Then I'm in the country in west Wales in the 1970s, writing about the country and the change in cultural production from hay to silage and the Common Agricultural Policy. Well, all the old slate farm kitchens were ripped out and replaced with modern German/Dutch design kitchens. There were six kitchen design shops in Haverfordwest in the 1970s because of the CAP directive that all the old kitchens should be replaced so farmers' wives could have an easier time and production would go up. So all the beautiful antique traditional stuff was ripped out and replaced by Formica and marble and stainless steel. And of course the next people who were coming along were these English people with aspirations for a Volvo estate and a house with three acres. So they were busy replacing, restoring the stuff that the Welsh people were throwing out, and there was always a middle-man involved in this, an antique shop, or a dealer in antiquities in a disused chapel, of course, which was another cultural indicator. I've written about all the massive changes that our culture has endured in the last fifty years because it is very interesting stuff and its not well documented, I don't think.

Mewn Heddwch

Rhyfelwr/Warrior. Hand-mixed oil on canvas. 84cm x 64cm

Biographical notes

Iwan Bala is an artist and writer. He is presently a Senior Lecturer at the School of Fine Art and Photography, University of Wales Trinity St David. In 1997 he won the Gold Medal for Fine Art at the National Eisteddfod of Wales and received the Glyndwr Award for his contribution to visual art in Wales. He has published seven books, in Welsh and English, including *Certain Welsh Artists* (Seren 1999) and *Hon, Ynys y Galon* (Gomer 2007) He has worked as researcher and presenter on S4C on many occasions.

His artwork is held in public and private collections, and he has exhibited widely in Wales and abroad, including four cities in China in 2012. He has worked collaboratively with poets, including Menna Elfyn and Twm Morys, and recently with musician Angharad Jenkins on an installation and performance, 'PROsiect hAlcw'. *It is as if...*, a book and DVD following the performances, will be published by The H'mm Foundation later in 2015.

Ivor Davies is an artist and art historian deeply interested in every aspect of art, He has used many media, including destruction as well as conservation. Academic directions at Lausanne led to a lectureship with the Art-History department at Edinburgh University; the first curatorship of the Talbot Rice Art Centre, a PhD on Russian art; some learned articles and a couple of books. In the eighties he edited *Link*, newsletter of the Artists and Designers in Wales and joined the radical movement, Beca. In the nineties he was Vice-President of the Cambrian Academy, and was elected President from 2012-14.

His work is in public and private collections, and he has designed mosaics for Westminster Cathedral in 2010 and 2012.

He will have exhibited internationally in about 200 collective and 100 solo exhibitions, including *Silent Explosion*, National Museum, Cardiff, November 2015-April 2016. The award he esteems most was the National Eisteddfod Gold Medal, 2002. He recycled the prize money as a new annual trophy.

David Alston is Arts Director at the Arts Council of Wales. He leads on arts development, strategy, international work and allied projects. His work has included the inception phase of the National Theatre of Wales, work on Wales at the Venice Biennale, work on the Creative Wales Awards to artists, work on securing and delivering WOMEX13 in Cardiff. Last year he led work on Arts Council of Wales's Inspire: Our Strategy for Creativity and the Arts in Wales, the Council's forward strategy for the arts. Previous to his work with Arts Council of Wales, he led The Lowry development in its opening years in Salford and in the 1990s was Keeper of Art and for a period, an Assistant Director in Amgueddfa Cymru National Museum Wales.

M Wynn Thomas is a Fellow of the British Academy and of the Learning Society of Wales, and professor of English and Emyr Humphreys professor of Welsh Writing in English at Swansea University. As editor of R.S. Thomas's unpublished estate he edited the posthumous volume *Residues* and recently published *R.S. Thomas: Serial Obsessive* (UWP, 2013).

John Osmond was Director of the IWA (1996-2013) He was a journalist with the *Yorkshire Evening Post* (1972-1982) and Welsh Affairs Correspondent with the *Western Mail* during the rest of the 1970s.

Between 1980 and 1982 he edited the current affairs and cultural magazine *Arcade – Wales Fortnightly*. Subsequently he worked with HTV Wales as a current affairs journalist and later as a documentary programme producer. He was Assistant Editor of *Wales on Sunday* between 1988 and 1990, after which he worked as a freelance journalist and television producer with his company Agenda Productions.

He was chair of the Writers Union of Wales in the late 1980s, and chair of the Parliament for Wales Campaign in the early 1990s. He is the author of many books on Welsh culture and politics, including *The Centralist Enemy* (1974), *Creative Conflict: the politics of Welsh devolution* (1978), *The Divided Kingdom* (1988) and *Welsh Europeans* (1996).

Christine Kinsey is an artist, who writes and integrates words into her visual language creative process. She has developed a group of female characters who inhabit her paintings and drawings and who follow the narrative line of a journey that began in her childhood in Pont-y-moel, in the industrial valleys of south east Wales.

Christine Kinsey was Co-Founder and Artistic Director of Chapter Art Centre, Cardiff, (1968 – 1976.) She has had three national and three international solo touring exhibitions and has paintings in collections internationally as well being represented in various public collections including The National Library of Wales, Aberystwyth and The Victoria and Albert Museum, London. The book *Imaging the Imagination* which she initiated and co-edited with Dr Ceridwen Lloyd–Morgan, was published by Gwasg Gomer in 2005. She is an Honorary Research Fellow of the Faculty of Art and Design, University of Wales Trinity Saint David, Swansea.

Professor Dai Smith was born in the Rhondda in 1945 and studied History at Oxford University and Literature at Columbia University, New York. He is the Raymond Williams Chair in Cultural History within the Centre for Research into the English Literature and Language of Wales, (CREW) at the University of Wales, Swansea which he joined in March 2005. He was Professor in the History of Wales at Cardiff University from 1985 to 1992 and Editor to BBC Radio Wales and Head of Programmes (English language) at BBC Wales from 1992 to 2001 when he was appointed Pro-Vice-Chancellor at the University of Glamorgan. He is currently Chair of the Arts Council of Wales and Series Editor of the Welsh Assembly Government's Library of Wales for classic works written in English from or about Wales.

He published a major authorised biographical work on Raymond Williams, Wales's most influential twentieth century intellectual figure. He has also begun research into key aspects of the cultural and creative history of Wales since 1945.

In the Frame: Wales 1910-2010 (Parthian, 2010) was on the 2011 Wales Book of the Year Long List.

Karl Francis Anonymous film maker and friend whose Dreams interpret Memory as does driving a fast car in Wales

And Wikipedia tells some truth; the opposite of which suggests

I create Welsh realism and poetry in film.

Who gave up Hollywood and Wizards of Was
Because I love film more than self
And because the mob who rule hate happiness I am
Faithful to God who is Love who
Guides my prayers.
I avoid all scapegoats
And am very good at liking all my character faults.
Because.
Change begins with liking self and Jesus helps
The prodigal
To forgive and love the enemy brings peace.

Wyn Morris Born in Gwaun Cae Gurwen in 1935 and educated at Pontardawe Grammar School and at the University Colleges of Wales at Aberystwyth and Cardiff. After his army national service in Hong Kong and three years teaching history in England, he returned to Wales to work in local government and then to various posts teaching in Further and Higher Education. In the early 1970s, he became head of the School of Trade Union and Social Studies at Gwent College of Higher Education. This School ran numerous day-release courses for shop stewards and other trade union activists in the Gwent area. It also pioneered the very successful one-year full-time Diploma in Trade Union and Social Studies which, over a period of many years, helped hundreds of trade union, labour movement and community activists into university education and further employment.

David Parfitt lives and works beside the Thames in West London. Here he paints portraits, and also the tidal Thames with its bridges and tower blocks, the towpath and the foreshore.
He was born in 1943 in Pontypool in south Wales, and grew up in Blaenavon. He went to Abersychan Grammar School and Monmouth School, and studied painting and drawing at Newport College of Art 1959- 1963 and at the Royal College of Art 1963-1966. His early paintings were of family and friends, and of the gaunt mountains and industrial valleys of south Wales – people and places have been his subject matter through his working life. He has taught in many art schools including the Royal Academy Schools where he was Senior Tutor 1987-1990 and Visiting Tutor 1994-1998. He was elected to the New

English Art Club in 1999 and exhibits regularly in NEAC Members exhibitions at the Mall Galleries, London. His work is represented by Messum's, 28 Cork Street, London W1.

Mick Arnold (Artist Painter) born Monmouth 1942, studied Newport College of Art 1960-64 (Painting) and Cardiff College of Art 1964-65. Throughout this time he was a contemporary and friend of Osi Rhys Osmond. From 1968-80 Mick taught Art in Germany and then moved to Brussels where he continued to teach Art until 2008. Mick and his wife Thea, also a painter and contemporary of Osi, now reside in Kent. Mick continues to exhibit and works from his studio in Margate.

Hedley Jones

Cardiff and Maidstone Colleges of Art, 1963-1967.
Worked in London and Cardiff in advertising; packaging design Revlon Cosmetics; product design Novolor Glass, 1967-1974.
Freelance designer 1974-89.
Part-time and visiting lecturer Swansea, Carmarthen, Newport and Cardiff 1976-1989.
Full time lecturer/division manager Carmarthen 1989-1995.
Vice Principal, Bournemouth College of Art 1995-1999.
Freelance designer 1999-Present.
BTEC Art & Design moderator 1987-1996.
WJEC Examiner A Level art & design 1985-2000.
WJEC Moderator Foundation Art & Design 2000-2012.
WJEC Chief Examiner/Moderator 2012-Present.

Noelle Francis was born in Cairo in 1942. She studied art at Ravensbourne College of Art and Cardiff School of Art. She continues to paint at her studio in Norfolk. She is married with 3 children and 8 grandchildren.

Susanne Schüeli, originally from Switzerland, lived and worked in Munich for many years, training hairdressers all over Europe. In 1994 she moved to Wales where she studied Architectural Stained Glass at the Swansea Institute. It was there that she met Osi. Today she works as a yoga teacher in the Iyengar tradition and runs her own studio.

Teilo Trimble is a former student of Osi at Swansea Institute of Higher Education going on to graduate from the international Film School of Wales. He is a filmmaker and artist and works at Theatr Arad Goch, Aberystwyth as a regional delivery partner for somwhereto_ .

Bella Kerr studied at Central School of Art, Middlesex Polytechnic (Hornsey College of Art) and Goldsmiths College and is a practitioner and lecturer in fine art, and currently the programme Director of the Foundation Art & Design course at UWTSD. Drawing has provided continuity in a practice that has spanned installation, small-scale multiples, film, and set design, shown in a range of contexts from screenings in major London galleries, to museums, and regional galleries. Recent work has been expressed in the form of large-scale installation, practice-based and written research, digital prints and participatory and curatorial work.

Steve Wilson is an artist living and working in West Wales. Steve has exhibited widely, including at the National Portrait Galleries, London and Edinburgh, Royal Academy of Arts, London and in private galleries both here in the UK and Ireland. He is also a campaigner for affordable, ecological housing provision for local communities. He was taught by Osi Rhys Osmond on the Foundation Course in Carmarthen, which he says was a formative experience and which still informs his practice 25 years on.

Sam Vicary studied under Osi at Carmarthen School of Art 1991, progressing to a first-class honours degree in Visual Arts at DeMontfort University and a subsequent postgraduate Painting Fellowship at the university campus in Lincoln.
She spent five years at Issey Miyake London working as UK Sales Manager and curating exhibitions at the flagship store in London W1. She also sourced artists and designer to work with Issey and exhibit in Japan. Eventually returning home, she established a programme of Visual Arts at Oriel Mwldan, Theatr Mwldan's new exhibition space in 2003. She is currently Marketing Manager at Small World Theatre.
In the last 12 months she has re-established her painting practise, exhibiting at Oriel Q, Narberth and with artist-

run projects Rhôd and Colony 14 Cardigan.

Tina Carr One half of the collaborative duo, Tina Carr (b. 1950) and Annemarie Schöne (b. 1947) have been working together for 40 years on many diverse projects combining both photography and video. Through longstanding collaborations, Carr and Schöne work with marginalized and disenfranchised communities to project a positive image that challenges negative attitudes and stereotypical views.

Together they have produced four books; *Pigs&Ingots* 1993, *Coalfaces* 2008, *From the Horse's Mouth – A Roma/Gypsy/Traveller Landscape* 2014 and *Tynescapes* 2015. To *Coalfaces* Osi contributed his very memorable essay, 'Cul-de-Sac: Through a Lens Darkly', which is now regarded as one of the most important comments on post-industrialisation in Wales.

Carr and Schöne's work is held in many public and private collections including the V&A, London, \'aoThe The Photographers' Gallery, London; The National Library of Wales, Aberystwyth; Deutsches Bergbau-museum, Bochum, Germany; The Science Museum, London and Northumberland County Archives.

Nathan Osmond Born Wattsville 1959
Interest in photography ignited by his brother in 1973
Studied at Gloucester College of Art and later at London Guildhall University.
Worked as a photographer in Advertising and Design in London for 16 years
Moved to Somerset in 1995 to lecture in photography at Somerset College of Arts. Lectured in photography at Plymouth College of Art from 2009- 2013 and at Bath College from 2011 to present. Work exhibited in various group shows at Association of Photographers Gallery.

Sara Rhys-Martin Daughter of Hilary Rhys Osmond.

Luke Osmond grew up in Pembrokeshire and after schooling in Llandysilio and Crymych he studied Foundation Art and Design at Carmarthen College of Art when Osi was running the course. He then went on to complete a degree in Fine Art Painting at Cardiff College of Art graduating in 1995. After working as an artist in Dorset he returned to Cardiff in 2001 to complete a PGCE in Secondary Art and Design. Since leaving full-time education he has been involved in art education at different levels. He is currently head of art at the Dragon School in Oxford, having previously taught at secondary level and post-16 education/ further education. He lives in Yarnton, a small village to the north west of Oxford with his family – he has been married to Kim, who he met at Cardiff, for 15 years and they have three boys; Gwion (16), Osian (14), and Aled (10). Although not quite as devoted a painter as Osi, Luke enjoys painting en plein air with his watercolours and due to the demands of the modern-day teacher, tends to undertake his personal creative output in the holiday season.

Simon Thirsk is chair and founder director of Britain's foremost poetry publisher, Bloodaxe Books, where he is responsible for finance, strategy and sales. He has lectured in journalism and marketing for the Chartered Institute of Marketing, worked as a journalist for twenty years, and has been a charity coordinator and literary festival organiser. He wrote a TV play about the poet Irina Ratushinskaya (broadcast on BBC2) and his 2010 novel *Not Quite White* was shortlisted for the Costa prize. He has an interest (and honours degree) in philosophy, lives in Bala and has learned Welsh.

Lynne Morgan Crompton
Curator of Oriel Q Gallery Narberth Pembrokeshire from 1995.
Lecturer at The University of Wales Trinity St David (formally UWIST) from 2004.
Art Teacher 1974-1988
Met Osi 1995

Linda Sontag I first bought a painting of Osi's on a visit to Wales, and when I came to live there briefly in 1995, some friends of his recognised his work on my wall and introduced me to him and Hilary. I now have four of his paintings, wonderful treasures. They are proof that though Osi has left the physical plane, his creative spirit lives on amongst us as vividly as ever.

Dr Rolf Jucker is currently the director of SILVIVA, the Swiss Foundation for Experiential Environmental Education. From 2008-2012 he was director of the Swiss Foundation for Environmental Education. Having gained an MSc in Education for Sustainability (EfS), he has worked extensively as a national and international learning for sustainability advisor and published widely on the subject, amongst others *Do We Know What We Are Doing? Reflections on Learning, Knowledge, Economics, Community and Sustainability* (2014) and *Our Common Illiteracy. Education as if the Earth and People mattered* (2002).

Ché Osmond is a Chartered Geologist working in the international mining industry, and did not follow his father's footsteps into the art world! But this was appreciated and welcomed by Ozi who came from a mining background and whilst not quite going down the pit like his father he understood and could appreciate this following. His career has taken him all over the world, from Armenia to Zimbabwe and numerous countries in between including Columbia, the DRC, Georgia, Guinea, Iran, Kyrgyzstan, Laos, Mali, Sierra Leone, Tajikistan and Russia. Outside of work he cycles, swims (sea not pool!), coaches a local junior rugby team, and occasionally writes private poetry. He now resides in Cornwall with his partner Josie and son Macsen.

Macsen Osmond Son of Nathan, grandson of Osi.

Colin Brewster. I am Osi's cousin, my mother and his were sister. My father and mother were Welsh and my father worked briefly as a miner. My family relocated to Bristol in early 1940 where my father worked for the Bristol Airplane Company. After studying Engineering, Architecture and Town Planning I completed a course in Graphic Design at the West of England College of Art in Bristol. I was a designer on many magazines at IPC in London for over 20 years, and an Art Editor on *New Scientist* magazine until my retirement at 65. Now I am a 'flaneur' and the countless galleries and coffee houses of London are helping to complete my education and life.

Ben Dressel is a native of Saint Louis, Missouri who first came to Wales at the age of two. After many family trips, summer holidays and a semester abroad at Trinity College, Carmarthen, he settled in Wales to pursue an

M-phil in Sociology at University College of Wales, Swansea. Upon completion of the degree in 1995, he was appointed resident director of Central University of Iowa's Wales Study Center at Trinity College, Carmarthen. During his tenure as Director he developed a Welsh Studies orientation involving extensive exposure to the culture of Wales through experiential education. His mentors in this venture were Nigel Jenkins and Osi Osmond. The 'Taith Gladgarwyr' Patriots Tour of Wales was a four day immersion into the history, landscape and culture of what all three considered to be a country of profound insights into the human condition.
He is currently a climber and surfer in exile, husband and father of twins, ex-patriot owner of Dressel's Public House in Saint Louis which, according to the late Nigel Jenkins, 'Is one of the finest pubs in North America.'

Megan Crofton grew up in Risca Monmouthshire. Attended Newport Art College from the age of 15 years, studied painting with Tom Rathmell.
Married Jack Crofton who studied sculpture at Newport, and had two sons, Michael and Justin. Moved to London in the early sixties.
After learning the bronze casting technique, Jack founded the Meridian Bronze Co. a small bronze foundry casting in the lost wax process in Greenwich. The foundry grew in size and reputation, always employing highly skilled craftsmen. The Foundry moved to larger premises, the Railway Arches in Peckham SE15, employing twenty or so craftsmen casting large monumental-size bronzes. Megan worked in the foundry as manager and director for almost forty years, casting for an enviable list of eminent and famous sculptors, with work seen in prominent positions in Britain and abroad.
Megan now lives in West Wales, with beautiful, stunning views over the sea and coast beyond.

Beverley Oosthuizen-Jones is the daughter of a Swansea boy, and the daughter-in-law of Osi and Hilary's close friend Ann Oosthuizen. She got to know Osi and Hilary during the many visits that she and her husband Jannie made to Wales over the last 20 years. Both worked for Christian Aid during the 1990s, and it was during that period that Bev asked Osi to make the 'Artistic Report' on Southern Sudan – a part of Sudan

which was profoundly affected by civil war. Beverley started her development work in Sudan in the late 1980s when she was posted to Port Sudan as a volunteer teacher trainer. She has been going back to the Horn of Africa ever since. She and the family are now based in Oxford, where their home is filled with Osi's pictures.

John Barnie is a poet and essayist. He was born in Abergavenny, Gwent and lived in Denmark from 1969-1982. He edited Planet: *The Welsh Internationalist* from 1990-2006. John has published several collections of poems, mixed poems and fiction, and collections of essays, one of which, *The King of Ashes*, won a Welsh Arts Council Prize for Literature in 1990. His latest books are a collection of poems, *The Roaring Boys*, and a memoir, *Footfalls in the Silence*, both published by Cinnamon Press.

Menna Elfyn is an award-winning poet and has published thirteen collections of poetry, children's novels, libretti for UK and US composers as well as plays for television and radio. *Merch Perygl* was published by Gomer Press in 2011, and her bilingual volume *Murmur*, Bloodaxe Books, in 2012. This volume was selected by the Poetry Society as Poetry Book Society Recommended Translation, the first ever book in Welsh/English to be chosen. Her work has been translated into eighteen languages for which she received an International Foreign Poetry Prize in 2009. A columnist with the *Western Mail* since 1994, she is also Professor of Poetry at the University of Wales Trinity Saint David and was recently made a Fellow of the Royal Society of Literature.

Richard Pawelko was born in Leeds and after graduating from Art School in Bournemouth he joined the BBC Film Unit. After a few years as an editor he left the broadcaster to join the Teliesyn co-operative which provided a springboard for his work as a director. History, arts, children's drama and entertainment productions formed the majority of his output. After forming Zip TV he went on to work for all the main television companies and made a low-budget feature. Osi presented fourteen films on painting for Zip TV looking at seascapes, castles, Christmas and the First World War.

Mary Simmonds was born in Cwmtawe and after graduating from the University of Bangor began working at the BBC in London in 1970. She worked in radio before moving to work in television production at BBC Wales leaving in 1976 to raise her two children. In 1986 she joined the independent TV sector and worked with the Teliesyn co-operative producing history, factual and music programmes for the UK broadcasters. In 2005 she joined Richard Pawelko at Zip TV. Amongst the programmes made by the company are the *Byd o Liw/World of Colour* series and *Celf Rhyfel/Art of War* featuring Osi as the presenter.

Bethan John is a freelance writer, specialising in nature conservation. Her particular interest is in how international conservation projects can empower some of the world's poorest and most marginalised communities. She has organised reporting expeditions to countries across Latin America, working with conservation organisations to build capacity within communications, while honing her skills as a storyteller. www.wildlandscreative.com

Mererid Hopwood studied Modern Languages in Aberystwyth and University College London, and has spent most of her career in education. She now works in the University of Wales, Trinity Saint David. In 2005 she was Children Laureate for Wales. She has won the Chair and Crown for poetry and the Prose Medal at the National Eisteddfod. She has also won the Glyndwr prize for her contribution to literature in Wales. She has translated plays from English and Spanish and in 2013 won the Tŷ Cyfieithu prize.

Ann Oosthuizen was introduced to Llansteffan by Hilary and Osi and has lived there since 1990. Born in South Africa, she moved to the UK in 1972 and to Wales in 1981. She has been a teacher and translator, an editor and a publisher. She has taught Creative Writing in London and in Carmarthen and her latest novel, *Sarah's Story*, received The Literature of Africa Award in South Africa. She is at present working on the memoir of Zegeye Asfaw Abdi, an Ethiopian social reformer.

233

Other publications from the H'mm Foundation

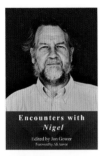

**Encounters
with Nigel Jenkins**
Edited by Jon Gower

CONTRIBUTORS:
Edwina Hart AM, John
Barnie, Stevie Davies,
Steve Griffiths, Angharad
Jenkins and Branwen
Jenkins, Noel Witts,
Deborah Llewelyn, Robert
Minhinnick, Peter Finch,
John Davies, Menna Elfyn,
Delyth Jenkins, Daniel G.
Williams, Dave Hughes,
Margo Morgan, Janet
Dube, Jane James, Steve
Griffiths, Ivor McGregor,
Benjamin Palmer, Dave
Oprava, Iwan Bala and
Twm Morys, Janice
Moore Fuller, Mike Parker
and Ceri Wyn Jones, Ifor
Thomas, Jane Fraser,
Martyn Jenkins, Carey
Knox, Steve Dube,
Humberto Gatica, Tom
Jenkins, D.J. Britton, Fflur
Dafydd, Anne Lauppe-
Dunbar, M. Wynn
Thomas, Jon Gower and
Peter Gruffydd.

ISBN 978-0-9927560-4-8

**A Fiction Map
of Wales**
Edited by John Lavin

CONTRIBUTORS:
Rachel Trezise, Thomas
Morris, Stevie Davies,
Cynan Jones, Francesca
Rhydderch, Joao Morais,
Jon Gower, Rhian
Elizabeth, Carly Holmes,
Lloyd Jones, Gary
Raymond, Tyler Keevil,
Richard Redman, Georgia
Carys Williams, Rhian
Edwards, Rhys Milsom,
Dic Edwards, Linda
Ruhmeman, Richard
Gwyn, Kate Hamer and
Robert Minhinnick.

ISBN 978-0-9927560-6-2

**Encounters
with R.S. Thomas**
Edited by John Barnie

CONTRIBUTORS:
Gillian Clarke, Fflur
Dafydd, Grahame Davies,
Gwyneth Lewis, Peter
Finch, Jon Gower, Menna
Elfyn, Osi Rhys Osmond,
Jeff Towns, Archbishop of
Wales Barry Morgan, M.
Wynn Thomas and First
Minister of Scotland Alex
Salmond.

ISBN 978-0-9927560-0-0

**Encounters
with Dylan Thomas**
Edited by Jon Gower

CONTRIBUTORS:
Rachel Trezise, Michael
Bogdanov, Kaite O'Reilly,
D.J. Britton, Dafydd Elis-
Thomas AM, Dai George,
Sarah Gridley, Sarah King,
Jeff Towns, George
Tremlett, Steve Groves,
Gary Raymond, Guy
Masterson, Jon Gower,
Horatio Clare and
Andrew Lycett.

ISBN 978-0-9927560-2-4

It is as if
Essays about recent work
by Iwan Bala, with images
and DVD of the PROsiect
hAlcw performances in
collaboration with
musician Angharad
Jenkins, based on the
poetry of her father, the
late Nigel Jenkins.

CONTRIBUTORS:
Iwan Bala, Dr Anne Price-
Owen, Osi Rhys Osmond,
Twm Morys, Aneirin
Karadog and Angharad
Jenkins.

ISBN 978-0-9927560-8-6

The H'mm Foundation is a newly formed organisation aimed at raising the profile of poets and poetry in people's lives. Inspired by the *Bardd teulu* (household poet) tradition of Medieval and Renaissance Wales, the foundation encourages business to engage with poetry in a number of ways, including the '*adopt a poet*' scheme.
The H'mm Foundation, Grove Extension, Room 426, Swansea University, Singleton Park, SA2 8PP.
info@thehmmfoundation.co.uk   www.thehmmfoundation.co.uk